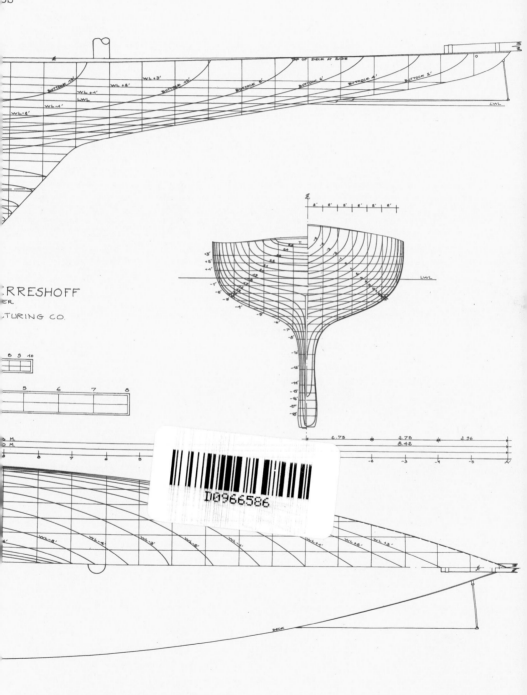

NCE
US

CRRESHOFF
ER

LTURING CO.

TEMPLE TO THE WIND

TEMPLE TO THE WIND

THE STORY OF AMERICA'S GREATEST NAVAL ARCHITECT AND HIS MASTERPIECE, *RELIANCE*

Christopher Pastore

THE LYONS PRESS
GUILFORD, CONNECTICUT
AN IMPRINT OF THE GLOBE PEQUOT PRESS

The Lyons Press is an imprint of The Globe Pequot Press.

10 9 8 7 6 5 4 3 2 1

Printed in the United States of America

Endpaper illustrations are courtesy of Chevalier and Taglang. From *America's
Cup Yacht Designs, 1851–1986*. Paris, 1987.

Library of Congress Cataloging-in-Publication Data

Pastore, Christopher.
  Temple to the wind : the story of America's greatest naval architect and his
masterpiece, Reliance / Christopher Pastore.
     p. cm.
  Includes bibliographical references and index.
  ISBN 1-59228-557-0 (trade cloth)
  1. Herreshoff, Nathanael Greene, 1848–1938. 2. Naval architects—United
States—Biography. 3. Yacht designers—United States—Biography. 4. Reliance
5. America's Cup (Yacht) I. Title.
VM140.H4P37 2005
623.822'3'092—dc22

                              2005012344

For Susie

CONTENTS

In 1903, *Reliance,* the largest America's Cup racer ever built, repre-sented the most sophisticated piece of naval and aeronautical engi-neering in the world. This was the same year the Wright brothers skidded across the Kitty Hawk dunes for less than three hundred yards. Propelled by the same principles of lift that applies to an air-plane wing, *Reliance,* at 143 feet, 8 inches long and carrying 16,160 square feet of sail—an area roughly the size of a large suburban super-market—was the most powerful lift-driven craft ever produced. The title came with one caveat: *Reliance* was so immense that some thought her too dangerous to sail.

With her topsail yard towering 189 feet, 6 inches above the water and sails stretching 202 feet from bowsprit to boom end, *Reliance* sailed fully powered, heeling to her rails, in only seven knots of wind—barely enough to fly a kite. To handle the immense loads pro-duced by her sails, the largest lines were made of four-inch-diameter manila rope as thick as a grown man's forearm. *Reliance* was suited with specially woven multi-ply cotton sails weighing roughly four tons and held together by several miles of stitching. Even the largest sails of the giant six-masted coal carriers were only a quarter the area of *Reliance*'s mainsail, the largest ever spread on any vessel. In addition to their weight, the force exerted on *Reliance*'s sails in a stiff breeze equaled that of over 1,200 straining horses. To counteract this load, *Re-liance*'s keel was filled with over a hundred tons of cast lead, extending 19 feet below the waterline. To sail her required sixty-four professional crewmen.

Designed and built by America's preeminent naval architect, Nathanael Greene Herreshoff, *Reliance* was the end result of years of experimentation. An introverted genius from the small seaside village of Bristol, Rhode Island, Herreshoff shattered the paradigms of naval architecture, developing the graceful, arching bow and stern overhangs now emblematic of classic yachts. During his career he changed the way sails and sailboats were made. Yet he also developed some of the fastest steamships afloat, including the first U.S. Navy torpedo boat. He infused his designs with wonders of mechanical engineering. And he employed construction techniques that allowed him to build bigger and lighter than ever before. During his lifetime, in his small home office, Herreshoff penciled thousands of drawings.

The Wizard of Bristol, as Herreshoff became known, created such graceful, fast vessels that he attracted the world's most powerful clientele, including Morgan, Hearst, Vanderbilt, and Rockefeller, among many others, as well as a rapidly expanding U.S. Navy on its way to becoming a world power. Partnered in business with his blind older brother, John Brown, Nathanael earned international acclaim. But fame came at a cost. He worked tirelessly his entire life. Under his older brother's authoritarian rule, he'd traded his childhood for drafting tools. And the years of resolute focus hardened him.

When in 1902 the order came for *Reliance,* Herreshoff didn't want to build the yacht. He was convinced he'd passed his prime, for *Constitution,* his last America's Cup design, had failed, consistently sailing slower than an older-generation trial horse. At the time, he'd also been hard at work calculating a new design rule, a complex mathematical formula that would render his towering, dangerous, turn-of-the-century yachts obsolete. Herreshoff declined the commission. But wheedled by a syndicate of wealthy New Yorkers resolved to defend the America's Cup from Sir Thomas Lipton, the fabulously wealthy British tea and grocery merchant, Herreshoff caved. After accepting the job, he retired to his study on the third floor of his home and sketched a plan for the most powerful sailing vessel ever created.

I discovered the story of *Reliance* while on a magazine assignment covering the Museum of Yachting's 2002 Classic Yacht Regatta in Newport, Rhode Island. There, I struck up a conversation with Halsey Herreshoff, the great designer's grandson. Our conversation was of boats, and sailing, and of his family's legacy. A few days later I met him and his brother Nathanael III for lunch at the New York Yacht Club in Manhattan. Maybe he extended the invitation because I had expressed sincere interest in our initial talk, or maybe it was simply because I was a fellow Rhode Islander, something of an enigma more than a hundred miles from the state's borders. As it turns out, the Herreshoffs had traveled to the city to research the yacht *Reliance*, the 1903 America's Cup defender designed by their grandfather. As president of the Herreshoff Marine Museum and the America's Cup Hall of Fame in Bristol,

Rhode Island, Halsey was planning a centennial celebration of the yacht for August 2003 and thought that I'd be interested in leafing through the library's collection with them.

I had a vague understanding of the boat's significance: I knew she was the largest and most architecturally extreme America's Cup yacht ever built, and I knew the image of *Reliance* had been minted onto the 2001 Rhode Island quarter. But as I sat down with the designer's two grandsons, both in their late sixties, and leafed through a pile of leather bound books—some filled with original newspaper clippings, others with stories and anecdotes about the owners and designers, and still others like the annotated personal scrapbook of J. P. Morgan—I realized that *Reliance* was not just a boat built to defend a silver cup, but the product of a dynamic cast of characters who had pooled money, talent, and incredible risk to create one of the most technologically advanced machines of its time.

Although *Reliance* proved extremely fast and responsive in trials, beating her 1899 and 1901 progenitors, her unwieldy proportions and unorthodox, scow-like hull shape, like that of a pumpkin seed, cast her as an unseaworthy freak. Why had such a boat been built? Why in 1903 would an estimated $175,000 ($3.5 million in 2005) be spent on something that might fall to pieces, potentially killing her crew? There's no doubt national pride and tradition were paramount. But after reading through the letters of *Reliance*'s managing owner Charles Oliver Iselin, I soon realized that these vast resources were put forth not only to meet Sir Thomas Lipton's challenge, but to deter him from ever returning to the America's Cup arena again. The syndicate had had enough of Britain's "amiable sportsman" and prodded Herreshoff to draft a design that would scare Lipton off for a long time into the future.

I felt a personal connection to Lipton's quest for the Cup. Upon finishing my final college exam in 1997, I drove straight from Maine to Newport, where I'd signed on as a deckhand on Lipton's 1930 America's Cup challenger *Shamrock V,* which at the time was working as a summer charter boat. I spent the next six months living and sailing onboard, and with each new group of guests I heard the abbreviated history of Lipton's challenges as retold by the captain. At 120 feet overall, *Shamrock V,* built to the J Class rule, was considerably shorter with less than half the sail area of *Reliance*. Nevertheless, *Shamrock V* was powerful and that summer I gained a feel for sailing a yacht of such grand proportions—hoisting her half-ton mainsail, the dizzying heights atop her 155-foot mast, and the teeth-clenching fear of climbing onto the boom to reef the giant mainsail at 2 A.M. in a thirty-knot gale.

If it hadn't been for the countless hours of polishing bronze, cleaning bilges, and sanding and varnishing teak, I'm sure the pangs of detachment would have been stronger when I left at the season's end. Ultimately, I couldn't help but be impressed sailing such a long, sleek yacht that spread so much canvas. When I later began to formulate an outline for a book about Nathanael Herreshoff and *Reliance* I kept these memories fresh in my mind. And I have no doubt that having this experience fueled my enthusiasm in my conversations with the Herreshoff brothers.

In the process of researching this book I spent many days in the wood-paneled library of the New York Yacht Club and then in Bristol, sitting next to a professional archivist as she catalogued Nathanael Herreshoff's yellowed letters in the Herreshoff Marine Museum's archives. I looked through *Reliance*'s plans housed at the Hart Nautical Library at MIT and sifted through company records and diaries and the enormous collection of Charles Oliver Iselin's letters housed at the Mystic Seaport Museum library. I then traveled to Northern Ireland to visit the Royal Ulster Yacht Club and then to Scotland, where I studied Lipton's personal scrapbooks in his hometown of Glasgow. At the Scottish Maritime Museum in Irvine I unrolled *Shamrock III*'s original linen line drawings. When I asked about *Shamrock III*'s designer, the legendary British naval architect William Fife Jr., I was told—much to my delighted surprise—that in an hour May Fife McCallum, one of his descendents and biographer and now researcher at the museum, would soon arrive and would be happy to answer questions. With May's directions I traveled to the village of Fairlie where the Fife boats were built and had a pint in the village pub while the locals pointed to sepia photos on the walls and regaled me with yarns of the old Fife yard. I then hopped a train to Dumbarton and visited the famed Denny Flow Tank and saw the former grounds of the Denny shipyard where *Shamrock III* was designed and built. Finally, I traveled to England, stopping at the National Maritime Museum and its library in Greenwich and then visiting the Royal Yacht Squadron in Cowes. After returning to New York and making many more visits to the New

York Yacht Club and Herreshoff Marine Museum, I set out to tell the story of America's greatest naval architect and *Reliance,* his masterpiece.

Throughout the book I have chosen to use nautical terminology. I feel that to call, say, the "starboard" side of a boat, the "right" side or the "bow" the "front" would detract from the tradition and profession that shaped a mind like Nathanael Herreshoff's and a yacht like *Reliance.* It also dulls the language. For those unfamiliar with nautical terms, I have included a glossary. Throughout the book I have chosen to use "she" instead of "it" when referring to boats. Although Herreshoff regarded his America's Cup yachts as machines designed for the sole purpose of defending the Cup, in his notes, letters, and diaries he always referred to them in the feminine. I defer to his judgment.

1

THE BLOCK OF PINE

May 1902–October 1902

Burdened by the request of a neatly folded letter, Nathanael Greene Herreshoff sat before his desk. There, in his office, on the third floor of his home, a three-story Second Empire style with mansard roof, perched on a spit of land called Love Rocks, he contemplated family, career, and reputation. From his office window, he could see his building sheds, machine shops, mill, and docks jutting into Bristol Harbor. It was May 23, 1902, and the spring sea breeze ceded as the sun sank over Poppasquash Point. On a piece of plain white paper, his personal stationery, he penned a letter in reply. It was addressed to Mr. Charles Oliver Iselin, a longtime business associate, friend, and member of the New York Yacht Club who had asked Herreshoff to build a yacht to defend the America's Cup. It was the weight of this request, folded in thirds, that sat so heavily on his mind. Any other designer would jump at the chance. It meant working at the leading edge of naval architecture. It meant testing new materials, new machines, pushing the limits of form and function. The project promised an enormous paycheck, and the knowledge gleaned from the work would trickle into every project he and his brother, the sole proprietors of the Herreshoff Manufacturing Company, had under way. This request would showcase the latest innovation in naval engineering, his ideas, his vision, granting him the poetic license to draw and build as he saw fit. Like Michelangelo in the Medici garden, he would be paid handsomely to sculpt a design from his own intuition, inspiration, and curiosity.

Nathanael Herreshoff's designs had restored Bristol Harbor to the grandeur of the early 1800s. The waterfront—Thames Street, Hope Street, the docks and landings—once again bustled like the days when Bristol privateers fought the American Revolution and War of 1812. His yard, an assortment of waterfront sheds, machine shops, offices, railways, and piers, had welcomed the wealthiest men in the world, fervent benefactors eager to commission Herreshoff's next creation. They or their representatives traveled from New York, Boston, and the great cities of Europe to a small town in Rhode Island, a peninsula jutting from the eastern shore of Narragansett Bay, where they found a surprisingly sophisticated shop for such a remote location. They found skilled workmen with unruly beards in canvas overalls and hobnail boots. They found an office of young draftsmen wearing coats and ties and wire-rimmed glasses. And then they found the peculiar proprietors, the brothers Herreshoff, John Brown and Nathanael, the former a shrewd, blind businessman and the latter a driven, laconic genius.

That their shop was tucked along the eastern shore of a shallow, isolated harbor didn't matter, for the two brothers—one tapping his tall commanding presence through the sheds with a cane, the other short with fiery introspective eyes—built the fastest sailboats in the world. Iselin knew this. Herreshoff knew this. But the thought of building another America's Cup defender, his fifth, was overwhelming to Nathanael. He thought about his wife who had fallen ill. His yard was overloaded with work, and he had been plagued with rheumatism, making his daily inspection rounds increasingly difficult. He also thought about how two years earlier in 1901 *Constitution,* his Cup defender, had been banished to the sidelines. The New York Yacht Club had decided his 1899 design, *Columbia,* was faster, and although *Columbia* had successfully defended, the whole affair left a bad taste in his mouth. He felt shortchanged, dismissed. He had spent hundreds of thousands of dollars to build a yacht relegated to the role of crew trainer, a trial horse, and he sensed a grumbling from his clients, those faint echoes of consternation. And so on the evening of May 23, 1902, he penned a reply to Iselin:

> [I] have quite decided not to design and construct another cup defender. It is nearly ten years since we joined hands in this work. I am quite a little older than you are, and I feel and know that my best years for such work have passed, and that it will be better to intrust the undertaking to younger minds.[1]

At fifty-four years old, Nathanael Greene Herreshoff had called an end to his affiliation with the America's Cup. He'd been working long hours almost every day since he was a child. With his brother he had built a successful business and earned a handsome living. But he was tired. The letter was short, only two pages. He closed with valediction, "Believe me. Most Sincerely Yours," and adorned the first letter of his name, N, with a long, looping flourish.

Iselin received the letter in early June. It's unknown how he took the news, but because there had not been an official challenge for the America's Cup—a formal letter expressing the desire to race—the topic was temporarily put aside. But in early June he visited Herreshoff in Bristol, where no doubt Iselin pressed him to design the American yacht. Throughout the summer the two conversed by mail, for Iselin was traveling in Europe and Herreshoff was working in Bristol. Iselin's persistence paid off and by the end of August Herreshoff had, with much hesitancy, conceded—and none too soon. On September 1, 1902, Iselin received a letter from the new secretary of the New York Yacht Club, George A. Cormack, indicating a challenge from Sir Thomas Lipton was imminent. Lipton, the extraordinarily rich tea and grocery merchant, had launched the previous two challenges and was preparing for a third. Cormack wrote:

> We have had information that must be considered reliable that Lipton's boat is underway and that his challenge will be conveyed by the Royal Ulster Club at an early date . . . Fife is to design the boat and Wringe is to sail her and that Fife is trying for a better all around boat more speed through the water & that he "Fife" intends going to the limit . . . [2]

Cormack acknowledged that Lipton would challenge and had hired the top naval architect in Great Britain, William Fife Jr., as well as Robert Wringe, the preeminent captain. Although Cormack's information was accurate, he made one incorrect assumption: "I think Herreshoff is anxious to design for you and have a final go at Lipton . . ." Iselin knew Herreshoff was ambivalent about designing a defender, but he also knew Lipton would return to New York with a faster boat and more polished crew. Lipton's phenomenal resources—from his unlimited bankroll to his designer to his captain to his head start in designing and building—would overwhelm any effort an alternate American designer could put forth. Iselin needed Herreshoff, who held the secrets of the last ten years in yacht design. Although Herreshoff doubted his own abilities, he possessed an unparalleled knowledge of architecture and engineering. He was eerily precise and could recall with savant-like accuracy minute details from any of a thousand intricate parts. Any future designs would build on his vast knowledge and if he had made mistakes in the past— perhaps *Constitution*—he would have learned from them. Another "younger mind" as Herreshoff suggested, would be reinventing the wheel and with Lipton's money and insatiable appetite for victory, shifting to another designer could be ruinous, forcing the New York Yacht Club to part with their beloved Cup. Competition for the America's Cup was no longer simply a series of races; it had become a proving ground for the latest in design and construction. Cup boats were vehicles for flaunting architectural and engineering prowess, and in the world of naval architecture Herreshoff was a veritable god.

After receiving a letter sent from Iselin on August 21, Herreshoff qualified his involvement in his reply:

> I appreciate very much your kind expressions and it is with pleasure I think of the grand sails and victories we have had together. It was, however, with much misgiving that I have consented to undertake the task, for I fully realize I have not the ability and endurance I had five years ago. And I know [what] is needed for the defense of the Cup.[3]

Herreshoff expressed his ambivalence to design the next defender, but in the next sentence, he hinted at the idea of building something new, something unique, something that'd never been done before. His diffidence aside, Herreshoff suggested a plan that would not only redefine the precincts of naval architecture, but would push the envelope of aeronautical engineering and redefine how engineers envision strong and light design.

Running on the same principles of lift as an airplane, a sailboat "flies" through air and sea, its sails driven by wind, its hull driven by water. Similar to the Herreshoffs, two brothers, Orville and Wilbur Wright, were experimenting with this idea of strong and light construction and foil shapes that could lift a human, like a bird, off the ground. Their designs, though functional, were still prototypes, their flights short and abrupt. Using the same mechanical principles, the

Herreshoff brothers were producing some of the largest "wings" in the world and their boats were driven by the most powerful and efficient lifting foils ever created.

When in 1900 Max Planck announced what would become known as Quantum Theory, he dismantled the former boundaries of physics. Likewise, Herreshoff, ever willing to challenge paradigms, had visualized a boat that would redefine the physical boundaries of mechanics, making "strong and light" his mantra, carving out a new realm of possibilities for lift-driven craft. He wrote to Iselin: "I have gone a little more on the extreme in scow form and power. I think it will fill the bill providing we can make it strong enough."...[4]

Later, in the same letter, Herreshoff indicated, "I now have a model very nearly completed . . ." He then detailed the percentage increase of dimensions the new yacht would have, compared to *Columbia* and *Constitution,* and continued, "If you have any doubts please let me know by cable, so I can modify the plans before we go too far."[5] This receptiveness to hear Iselin's feedback was uncharacteristic of Herreshoff. He'd turned down commissions from some of the wealthiest men alive because they had suggested changes to his designs. He designed the way he designed. If you asked for a seventy-foot yacht, you received one of the most precisely designed and built seventy-footers in the world. But if you wanted to suggest how he should organize the staterooms or where the jib halyards were led, your contract was cancelled and your name was placed on a blacklist along with those few others who had made the same mistake and proved unworthy of owning a Herreshoff yacht.

That Nathanael offered to hear Iselin's advice is indicative of his respect for the man. Iselin had proven to be a masterful yacht manager who, in his three defenses as managing owner, had overseen everything from building contracts and crew organization to securing funding and tuning up and racing the chosen defender. In 1887 he sailed aboard *Volunteer* and successfully ran the syndicate backing *Vigilant* in 1893. He then tactfully allayed loud protests from the Earl of Dunraven in the *Defender* defense of 1895 and then successfully managed the *Columbia* defense against Lipton's *Shamrock* in 1899. Although Iselin had not been involved in the 1901 Cup defense, perhaps *Constitution's* failure emboldened him to speak his mind. When Iselin received Herreshoff's letter in Berlin, he looked over the specifications and wanted more.

Within days, Iselin had contacted Commodore Lewis Cass Ledyard and Edwin D. Morgan from the New York Yacht Club. They quickly traveled to Bristol to discuss the design and Iselin's proposed changes. Ledyard and Morgan had been talking with Lipton. The challenge would be held in yachts ninety feet on the waterline. That was the only restriction. From there, Herreshoff could design and build as he pleased. On September 25, 1902, referring to this meeting, Herreshoff wrote to Iselin: "[T]hey are both of the same opinion as you ... to make a more powerful vessel than before and more extreme in type. I think your expression, 'Pikes Peak or Bust' about covers the feeling."[6]

Herreshoff's letter was enthusiastic. A license for bold experimentation was, after all, what made designing for the America's Cup so tantalizing. Iselin was assembling a cadre of millionaires to fund the project. Herreshoff would put smaller boats, for which he had taken orders, on hold—but these boat owners would ultimately reap the knowledge gained on this new boat, this ninety-foot-on-the-waterline blank canvas. He thought of his previous yachts, those aspects he liked. From winches, blocks, and sheaves to decking, spars, and sails, the Herreshoff Manufacturing Company would design and build it all. From tiny hand-tooled shackles and deck hatch hinges to belaying cleats and chain plates, the machine shop would make improvements on everything they'd ever built. Every piece would be stronger and lighter. The hull itself—stronger and lighter. The sails, mast, gaffs, and booms—stronger and lighter. And it would trickle down into every project Nat and his brother took on, from rowing skiffs to 150-footers.

Architects in New York had only two years prior completed the Park Row Building, a thirty-two story behemoth of brick and mortar, the tallest building in the world. But it didn't move, it didn't have to plow through waves and outmaneuver opponents. It didn't have to be so streamlined, so efficient, that every working part, thousands of them, flexed in unison, each absorbing the energy of the next, each with the sole purpose of turning potential energy into kinetic energy, transferring hundreds of thousands of pounds of force into motion, thwarting drag, generating lift. Designing a sailing yacht is like designing a musical instrument. Every piece influences the end result. The strings of a violin, the aging process of its wood, the wear on the fingerboard, all add to its tone, its ability to be played, and the resultant music. Likewise, the myriad pieces of a racing yacht must dovetail into one unified system intentionally designed to make a yacht sail fast and true, so that with each puff of wind, set of waves, or tiny movement of the crew, the boat remains in perfect balance.

This ability to visualize, design, and build such meticulous structures in which a hull, rig, and crew meshed in perfect harmony with wind and water had made Herreshoff the preeminent designer of his day. His past designs had produced yachts of such precision that some wondered if he had in him a touch of magic. In fact, in recent years his nickname Captain Nat had, by those who revered his gift as something truly unique, been supplanted by a new one: the Wizard of Bristol. But his ability to craft the fastest boats in the world came not from some mystic power, but from his innate understanding of proportions. If he added more sail, he might add more depth or ballast to the keel. If he added more depth, he might add more rake to the rudder post. If he added more beam, he lengthened the waterline, maintaining a constant prismatic coefficient. And whereas many designers made these bold adjustments as rigid tradeoffs bound by formulae, the Wizard used his intuitive architectural foresight to suffuse this give-and-take process into every nut, bolt, line, and shackle, so that each piece would continue working in concert with the next.

Part of the reason he normally refused design input was that every component of his yachts were so intertwined with the next that to move a hatch cover or crew cabin would snowball into an endless cascade of design changes, myriad microadjustments needed to disperse loads or ensure stiffness or required flex. Each facet of a Herreshoff yacht was so interdependent with the rest of the vessel that they assumed an almost lifelike quality in which every piece played an organic role. Each yacht was a towering manifestation of his mental picture, and to make changes would diffuse that spark of genius. But Iselin, E. D. Morgan, and Commodore Ledyard had made their suggestions in the early stages of his design process. And perhaps Herreshoff felt he owed them this, for their last boat of his design and build, *Constitution,* had been a flop. And perhaps he thought he needed their advice. He had, after all, written that he wasn't the same designer he once had been, that perhaps he'd lost his gift, that he was no longer the brilliant young architect with endless ideas and an insatiable thirst for competition.

He was now being asked to stretch those proportions, to create a boat more powerful, more "extreme in type," a boat that could not only defeat Lipton's third challenge, but defeat him with such authority that he would never challenge again. Although Lipton had been embraced by yachtsmen and the American public alike as an honorable sportsman and magnanimous showman, his back-to-back challenges were costing the members of the New York Yacht Club heaps of time and money. The first *Columbia* defense had cost roughly $250,000 all told; the second, including the cost of building *Constitution,* almost $300,000. Members of New York Yacht Club were tired of shelling out huge sums to defend their Cup. They would defend it at all costs, but eager for a break, preferred to lock it away behind glass on its trophy case shelf. In his September 1 letter to Iselin, George Cormack confirms the club's sentiments: ". . . for should [Lipton] fail this time I am sure we will be left in peace and quiet for some years."[7]

Could Herreshoff stretch the dimensions of his initial vision to create the requested "extreme" vessel? Could he build a boat perfectly in tune with itself at such monumental proportions? As letters passed between Cormack and Lipton, Iselin and Commodore Ledyard, Herreshoff and Iselin, Herreshoff and Ledyard, they fleshed out the details of what was needed. Herreshoff knew his boat would be bigger and more powerful, but how extreme could he go? That question depended on who would stand at the helm, who would hold the wheel and hire and train the crew. For even an experienced helmsman, a yacht of the proposed dimensions could, in a breeze, turn into a wild bronco, spinning out of control, potentially damaging the boat and injuring crew. There was one person alone who could steer the design that swirled in his head as he returned from his workshop rounds, walked through the door of his home, placed his hat on the rack, and entered the gas-lit dining room where dinner waited. The helmsman he hoped for was the most talented in the world with a gift for taming the largest, most-powerful yachts. The man Nat had in mind had twice defended the America's Cup with a Herreshoff yacht, and between them there existed a strong mutual respect. But ultimately, the decision over who would drive was Iselin's. And for Herreshoff the dinner table was the only time of day when he could forget his all-consuming work and sit quietly.

Like every night, his wife, Clara DeWolf Herreshoff, served dinner promptly for him and their six children. They ate in silence. He liked to be left to his thoughts. When they finished dinner each night, he climbed the stairs of their four-story, red shingled home perched on a spit of land called Love Rocks. On the third floor, just below the attic, he kept his personal workshop remote and quiet, except for the occasional squeak of a rooftop weather vane the shape of a Maltese cross with a blue background, his private yachting signal.

His office allowed him the solitude he needed to draft his designs. Philosopher Gaston Bachelard once wrote that the house is a place to daydream, and that the attic or top floor, "bears the mark of ascension to a more tranquil solitude."[8] Herreshoff plunked down in his chair, at his desk, and allowed his eyes to wander the room—a room with walls neatly lined to the ceiling with half models of his previous designs; a fireplace with its mantel filled with framed pictures, a barometer, and various odds and ends; bookshelves stuffed with books; tables piled with various plans and scraps of paper; a large wooden chest filled with tools; and his workbench on which was mounted a vise, a lathe, a moveable lamp. Perhaps the magic came from his daydreams in this room at the top of his house, a room festooned with models representing the last thirty years of yacht design. He simply had to swivel his head to see the progression, to follow his own line of thought. He simply had to gaze from one of the large four-paned windows to see the yard, piers, and myriad boats, to witness how the objects of his thoughts had come to fruition.

The act of designing a yacht or house usually begins with a set of drawings made by an architect. These drawings, two-dimensional representations of the architect's vision, are then scaled-up and executed by builders. House drawings largely comprise an arrangement of straight lines and right or 45-degree angles. To design a yacht, conversely, is to design a vehicle intended to move through fluids—water and air. To design a yacht, and particularly a fast one, is to assemble lines into a shape that will minimize drag through those fluids. Whereas a building might take on a cubelike structure with eight well-defined 90-degree corners, a yacht must take on a more streamlined shape comprising thousands of curves, an infinite number of infinitesimal corners, that fall into perfect alignment. Because a yacht's hull shape is wholly dependent on how it will move through the water, most yacht designers spent days working out the figures for various wave-line theories, that is, how the length and shape of the vessel meshes with the type, size, and location of the waves the hull will make. All displacement hulls—meaning hulls that push through water, unlike, say, speedboats that skim across the top—create two waves, one at the bow and one at the stern. The greater the distance between these waves, generally, the less they conflict with each other, and the faster the yacht is capable of sailing. This maximum speed as determined by this wave-line theory is called the yacht's hull speed. Longer yachts have higher hull speeds. But when designing to a certain length as prescribed by certain racing-rule parameters, it is possible for the architect to augment the shape of the boat so as to create a longer separation, even if only by a few fractions of an inch, between the two waves, resulting in a faster yacht. These changes in hull shape, however, are highly complex and require hours, if not days, of computations and theoretical testing. This is where Herreshoff excelled.

Although he used complex math in many of his calculations, particularly when creating engines, rigging, and machine parts, he took a different approach with hull designs. To craft a yacht's foundation he built models. Instead of relying on empirical data, he used his eyes and hands to forge a shape purely on feel. For most yacht designers this would be unthinkable. They were bound to the system of creating drawings and sending them to the owners and builders for approval and changes. These drawings passed back and forth via courier countless times with endless changes implemented even during the building process. Herreshoff didn't accept suggestions. He designed his yachts on the top floor of his home and built them next door. Although his models were transcribed to paper, providing his foremen and builders with a template and schedule, the process of creation was solely his. His benefactors trusted it; in fact they sought this wisdom, this unfettered confidence. And although Iselin prodded him to go more extreme from his first model, he knew the design characteristics of "extreme" would be solely his. Perhaps building a yacht of such epic proportions was now enticing, even tantalizing—something the dutiful, obedient younger brother, the overworked designer who'd two years earlier been blamed for *Constitution*'s failure, couldn't have done without a nudge.

The contract for hull No. 605 was logged into the Herreshoff Manufacturing Company's construction book on October 16, 1902. That night, after sketching a shape on a pad of 10½- by 8-inch paper, noting the overall length, waterline length, and draft, beam, and freeboard,

Herreshoff left his desk and took a seat at his workbench. According to his son, L. Francis Herreshoff, his designs always began with this rough sketch, providing a framework from which he would begin his half-hull model, a three-dimensional representation of the yacht's hull from bow to stern, sheer line to keel, terminating at the yacht's centerline.

The rough model consisted of a solid block of white pine roughly cut to the overall shape of a yacht hull, wide at the deck, tapering to the keel. Having built these half models since he was a boy, Captain Nat worked quickly with sure hands, his ideas taking form as he worked. L. Francis later wrote: "Model making is so much akin to sculpture that when well done, it is a higher means of expression than the arts that are all on one plane, like drawing or painting."[9] Like his father, L. Francis sought expression through the empirical, through engineering, through building. Not one to dwell on inspiration from the arts, Nathanael would have built his model not as a poetic gesture, but for pragmatic reasons: to design and build a vessel. But as he planed the centerline surface of his model and, using pencil, outlined No. 605's profile, he knew exactly what form his yacht would take. Underlying his terse, anatomic approach, there was a vision and perhaps revelation buried beneath the grain. Michelangelo once said that his statues were already there, locked inside his slabs of marble; he simply had to carve away the excess to see them. Similarly, Herreshoff's No. 605 was trapped within his block of pine. He only needed to carve away the excess, shave away the splinters, excavate the yacht he'd been thinking and dreaming about—the yacht that had haunted him, the one he thought he was too old to build.

Securing the model in his vise, Herreshoff laid a batten—a flexible ruler—along the top of the block. Then, by eye, he marked with a pencil the sheer, the line marking the profile of the deck as seen from the side. Using his drawknife and heeding the line, he carved the excess wood away. Next, standing over the model, as if looking at the deck from the top of the mast, he bent his flexible batten into the curve of the deck line and traced it with his pencil. He carved the excess wood away, and the block assumed a rudimentary hull shape. From the side one could see the sheer profile; from above, the plane of the deck, an elongated teardrop dripping from both ends. Like Michelangelo's *Captives,* a figure emerged—a rough-cut semblance of a body half-exposed, half-anchored in its primordial form.

Next, he made a template. To do this, he laid his original sketch of the midships cross section over a thin piece of soft pine. Using a needle to poke holes through the paper and into the wood, he traced the cross section. Connecting these dots with pencil, he then cut out the template. Once placed against the rough-cut model's hull, it was used as a guide, indicating where wood should be chipped away. Once he'd carved an approximate shape of the cross section, he dusted the template with chalk, which when placed against the hull marked the high spots. He then carved away until it was fair.

Once the centerline cross section was complete, representing a profile view from the deck to the bottom of the keel, Captain Nat, relying on his phenomenal sense of proportion, carved away his captive hull. He chipped and shaved excess wood, all the while taking into consideration the countless factors that would brand this hull a success or total bust. He thought of the mast, boom, and sails, the web of lines and blocks, the placement and weight of lead in the keel, the crew, the winches, the steering column, and the wheels. He thought of the hull materials—the rivets, bronze plates, and frames of nickel steel. These countless details swirled in his head as he bent over his vise, pushing swift, confident strokes of the pairing gouge. White curls of wood fell to the floor. But how much is too much? How does one scrape into the unknown?

That Captain Nat's models lined the walls of his workroom was no coincidence. Each shape represented a step in architectural evolution. No. 605 was the end result of years of work, borrowing pieces from his triumphs, avoiding the pitfalls of his failures. But one model was not on the wall—yet the image was branded in his mind as he completed the overall shape of hull No. 605 with his wood planes, a set of ten Stanley No. 101s.[10] Fairing the long, flat bow section and the flat, wide stern, he saw the scow shape he'd promised Iselin and recalled that earlier incarnation of the design he sought, the shape now almost fully exhumed from the block. He'd seen a failed attempt at an extreme scow during the America's Cup trials of 1901. Thomas W. Lawson of Boston had entered a yacht to compete with Herreshoff's *Columbia* and *Constitution*. Designed by Bowdoin Crowninshield, the yacht was enormous, with a towering rig and unorthodox hull shape; but she leaked and was plagued with frequent breakdowns. Large and unwieldy, the yacht proved out of control with frequent spinouts, and the helmsman and crew were unable to maintain control. Although chided as an interloper by the New York Yacht Club and then brushed aside as a hopeless failure, *Independence* had caught Captain Nat's attention. If the lines of *Independence* could be balanced, her shortfalls corrected, he knew he could build something unprecedented. He saw the giant scow's potential, and with Iselin's urge to push bigger and more powerful—a license to cut loose—he saw the shape of No. 605.

Using his special modified blades, Captain Nat slid the plane across the model, peeling a thin rind of pine with each stroke. L. Francis noted, "some of the planes were concave crossways, and some convex crossways, and some curved both ways fore and aft."[11] He ran his fingers over the increasingly smooth shape—a perfect union of continuous muted curves aligned with precision, with a mathematical accuracy that subsumed even the most intricate details of its future construction. Using battens rubbed with chalk, he scoured the model's surface, identifying uneven spots to be faired with his planes. He was meticulous with this process, for his design plans would be taken directly from this scale representation. Any irregularity would be passed to the final product. It had to be perfect. A tiny bump brought to full scale became a costly mistake. And so he faired the hull to perfection, carefully sliding the planes over each irregularity. While building the model for No. 605, he spread this process over two days. His son later wrote, "I remember well watching my father cut this model and he did most of it in two evenings, but he was an extremely fast worker . . . and seemed to know before hand what shape was wanted."[12]

With adroit command of the planes, Captain Nat worked the hull until it was nearly smooth. Then, using a small square of sandpaper, he began to meld the myriad curves into one hydrodynamic body. L. Francis observed, "He held [the sandpaper] a certain way with the tops of his four fingers on top, and the thumb holding the partly turned up edge. As the sandpaper traveled back and forth his sensitive fingers could detect the slightest irregularity which he worked over until the whole surface was entirely fair."[13] When the model was complete, Captain Nat, wiping away the dust, applied a coat of shellac. The finished model of No. 605, held by the vise at a 45-degree angle, soaked the sealer into its grain, slowly drying overnight.

At a glance, the newly finished model looked like the others lining the walls: his office was full of sleek, narrow half-hulls, each of a fine polish, the wood grain dark and inviting like the desks of an ancient reading room. But that model, its thin keel and tapered rudder slicing upward, held something infinitely different, for Herreshoff had infused it not only with knowledge and vision, but his doubts, his misgivings, and even his failures.

2

THE TOWN OF BRISTOL

Winter 1857

Gripping his hammer's handle, John Brown Herreshoff, with an accurate thump, drove the final quarter inch of iron nail through plank and frame. At age fifteen he was a gifted, indefatigable carpenter. His twelve-foot sailing skiff, to be named *Meteor,* was skeletal but taking shape. Inspecting his work, he sat on a small cask of nails, his boots scraping rough-cut floorboards. The room smelled of whale oil and pine pitch. This was his first boat, his first big project, and it consumed him. Glancing with his one good eye, he assessed the work yet to be done. He had plans to finish that winter and launch *Meteor* the following spring.

The next day, however, while playing with his brother, Charles, he was struck in his good eye with a stick. John Brown's parents put him to bed. The same doctor who'd tended to his other eye, in which he'd lost vision from a cataract, arrived in the morning and diagnosed the blindness permanent. *Meteor* sat in the workshop unattended. For John Brown the world had gone dark. Retiring to his room, he fell into depression, locked himself away, and during the long Rhode Island winter of 1857, took meals alone.

After four dormant months, the ice of Bristol Harbor, announcing spring, groaned with each change of tide. Red buds dotted the elms of Hope Street. And as the days grew longer John Brown grew anxious. He'd always enjoyed working with his hands. His father, Charles Frederick, full-time hobbyist and gifted woodworker, had instilled in him a love of building and design, and they had grown close. He'd been a gifted student, a hard worker, and obedient son. Now he felt isolated and alone, cursed by his blindness and ambition. One afternoon, exasperated by his self-inflicted isolation and encouraged by his father, John Brown left his room and felt his way down a corridor lined with his brothers' and sisters' bedrooms. Brushing his hands over beaded oak wainscoting and glass doorknobs, he reached the end of the hall, lifted the iron latch, and opened the door of his workshop. He felt his way down the tool bench, identifying each piece. He ran his fingers down *Meteor*'s dust-covered frames and felt nail heads and hammer dents along her soft pine strakes. He felt the cold of the floor and smelled that workshop smell of oil, and sawdust, and paint. John Brown knew there was much to be done.

The same insatiable fascination with boats and carpentry that had drawn his father to woodworking now consumed him, despite his disability. Resuming construction on *Meteor*, John Brown learned to work by feel. He trained his hands to precision. As the fourth of nine children, he had always been a servant to his older siblings. Now holding rank, he employed the services of his younger brother, the seventh born, to complete the drafting and serve as his attendant. This was the same brother who'd helped John Brown spin cotton strand into rope and peddle it to merchant ships in Bristol Harbor, the same brother on whom John Brown heaped responsibility without a word of protest. Quiet and intelligent, the nine-year-old Nathanael sat at John Brown's drawing table and dutifully obeyed.

For the next five weeks John Brown and Nathanael worked tirelessly to complete *Meteor*. The older brother taught the younger everything from sharpening saw blades to tempering tools. He taught him to interpret building plans and translate model sections to full-size drawings. And he did this the only way he knew how: with his hands, interpreting form and function by feel. As the boat took shape, Nathanael, following his brother's lead, ran his hands along each section, discovering tiny flaws with the tips of his fingers. He guided John Brown's hands at the lathe. He not only witnessed the transformation of raw materials, he learned how a series of drawings, a web of measured lines on paper, was manifest in something three-dimensional. John Brown's laconic minion discovered a language through which he could express himself. Like a young musician who discovers perfect pitch or scholar with photographic memory, Nathanael had, within those few weeks, learned he could see and feel and almost taste a design. Even John Brown realized that his serious little brother, too short to reach the slanted drafting table but explaining blueprints with pinpoint accuracy, had an uncanny gift.

Launched in July, *Meteor*, a white V-hulled lapstrake skiff, looked sleek. With John Brown trimming the sheet and Nathanael at the helm, the brothers sailed from Bristol Harbor to Sandy Point on Prudence Island's eastern shore and back, roughly seven miles. *Meteor* proved extremely fast. Following John Brown's directions and answering his questions, Nathanael described the sail's influence on his ability to steer. With each puff of wind, the tiny boat heeled to her leeward rail. John Brown, feeling the leading edge of the puffs wash over his face, anticipated the movements, bracing himself, while calmly talking to his brother. With each burst of wind, the tiny boat heeled, and Nathanael, sitting to windward with both hands on the tiller, described how it pulled. *Meteor* pleaded with her young helmsman to steer into the wind, but Nathanael defied the inclination. At Sandy Point, Nathanael bore off, steering toward home, John Brown paying out the sheet as *Meteor* tore an arcing swath of a wake. Nathanael guided *Meteor* past Hog Island and, with their father Charles eagerly waiting, to the dock on the eastern shore of Bristol Harbor. With the boat's motion and his brother's feedback, John Brown determined *Meteor* had a heavy helm, meaning the shape of the hull and sail plan made steering difficult. *Meteor* was a good boat. She was fast and beautiful, but John Brown, taking Nathanael's arm in the crook of his elbow, told him next time they'd do better.

By the summer of 1857 trade in Bristol had slowed dramatically. In less than thirty years, the colonial seaport village had witnessed its harbor, once teeming with over a hundred privately owned merchant freighters, slave ships, and coastal schooners, practically abandoned with the rise of the whaling industry. Although a few whaling ships had been built and rigged there beginning in 1825, Boston, New Bedford, and Nantucket had eclipsed Bristol's presence as a maritime hub. Twenty miles south of Providence and equidistant to Newport, Bristol, a lobster claw-shaped peninsula on the eastern edge of Narragansett Bay, nevertheless turned out sixty vessels between 1830 and 1856. But as some of the town's wealthiest benefactors began shifting capital from shipping to textile mills for cotton production and with a quickly expanding network of railroads making ground transportation between Boston and New York economically viable, ship building all but ground to a halt.

Originally part of the Plymouth colony, Bristol was named because it was hoped the town, like its English namesake, would become a notable seaport. Before the Mayflower Pilgrims landed in Plymouth, Massasoit, the sachem or chief of the Wampanoag, ruled the land. Although he and his people often moved from place to place, following food, one of his villages was located on the slope of Mount Hope, the easternmost point of what would become the town. Massasoit was a great friend of the colonists, and after his death, his first son Wamsutta followed this amiable compact.

In 1675, however, Massasoit's second son, Philip, waged war on the colonists, fighting head to head with forces of Captain Benjamin Church, considered at the time to be one of the greatest Indian fighters on the continent. For a year Church's forces overran the Wampanoag, and although Philip had organized a massive revolt, traveling from tribe to tribe, rallying their warriors for the cause, they were ill equipped to battle English firepower and disease. On August 12, 1676, at Mount Hope, a gently sloping hill on the shores of Narragansett Bay, King Philip made his last stand. And there he was shot and killed.

Although half the English settlements in the Plymouth and Massachusetts Bay colonies had been attacked during the fourteen-month campaign, the spoils of war afforded the Plymouth Colony nearly seven thousand acres in the area surrounding Mount Hope. Within four years the colony unloaded the land to four Boston investors, John Walley, Nathaniel Byfield, Stephen Burton, and Nathaniel Oliver, for fifteen cents an acre. The quartet, registering the title on September 24, 1680, touted their new town of Bristol as the colony's seaport to the west, a sister to Boston. Hoping their fledgling village would one day become as prosperous as the English slaving port, Byfield, Burton, and Walley (Oliver sold his share within a year to a sailor named Nathan Hayman) settled the land and set out to organize and market their makeshift burg to other settlers of Plymouth Colony.

Byfield soon built a farmhouse overlooking Bristol Harbor on a peninsula called Poppasquash, a corruption of Papoose-squaw, meaning a place where Indian women and children hid during times of war. He then built a second home in town. Oxford-educated and the richest of the landowners, Byfield became Bristol's de facto mayor. He dictated, top-down, what he wanted in his new town. He mandated the streets be laid at 90-degree angles, that a town commons be built and maintained, and that all houses be two stories tall, with no less than two rooms on a floor. Byfield had a clear-cut vision for Bristol. It would be aesthetically pleasing, neat and orderly, and above all prosperous. He set four roads parallel with the harbor, and another nine evenly spaced, crossing them, and running to the water's edge. Although the three town proprietors divided the best lots among themselves, they offered a free in-town house lot and ten acres of backland to the first sixty settlers.[1] With an offer of free property, the town filled quickly and the newcomers built roads and cleared fields. Trees—thousands of them—were felled and used for building docks, houses, and firewood.

With its roads still in a fledgling state, Bristol relied on its large, sheltered harbor, which quickly became an important coastal trading seaport in Narragansett Bay. Deacon Woodbury built the first shipyard at the head of the harbor and Byfield commissioned its first ship, appropriately named *Bristol Merchant*. By 1686 *Bristol Merchant* was making runs to the Guianas, shipping Bristol red onions and Narragansett Pacers, a breed of horses lauded for its steady, arrow-straight gate, and returning with molasses and mahogany. Byfield's involvement in maritime trade soon grew, and Bristol's waterfront expanded. By 1690 Bristol citizens owned fifteen vessels engaged in foreign commerce.[2]

Bristol became a popular point of trade for small coastal packets and a haven for local fishing vessels. But as more money flowed into the town, larger ships followed. When King George's War broke out in 1744, Bristol sailors, including Simeon Potter and his business partner and brother-in-law, Mark Anthony DeWolf, sought their fortunes privateering: the seizing, by force, of enemy vessels by government authority. This was an incredibly lucrative business, considering at the time a 300-ton ship without cargo could fetch upward of $100,000.[3] In the name of King George II, DeWolf and Potter, pillaging the vessels of Spain and France, became rich men and firmly established a Bristol tradition.

But by 1746 the political climate had shifted. Bristol officially became part of Rhode Island, forming a more continuous municipal link between Providence and Newport. A considerably more liberal colony founded by Roger Williams in 1636, Rhode Island was a haven for those fleeing the Bay Colony's protracted puritan bureaucracy. The state was small, and lacking the funds and political connections with Europe that Massachusetts had, cash became its principal motivator. And as tensions rose between the American Colonies and Britain, even

Potter and DeWolf's allegiance followed the buck. In the twenty years leading up to the American Revolution, 123 privately armed ships hailed from Rhode Island ports.[4] The infamous Bristol privateers owned their fair share. Financially, they were making a killing, and with war looming, British ships became fair game.

With the burning of the eight-gunned British schooner *Gaspee* on June 8, 1772, in Narragansett Bay, Rhode Island played host to arguably the first armed conflict of the American Revolution. Simeon Potter and a gang from Bristol helped light the fire. John Brown of Providence led the assault. Brown's actions made him a hero, but it was his unflappable mien in the face of impropriety that made him one of Rhode Island's wealthiest merchants. He owned privateers and slave ships, and despite the Quaker influence of his younger brother, Moses Brown, he firmly believed his business as legitimate as any. A principal owner of the Hope Furnace Company in Cranston, Rhode Island, which manufactured cannons for the Continental Army, John Brown was said to be a patriotic supporter of the fight for American independence. He had the foresight to purchase large shipments of gunpowder before the Revolution began, selling it to the army when it was needed. His involvement earned him the regard of George Washington, who presented John Brown portraits of himself and Martha. While Moses Brown was influential with respect to Rhode Island education, founding the Friend's New England Boarding School (later renamed the Moses Brown School), he was also a successful banker and businessman, financing Samuel Slater, who used his knowledge of British textile production to establish the first water-driven mills in America.

The Browns were rich and influential, but their businesses were only as successful as the men they hired to run them. Moses Brown found the genius Slater, who smuggled intricate mechanical plans by memory and re-created them on a river in Pawtucket, Rhode Island, launching the American Industrial Revolution. In 1793, three years after Rhode Island ratified the Constitution, John Brown met another young hopeful who had traveled from New York to discuss the importing business. He was bright, energetic, and well-spoken. John Brown liked him immediately, inviting him to his large brick mansion on the corner of Power and Benefit streets in Providence.

Karl Freiderich Herrschhoff II was tall and broad shouldered and had been raised in the court of Frederick the Great of Prussia. He could tell a story, sing well, played the flute, and could speak seven languages. And although his business propositions for John Brown fell by the wayside, his overwhelming charm caught the eye of John Brown's second daughter Sarah, who was also a musician. For nine years he made trips from New York to Providence, traveling by coach. In John Brown's home, Karl and Sarah played music together. Karl Freiderich proposed marriage but met with hesitation from her father, who saw the marriage of his daughter to this unknown charmer a rather risky gamble. He was a great entertainer but not a suitable son-in-law. The young Herrschhoff had no family or fortune to speak of. His mother, Agnes Muller, had died soon after he was born, and his father, Karl Freiderich, stricken with grief, wandered into the mountains of northern Italy never to be seen again. Rumored to be an illegitimate son of Frederick the Great, Karl Freiderich Jr. was placed in the care of a professor in Potsdam. The Prussian king then arranged for the boy's education in Dessau. When the monarch died in 1787, Karl Freiderich left to seek his fortune.

Although highly educated and able to command a room, Karl Freiderich's business sense had not led him to any exceptional income, making John Brown even more hesitant. But over time John Brown softened, and on July 2, 1801, Karl Freiderich and Sarah were married in the drawing room of the Power Street house.

The newly married couple soon settled on Point Pleasant Farm on Poppasquash Point in Bristol, the original country estate of Nathaniel Byfield, built in 1680. One of John Brown's several country estates, the house and land had been confiscated from an American Tory during the Revolution and granted to John Brown for money he had given the federal government to help finance the war. The house had two stories with a large fieldstone fireplace, beamed ceilings, and sloping floors— the kind that gave a home character and charm—and was considered, even at the turn of the eighteenth century, a venerable antique. The house had sheltered Rochambeau's soldiers during the Revolution, some of whom were buried on the grounds. The beach sand-dusted walkways were lined with tufts of purple and pink mayflowers, yellow goldenrod, and bushes of elderberries and huckleberry. A veranda on the east side of the house overlooked Bristol Harbor and downtown.

With understated elegance, the house blended perfectly with its sur-
roundings, exuding refined taste without opulence. From the far side
of the harbor, its roof flowed seamlessly with the tree line.

Around this same time Karl Freiderich simplified his name to Carl
Herreshoff, and settled in to the role of master of his manner. John
Brown's intuition had been correct: although Herreshoff could dazzle
a room with the parlance of a prince, he was a dandy, more fixated on
sumptuous clothing and fine wine than earning a living. By the time
Sarah had the last of their six children—Anna, Sarah, John Brown,
Agnes, Charles Frederick, and James Brown (who died in infancy)—
her husband's indolence had tempered her dedication with resent-
ment. She likely felt he was robbing her family of a future, a
sentiment her father and his brother no doubt shared. Eventually he
tried farming, raising sheep, and mining in the Adirondacks, but they
all failed. During the spring of 1819, he climbed Thendara Hill near
his Adirondack mine and shot himself in the head.

As a member of the House of Representatives, John Brown stood up
in Congress in 1800 to oppose the passage of an act that would ban
the slave trade. His argument that England should not be allowed to
reap all the profits fell on deaf ears. By 1808 slave importation to the
United States was illegal. Although trading Africans was still rampant,
most New England merchants had diversified. Boston and
Providence were profiting in the China Trade. Salem had developed
strong ties with the East Indies. Nantucket and New Bedford had
cornered the market for whale oil. With a relatively shallow harbor
surrounded by dirt roads and forest, Bristol lacked the infrastructure to
distribute large consignments. But as America entered the War of 1812,
Bristol, with its fast and vast fleet of privateers, seized the opportunity
to make money.

Again, the DeWolfs became Bristol's principal employer.
James DeWolf's 120-foot brigantine *Yankee* took more prizes than any
other American privateer in history and destroyed nearly one million
pounds sterling of British property, bringing in over a million dollars
into Bristol.[5] After the war, however, the tiny port town foundered.
Privateer captains who had once commanded 200 men, earning fan-
tastic wages, now clerked in Bristol's chandleries. Marines who'd lived
a swashbuckling existence were now earning paltry wages hauling

cheese, candles, and soap. The freewheeling days of the *Yankee* were over, and Bristol felt the loss.

Determined to capitalize on his dormant fleet, George DeWolf continued to support various slavers and privateers. With the rest of Bristol commerce waning, the town invested heavily in his highly lucrative ventures. But in 1825, he failed to deliver a cargo of Cuban sugar in which the town had invested heavily. When word came, the DeWolfs left that night. The next day Bristol collapsed. Entire families, destitute and with no other choice, fled west, joining the migration that so many others had taken from New England towns. The DeWolf descendants wouldn't return for twenty years. Eventually, one would marry a Herreshoff.

Though destitute, Bristol was flanked to the west by the islands called Prudence and Patience and to the east, a peninsula on top of which sat a small mountain called Hope. If geographical features alone could shift the karma of a town swaged to a legacy of impropriety, it did. Alone with her five children on Poppasquash Point, her husband having squandered their savings and taken his life, Sarah Brown Herreshoff made do with what she had. The once trimmed hedges burst into bittersweet-choked snarls; the manicured lawns had gone to seed. Though money was tight, Sarah had invested wisely during the War of 1812 and had earned enough to maintain her modest yet upper-class lifestyle.

Now financially firm, Sarah provided the best for her children, taking it upon herself to teach them reading, mathematics, and music. Her fifth child, Charles Frederick, although not particularly drawn to his studies, preferring to roam the forested Indian trail connecting Poppasquash Neck with town, proved himself an apt pupil.

Fascinated by the docks, sailors, and bustle of the waterfront, Charles Frederick learned the ways of the harbor. It was a commonplace competition in Bristol to race to the top of a ship's rigging, the first one placing his cap atop the topmast the winner. He quickly learned how boats were rigged, how sailors spoke, and the way a boat responded under sail and oar. At twelve years old he built his own small sailing skiff, exhibiting a mechanical gift beyond his age. This gregarious curiosity combined with an academically disciplined upbringing eventually earned him entry to Brown University when he was fifteen.

There's no doubt family ties also had a prominent role in his acceptance. John Brown and his brother, Moses, had been instrumental in moving Rhode Island College from Warren to Providence, where on May 14, 1770, John Brown laid the cornerstone of University Hall. In 1795 the struggling school announced it would grant whoever donated six thousand dollars the privilege of renaming it. When no one stepped in, they lowered the ante to five thousand in 1803. A year later, Nicholas Brown, Jr., John Brown's nephew and Charles Frederick's second cousin, donated the sum and the name was changed to Brown University.

Charles Frederick had been at school one year when the DeWolfs fled Bristol, leaving the town in a state of panic. He nevertheless finished at Brown, graduating with the Class of 1828, and then returned to Point Pleasant Farm, where, resting on the good fortunes of his mother's investments and his late grandmother's windfall, he spent his time farming onions and beets and converting former slave quarters, a brick outbuilding on the Poppasquash estate, into a woodworking shop. He was a rugged young man with thick wavy blond hair, broad shoulders, and a chiseled profile. He had a penchant for working with his hands and spent his days repairing the house and grounds that had gone into disrepair. It was more a hobby than a profession, something that gave him tangible purpose, but he enjoyed it nonetheless. He tended to his small garden and even sold the small batches of onions to exporters. He quenched his boyhood curiosity with boats by building skiffs in his workshop, often visiting town to talk shop with merchant sailors and local craftsmen. On one of these excursions he met Julia Ann Lewis, the daughter of the wealthy merchant sea captain Joseph Warren Lewis of Boston who summered in Bristol with his family.

Thin with high cheekbones and long blond hair, Julia Ann was striking and a gifted musician to boot. She always traveled with her harpsichord and could play well. Charles Frederick was smitten, and the two hit it off famously. With the consent of both families they were married on May 15, 1833, in Boston and soon after moved to Point Pleasant Farm. A year later they had their first child, who they graciously named James Brown, after Charles's uncle, custodian of the Brown family fortune.

During the next twenty years Charles Frederick and Julia Ann had nine children. Two years after James Brown came Caroline Louisa, and two years after that Charles Frederick. In 1841 came John Brown and three years later Lewis. A year later in 1845 Sally Brown was born. Three years later in 1848 came Nathanael Greene followed by John Brown Francis in 1850. And finally in 1854 Julian was born. Living a charmed existence with ample funds to support the family, Charles Frederick continued to spend most of his time dabbling in carpentry. Although he never worked, he didn't have the frivolous spending habits of his father and dressed simply. He was wealthy, but that he worked with his hands—even if it was for his amusement—earned him the townsfolk's respect.

He enjoyed improving upon the designs of common tools. He built a mowing machine and a rotating stovetop, which allowed pots to be rotated over the fire when necessary. He built swinging fence gates and frames for harrows. He tinkered and fiddled with anything he thought needed improving. But it was his boats that garnered the bulk of his attention and even turned a few heads in the harbor. The year he and Julia Ann were married, Charles Frederick built a twenty-three-foot, gaff-rigged catboat, which he named *Julia,* after her. He felt a part of Bristol's and his family's seafaring tradition. With a large cockpit and small forward cabin, *Julia* held his growing family as they sailed around Narragansett Bay, visiting the summer estates of friends and relatives in nearby towns.

Although his eldest son expressed interest, Charles's love for boats was most strongly embraced by his second eldest son, John Brown, who even at a young age took a liking to all things nautical, including the traditions. Charles demanded that shoes were clean and their soles properly fastened, lest a loose nail scratched the varnish. Washing hands before furling sails was compulsory. Having sailed transatlantic passages with her father, who owned more than eighty packets making frequent trips between Boston and England, Julia Ann also had a keen eye for sailing vessels. Both she and Charles were well versed in nautical terminology and they spoke it freely and frequently. Like learning a foreign tongue, their children, at a very young age, absorbed this nautical lexicon, the motion of a well-balanced boat, the eye for detail, the rules of seamanship, and the sense of excitement, power, and absolute freedom that results from the simple act of filling sails with wind.

It was in 1848 that their seventh child Nathanael Greene Herreshoff was born. He was named after General Nathanael Greene, second in command to George Washington during the Revolution. The General was a friend of John Brown's, and the families had remained close. In fact, Charles often sailed with his family aboard *Julia* six miles south to visit the late General's estate on the western shore of the island then known as Rhode Island (now called Aquidneck Island). Like his six older brothers and sisters, Nathanael began his childhood on the Point Pleasant estate on Poppasquash Point. But unlike the rest of his family, he was quiet and introspective. He had dark hair and dark eyes and carried a thin, frail frame. He was intense and restless even at a very young age. As a small boy, one summer night, as the tale is told, he climbed out of bed and walked down to the shore, where he nestled in the sand and fell asleep only to awake to the incoming tide. Although Nat was filled with an independent spirit, freedom was hard to find in a house filled with so many siblings. Being so small and frail his older brothers kept him tight by their side. Eager to please them, he bowed to their wishes. When John Brown built a ropewalk, Nat spent hours spinning the wheels, twisting yarns. When John Brown began to build his first boat, he conscripted Nat.

In 1856, the same year John Brown began *Meteor,* Charles moved the family from Point Pleasant to a house in town at 142 Hope Street. Shaded by two giant oaks in the front yard, the colonial clapboard house was surrounded by a white picket fence, its front door framed by four shuttered windows and a wooden porch with slatted railings. Elegant in its simplicity and larger than it looked from the main road, the house wrapped around to a wing of children's bedrooms, at the end of which was an old summer kitchen that they converted into a workshop. After hauling the unfinished *Meteor* to the new house, John Brown went blind. By spring his father had convinced him to return to work. He ordered Nat to help. Although trapped, beholden to a boy nearly twice his age, Nat couldn't deny his brother. He was blind, alone, and unable to see the one thing that mattered to him. Nat never sulked. He simply obeyed. Each day after finishing school, he walked home, took his older brother by the elbow, and went to the workshop.

THE WORLD OF WORK AND WAR

July 1844–Spring 1874

By the middle of the nineteenth century Bristol, like the rest of America, was experiencing the tribulations of rapid change. The Panic of 1837, a severe depression lasting until 1843, left the republic exasperated and questioning its teetering economic system, which had inched precariously close to total collapse. But with President Martin Van Buren's establishment of a federal reserve, the economy clawed back and by the mid-1840s, with John Tyler (1841 to 1845) and subsequently James Polk (1845 to 1849) holding the presidential office, the economy rebounded. Cyrus McCormick patented and distributed his grain reaper; the cast-iron stove replaced fireplace cooking; and by 1845 roughly eight thousand miles of railroad linked coastal cities with the burgeoning American interior. Fifty-two transatlantic packets maintained scheduled runs between America's major ports—New York, Boston, Savannah, New Orleans, and Charleston—and Europe. Steamships had also made their debut, but with boiler and paddlewheel technology still in its infancy, the American clipper ship took center stage. The fast, heavily canvased sailing vessels not only dramatically increased the speed of oceangoing commerce, but they also established America as a major naval power. That power, and perhaps hubris, prompted President Polk on May 13, 1846, to declare war on Mexico. By 1848, the year Nat was born, Mexico had ceded California, the Texas lands north of the Rio Grande, and New Mexico (now, Arizona, Nevada, Texas, Utah, and part of Colorado).[1] In less than three years, the United States had grown by more than a million square miles.

It was during this period of expansion and economic growth that on July 30, 1844, industrialist John Cox Stevens and seven friends formed a club in the main saloon of his schooner *Gimrack*. By 1850 the New York Yacht Club was small but firmly established, and Stevens, as principal founder, was named commodore. That year he commissioned the construction of a yacht he believed would reflect the progress made during the American Industrial Revolution. He planned to show the yacht at England's Great Exhibition of 1851, an international fair billed by Prince Albert, Queen Victoria's husband, as a celebration of science, art, and industry to be held in London's Crystal Palace. That spring while his yacht lay in frame at the shipyard of William H. Brown on the East River end of 12th Street in Manhattan, Stevens received a letter of invitation from Thomas Grosvenor Egerton, second Earl of Wilton and commodore of the Royal Yacht Squadron in England.

Stevens wrote back, indicating he would "offer to convey to the gentlemen of the Royal Yacht Squadron, and to yourself, the expression of our warmest thanks for your invitation to visit the Club House at Cowes," indicating that he would "take with good grace the sound thrashing we are likely to get by venturing our longshore craft on your rough waters." Although the Earl of Wilton had not directly challenged the Americans to a race, Stevens was eager to test his new yacht.

Christened *America,* the yacht arrived in Cowes on southern England's Isle of Wight, approximately seventy-five miles south of London, to a congested harbor filled with small coastal fishing boats, square-rigged merchant ships, private yachts, and steamers. The excitement of the upcoming Great Exhibition and *America*'s arrival permeated the village. In dark, woody waterfront pubs, sail lofts, and the well-groomed patios of the Royal Yacht Squadron's clubhouse, a castle at the mouth of the harbor, conversation revolved around Stevens's 102-foot gaff-rigged schooner.

With two swept-back masts and low-to-the-water rails, which gave it a sleek profile, *America* resembled nothing in English waters. Crowds lined the shore and small boats sailed or rowed across the harbor for a closer look. *America*'s racy appearance piqued curiosity, but it was Stevens's challenge to race any yacht in the British Fleet that set the throngs murmuring. In a time when the United States was just starting to assert itself as a fully independent nation, one flourishing in the wake of its industrial boom, a challenge to England, the nation with the most established and powerful maritime tradition in the world, had weighty implications.

Most of the world's commerce still depended on wind power. The whaling industry was at its apex, and the United States and its whalers from New Bedford and Nantucket had so far dominated the trade in all corners of the globe. Ground fishing had just begun its transformation from a localized inshore, small-scale industry into an international offshore business, with square-rigged ships sailing clear across the Atlantic in search of cod. With some of the richest fishing grounds in the Atlantic, namely George's Bank off of Cape Cod and Grand Banks off Newfoundland, the United States had, because of its proximity, asserted itself a world maritime leader. When it came to speed, the U.S.-designed clippers, were unparalleled.

But British experience and tradition went a long way. The Royal Navy and Merchant Marine were still the largest in the world. And yachting, the sport of royalty, the game of kings and princes, dukes and earls, had never been legitimately contested outside of Europe.

Confident in *America*'s speed and intent on finding a sparring partner, Stevens wagered a staggering £10,000—enough to build the equivalent of two *Americas*—to any yacht of any size that would race him. But no one would bite. The *Times of London* compared the English yachtsmen with a flock of panic-stricken birds: "Most of us have seen the agitation which the appearance of a sparrow hawk in the horizon creates among a flock of wood pigeons or skylarks . . . they all at once come down to the ground and are rendered almost motionless by fear of the disagreeable visitor."[2] With her competition stock-still and huddled, *America* and her owner's wager loomed quietly on the horizon.

By August, with still no one to accept his challenge and with the invitation of the Earl of Wilton, Stevens entered *America* into the Royal Yacht Squadron's fifty-three-mile annual race around the Isle of Wight for the Hundred Sovereign Cup. Because of the Great Exhibition, the Earl opened the competition to non-British vessels. *America* was the only foreign yacht to accept. On August 22, 1851, with fifteen vessels ranging from the 47-ton cutter *Aurora* to the 392-ton *Brilliant, America,* weighing in at 171 tons, started the race late when her anchor fowled as the starting gun fired. But *America* slowly gained on the fleet, her sails, made of tightly woven American cotton, allowing her to sail closer to the wind and considerably faster. Just after the sun set over the Solent and with the towering white cliffs of the Needles off their stern and to starboard, *America* crossed the finish line at 8:37 P.M. to a barrage of cannons and fireworks. *America* had won the Hundred Sovereign Cup, a gaudy two-foot silver ewer, which from then on would assume the foreign winner's name, *America*'s Cup.

The Cup, which had once been one of the Royal Yacht Squadron's coveted prizes, spent the next five years tarnishing in Stevens's closet.

Saved from being tossed out by his butler, it was later handed over to the New York Yacht Club, which by now had become more established. They considered melting it into commemorative coins, but then demurred and instead canonized the ewer into a perpetual trophy. In 1857 the New York Yacht Club wrote what it called, a "Deed of Gift," a 250-word document inviting all foreign recognized yacht clubs to compete for the Cup. Subsequently modified, the Deed of Gift also prescribed the rules for future Cup challenges.

As the New York Yacht Club matured a new class of young entrepreneurs earned their fortunes. Some looked west, and others turned to international sea trade. As markets in China, Europe, South America, and the American West Coast expanded, so too did the demand for larger vessels over 100 feet long and 400 tons. Before 1830, smaller vessels were built by groups of local workers in makeshift yards, and these boats were built to the length and draft their harbors could handle. But as tonnage requirements increased, ship construction became concentrated in larger ports in organized yards using sophisticated machinery.[3] Between 1830 and 1856 roughly sixty ships were built in Bristol. After 1856 the harbor fell dormant.

It was during this period of commercial lassitude that Nat and John sailed *Meteor* around a quiet Bristol Harbor. Growing accustomed to his disabilities and with his brother at his beck and call, John honed his woodworking skills. In 1859 Charles Frederick purchased a dilapidated shed perched on the stone wharf across the street from their home. The building had been an old tannery that had once produced saddles, harnesses, and breeches and had presented itself at an irresistible price.

The boys installed three new lathes and an assortment of tools purchased with their father's help. Each morning, John and Nat crossed Hope Street, a rutted dirt road snaking around the harbor's edge, and went to work. Opening the waterfront barn doors, the small workshop flooded with light. An 1864 painting by their neighbor Charles DeWolfe Brownell shows a simple single-pitched roof resting atop clapboard walls. Launching rails descend from the shop's main doors. Although the rails were added later, the painting shows the shop, partially shaded by a willow and two elms, as it looked when they first moved in. Nat noted:

The building was about 32 feet by 55 feet with low studding and the upper floor, at or near the plates, and a barn pitch roof above that, having roof sash in [the] middle part, and a window (or door) at each end. The floor was supported from the roof, so [the] lower part was clean of posts. The roadway leading to [the] wharf had quite a grade, so the floor at mid-length was even with it and much below near the east end.[4]

The first thing John Brown built was a walking stick notched with measurements. He became adept at determining an object's dimensions by quickly laying the stick alongside or by rocking it carefully around the length of a curve. The stick served him well, but his brother's surrogate eyes were better. Nat obeyed John Brown's orders. When the elder had ideas, Nat executed them. Day after day, they trudged, arm in arm, through the swinging gate of the picket fence, across Hope Street, and to the workshop. "At the age of nine years I began to be my brother's companion to lead him about," Nat recalled, "or I should more properly say to be dragged about."[5]

Trapped in darkness, John Brown assuaged his frustration by working, keeping young Nat in the workshop for long hours. "I was only a light puny boy," Nat wrote later in life, "and it was a tough job for me and real brutal at times, for John had a violent temper when things did not go right. However, with this training I learned to do many things that were very useful while others of my age were playing games. I not only became quite skillful in small boats, but learned to use small tools . . . and at 10 could temper all small tools, [such] as drills—taps & dies, for they had to be made in those days."[6]

Although apprenticed to a master still learning his trade, Nat felt at home in the shop. He quickly learned to draft designs on paper. He was empirical and exact, or at least his brother made him that way. Although John Brown had proved himself an architect with god-given talent—enough to visualize the myriad components of a boat without seeing them—he knew his younger brother had the same gift with the advantage of sight. Nat was a ten-year-old with an innate sense of trigonometry and calculus. John Brown could only marvel when he ordered his brother to execute a complex computation, and the young wiz spit out answers. For Nat, taking measurements from a model and scaling them up to size, a process called laying down the lines, was a natural exercise for his meticulous mind. He easily visualized how a boat's individual parts functioned as part of a whole. Perhaps the heavy helm on *Meteor*'s maiden voyage could be fixed by moving the mast aft an inch or two. Or perhaps they could add more area to the keel.

Making a few minor changes to *Meteor*, John Brown and Nat entered a number of races in Bristol Harbor and beat every boat of comparable size. In the fall of 1859 John Brown, lying awake at night, devised the plans for a new, bigger boat. In the workshop, he conveyed his thoughts to Nat, describing each piece, its length, breadth, and how it would fit into the web of lines that would become *Sprite*. At eleven years old, Nat, an experienced draftsman and now accustomed to his brother's work style, could quickly sketch drawings as his brother impatiently rattled off ideas. "I had the job of getting sections from the model and of tabulating expanded measurements for the moulds," wrote Nat, "also making drawings for [a] sail plan."[7]

Their father Charles had helped shape this boatbuilding team, providing the tools, equipment, and raw materials. Although these three had forged an intimate working relationship, Nat was also very close with his mother. He obeyed her every wish and often confided in her. In front of his brother and father, Nat was serious and high strung. With his mother he was sensitive and hinted vulnerability. He could open up to her. Perhaps she was the only one who thought of him as a child and treated him as one. She had compassion, and perhaps he desperately needed someone to whom he could vent his frustrations.

John Brown, Nat, and their father worked tirelessly throughout the winter and spring on *Sprite*, and on June 28, 1860, she slid into Bristol Harbor. Twenty feet long with a nine-foot beam, "*Sprite*," as Nat described her in his diary, "was very fast, and easily the fastest sailer in the Bay. But she was a brute to steer, due principally to the very long boom, wide and weak rudder."[8] A few weeks later, taking on a few friends for crew, they sailed *Sprite* and *Julia* to New York to see the new steamship *Great Eastern*, a 22,500-ton British behemoth—the largest in the world—that had just finished her maiden voyage from Southampton. That Charles was willing to make a special trip to see this ship showed his mounting enthusiasm for the art of naval architecture. Two of his boys, the most nautically inclined of the clan, had embraced the pilgrimage with the same conviction, and with the successful voyage of *Sprite* their confidence grew. By this time, their tinkering shed had come to look like that of a true boatbuilding shop. A photo from this time shows timber stacked on the stone wharf, a small rowing skiff propped on blocks. The main door of the shed swings up, like a rabbit trap, propped open with a block and tackle used to lower the door closed each night.

In 1861 the Civil War began. Being of a prominent family, Nat's oldest brothers, James and Charles Frederick, circumvented conscription. Nat's older brother, Lewis, was born blind, so he and John Brown were exempt. At twelve years old, Nat's only exposure to the war was through his fellow townspeople, the town record showing 305 who served.[9] The most famous was General Ambrose E. Burnside, whose prodigious tufts of facial hair became fashionable, earning the name "side burns." Burnside marched 120,000 Union soldiers into the hills outside of Fredericksburg, Virginia, and in a reckless frontal assault of Lee's stronghold, led 9,000 men to their deaths. A Union soldier reported northern troops seemed to "melt . . . like snow coming down on warm ground."[10] Burnside secured infamy when his Bristol-based rifle company produced a large consignment of shoddily built guns, notorious for blowing off fingers. With the war raging and the price of everything from nails to coffee skyrocketing, the harbor grew eerily dormant. Not a single boat was built in Bristol until 1863, when the Herreshoff brothers turned their hobby into a trade.

After launching *Sprite,* which consistently proved fast on the racecourse, John Brown began building small rowing and sailing skiffs on spec, his father helping with the hull designs, his brother with the rig and sail plans. The boats sold quickly although they built them slowly, for their family workforce was small. In 1863 John Brown, now age twenty-two, hired a few local workers to help fill mounting orders. But with the businesses barely turning a profit, he took on Dexter Stone as a partner in 1864, much to Nat's disliking. With the partnership, however, came an infusion of capital, allowing them to buy the old Burnside Rifle factory next door. A year later they lengthened the tannery and built their own mill, allowing them to cut lumber specific to their needs. "These gentlemen carry on the business of yacht and boat building on a scale probably unequalled in this country," wrote the *New York Tribune* in April 1866, "conducting on their own premises, nearly every operation necessary to convert the raw materials—wood and iron—into boats. . . . In their blacksmith shop, block shop, spar-yard, and rigging loft, the various adjuncts of the vessels are turned out so that their establishment is almost a miniature navy yard."[11] In a short time Herreshoff and Stone had built a name for themselves, but in doing so, alienated Nat. Adamantly opposed to Stone joining the business and largely ignored by his brother, the brooding fifteen-year-old retreated into his own projects.

In the corner of the shop, he began experimenting with steam. He spent long hours alone, designing and machining parts, and he ultimately built a small rotary engine. He then designed and built *Violet*, a twenty-five-foot, gaff-rigged sloop. It was the first boat he'd designed completely on his own. Nat had a clear vision of what he thought a sailboat should be. But whether he knew it or not, he built it the only way he knew how—by feel, as his brother had taught him. He built a model that felt right in his hands and then scaled it up.

The yacht sailed well, but when he lined up *Violet* with his father's latest *Julia* he was sorely beaten. Upon reaching the dock, he stormed into the workshop, pulled out *Violet*'s model, and, pulling the hatchet from its mounts above the workbench, hacked it to pieces. Incensed, he vented to his father that by destroying the model no one could ever build another failure like it. To his father, the fury mounting in young Nat was alarming.

Nat had attended public elementary school in Bristol and had continued on through high school, from 1861 to 1865, working with his brother every free moment. By the time John Brown had partnered with Stone, Nat was fed up. He had forgone the freedom of youth to serve his brother. He had held the crook of his arm countless times and guided his hands at the lathe. Fortunately for them, Herreshoff & Stone Yacht and Boat Builders dissolved after two years, and Stone left the business in 1866. Still disgruntled and with the Civil War having ended, Nat decided to leave Bristol and Rhode Island, forgoing his family's legacy at Brown and attending the Massachusetts Institute of Technology in Boston to study mechanical engineering. Alone, John Brown, with his father's help, continued building skiffs and rowboats in the shed across the street.

James Brown Herreshoff, Nat's eldest brother by fourteen years, was becoming rich as an engineer. As a teenager on Point Pleasant, James had been the outgoing one of the bunch, leading Nat, John Brown, and Lewis, on excursions down the Poppasquash Indian trails. Even as a young boy, he experimented with windmills, a number of his designs sprouting up around the farm. With the same intuitive sense of mechanical engineering that boiled in his brothers' blood, he later developed a tension regulator for sewing machines. After graduating from Brown University in 1853, James took a job at the Rumford Chemical Works, where among other things he developed between 1855 and 1862 Horseford's Substitute Cream of Tartar, which later became known as baking powder. Although Rumford Chemical Works maintained patents on many of his achievements, he maintained rights to his baking powder, making him a wealthy man.

James invested his earnings into the fish oil business, harvesting and rendering into oil the teeming schools of menhaden, known as pogies, that poured into Narragansett Bay each summer. After learning the art of manufacturing, he diversified into paints and toothpaste. Reaping substantial profits, James gave John Brown money to expand his boat-building business, which until that point, though earning local praise, was barely making ends meet. The Herreshoff skiffs were lauded for their graceful designs and durability, but with most of the country slogging through post-war slump, money was tight. John Brown needed to diversify and it was exceedingly evident that he needed Nat to do it.

After entering a mechanical engineering course of study at MIT, Nat plodded through his work. He was a nonmatriculated "special student" attending courses in physics, chemistry, and mathematics. Although he had far more hands-on experience than his fellow students, Nat's academic contributions were middling at best. He did, however, gain the attention of his professors when during an analytic geometry class he described a certain curve he'd used in designing his rotary engine. Curious, for curves of this type had yet to be used on engines, the professor asked for a demonstration at the next meeting of the Society of Arts at MIT. Nat had the engine sent up from Bristol and earned a round of applause when he fired it up. While his brother had pushed him aside for a new business partner, the brooding sixteen-year-old had built an engine that impressed some of the most brilliant engineers in America.

In Boston Nat forged ties with the local yachting community. He had earned a name as a skilled helmsman, having won numerous races in southern New England and his designs having become somewhat of a curiosity. He was invited to attend the first formal meeting of the Boston Yacht Club on November 21, 1866, in the Parker House and was asked to develop a rating and measurement system so boats of various sizes, designs, and tonnages could compete against each other in club races. On December 5 he was elected a member. By 1867 he had devised a table of allowances in minutes and seconds per mile. There had been a previous rating system employed in England that left boats largely mismatched. Nat's system, published in the Boston Yacht Club's first club book, would allow twenty-footers to race fairly against fifty-footers. In Nat's system, all boats were timed from the start until they finished. Then each yacht's time and respective rating number (determined by the yacht's size) was plugged into his table. By combining the actual time with a yacht's rating, Herreshoff's table calculated a "corrected" time. The yacht with the fastest corrected time won. The table simply provided a method for comparison. For example, twenty-foot yacht A (the slower boat because of her smaller size) sails swiftly around the course, with flawless crew work, in one hour. Fifty-foot yacht B (the faster boat because of her larger size) sails around the same course with faulty sail trim and sloppy crew work, but because she is a bigger, faster boat, crosses the finish line in only forty minutes. After plugging their elapsed times and rating numbers into Herreshoff's table, the race committee determines the yachts' corrected times. Because yacht A sailed cleanly to her rating potential, she has a faster "corrected" time than yacht B and therefore wins the race.

Although he'd become a rising star in Boston, Nat most likely received pressure from his family to return home. After splitting with Stone, John Brown jumped, perhaps prematurely, into a marriage with Sarah Lucas Kilton of Boston, with whom he had a daughter. Soon after they divorced. Although John Brown had kept the business afloat, he now realized Nat was indispensable. With a job offer at the Corliss Steam Engine Company in Providence, the leading engine manufacturer in the country, Nat left MIT without earning a degree.[12]

He worked as a first-year apprentice at the Corliss Company, drafting plans and overseeing engine installations, their calibration, and final valve adjustments. Although he maintained a room in Providence, after a day's work he often traveled two hours by horse-drawn coach to Bristol, where he would work late into the night and all day Sunday drafting designs for John Brown. During those years, among other designs, Nat drafted plans and oversaw the construction of the steam-driven menhaden trawler *Seven Brothers,* which proved so effective she set the standard on Narragansett Bay. He also quietly toyed with a small thirty-seven-foot sailboat he called *Shadow,* which combined the wide beam of the classic American shape with the deeper draft of the British type. Although Nat's whimsical experiment proved fast, this "compromise model" didn't garner a following. No one, including him, knew that *Shadow* was fifteen years ahead of her time. Seven days a week, Nat hunched over his drawing table, working quietly. Although exhausted, he dutifully carved models and tailored blueprints. "I was," he recalled, "well occupied evenings by making for John all his drawings and many of the models of his craft."[13]

A few years earlier, Henry David Thoreau, touting the transcendentalist message, had taken to the woods near Walden Pond. His prophetic book pitied the harried worker hobbled by the conventions of society. "The mass of men lead lives of quiet desperation," he wrote. "There is no play in them, for this comes after work."[14] By 1874, after working every waking moment for six years, Nat, wallowing in the quiet desperation Thoreau had so aptly described, physically and, as one Herreshoff descendant contends, mentally broke down.

4

THE BUSINESS PLAN

Autumn 1869–January 1878

America's 1851 victory in the race around the Isle of Wight pushed yachting into the public eye. Although racing small centerboard catboats, like Nat and John Brown's *Sprite,* had become popular, larger yachts were rare. Competitive sailing had stopped during the Civil War, but as business recovered so did yachting, and a number of big schooners were built along the Eastern Seaboard. Although the New York Yacht Club had established itself as the hub of competitive big-boat racing, a handful of clubs had formed in the area, including the Brooklyn Yacht Club, Atlantic Yacht Club in Brooklyn, Boston Yacht Club, Eastern Yacht Club of Boston, and Seawanhaka Corinthian Yacht Club on Long Island Sound. Strong competition arose between them, and although by 1876 there was some effort to standardize the various clubs' rating systems and racing rules, many staunchly maintained airs of exclusivity, their members insisting they remain independent.

It wasn't until 1869 that James Ashbury of England wrote a letter to the New York Yacht Club, challenging them to race yachts "of a tonnage not to exceed ten per cent of the Thames measurement (188 tons) of the *Cambria* [his yacht]." A series of letters passed across the Atlantic before the initial challenge was reworked to coincide with the America's Cup Deed of Gift. Ashbury and his American friend James Gordon Bennett, aboard the 123-foot *Dauntless,* raced from Gaunt Head buoy, near Head of Kinsale, Ireland, to the Sandy Hook Lightship (*Cambria* won by 1 hour, 43 minutes), and prepared to race a fleet of American ships, including the keel schooners *Fleetwing, Dauntless, Restless, Rambler, Alarm, Taroltina,* and the centerboarders *Tidal Wave, Silvie, Madgies, Phantom, Madeleine, Idler, Magic, Jessie, Halcyon, Widgeon, Calyps, Josephine, Era, Fleur De Lis, Alice,* and *Palmer.* On August 8, 1870, Ashbury's *Cambria* was sorely beaten, finishing tenth; the 84-foot *Magic* won.

Ashbury took the defeat in stride and was so impressed with the American enthusiasm for yacht racing—an enormous fleet of spectators had turned out to watch—he issued a second challenge for 1871. In doing so, he argued for one concession: that the New York Yacht Club not defend with its entire fleet. His request was honored, but the New Yorkers reserved the right to select a defender from its fleet before each race. This new format was a marked change, and one-on-one "match" racing became standard format. Ashbury ordered a new yacht, the 115-foot, 264-ton *Livonia,* and sailed for America, representing the Royal Harwich Yacht Club.

Livonia lost the first two races to Franklin Osgood's new 107-foot schooner *Columbia.* Chosen for the conditions, James Gordon Bennett's *Dauntless* was scheduled to defend for the third race, but was disabled in a pre-start accident. Once again, *Columbia* stepped in, but this time, her volunteer crew broke down in heavy winds, losing to *Livonia* by more than fifteen minutes. Vice Commodore William L. Douglas's *Sappho* won both the fourth and fifth races, capping a successful defense of the Cup. Although Ashbury filed protests, claiming he'd won on the grounds that *Columbia* had rounded a mark in the wrong direction and that *Livonia* had been shortchanged by a shorter than seven-race series, his objections fell on deaf ears. Silence from the New York Yacht Club prompted a flurry of terse letters, indictments of unsportsmanlike conduct, and a slue of searing articles by the British press. Word spread that the British Navy would be sent to recoup Ashbury's trophy. Although the New York Yacht Club maintained its entitlement to the Cup, the fiery media attention prompted the club to reassess its policy of reserving the right to defend using its entire fleet. The Cup had reached the public eye, had cultured a new and potent strain of nationalism, and raised the pulse of international yachting competition.

While Americans dominated a sport borrowed from British royalty, a young man the same age as Nat from Glasgow, Scotland, resolved to master a game he'd learned in America—the freewheeling world of commerce. He came from humble beginnings, without capital or connections. But he was intelligent and clever and had an insatiable drive to succeed. After four years of traveling and working odd jobs in the United States, he sailed from New York for home, intending to make his mark. After his steamship docked at Glasgow he ordered a horse-cab and on its roof tied the barrel of flour and rocking chair he'd brought for his mother. He asked the driver to roll slowly up the Clyde bank to his parents' small flat so that all could witness his triumphant return. In his pocket, the young man carried the five hundred American dollars (a store clerk's yearly salary) with which he planned to stoke his fortune.

Thomas Johnston Lipton was born in Glasgow in 1848, the son of Irish immigrants who had fled County Monaghan for Scotland during the potato famine. His father was employed in a calico printing mill. His mother managed the house and watched over young Tommy and his older brother and sister, who were both plagued by illness. They were poor, but not destitute. The Lipton's four rooms, as he recalled in later life, were meticulously clean, and Thomas grew up eating home-cooked meals and wearing handmade clothes while his parents scrupulously saved what they could. When Tommy was nine, the year he began school, his nineteen-year-old brother died of consumption.

In 1864 he and his family moved to Crown Street in the Gorbals, the rough side of town, where his parents invested their savings in a small ground-floor grocery store next door. The tiny shop, which could hold no more than a half dozen people at a time, specialized in hams, eggs, and butter shipped from Ireland by a peasant farmer friend of Mrs. Lipton's. The shop did reasonably well and for Tommy was an enormous source of pride. He helped by running errands, making deliveries, and cleaning and polishing the counter and windows. He enjoyed the exchange with customers, stocking shelves, and bartering for supplies.

When picking up shipments for the shop, Tommy developed an interest in the Broomielaw, Glasgow's waterfront. Combing the docks, he took particular delight in asking ships from where they'd traveled. His forthright style was well received by the sailors who regaled him with stories of foreign ports, exotic islands, and that which most piqued his interest, America. He soon purchased a world map, on which he located the various places mentioned in their yarns. There, he marked ports, calculating distances and durations of particular journeys. On many evenings he sat in his room, an oil lamp burning dimly as he pored over the map, dreaming of their stories, memorizing names of cities, rivers, and mountains.

In addition to the commercial vessels, Tommy had a special interest in the sleek sailing yachts that every so often visited the harbor. After studying their towering masts, tidy decks, and gleaming varnish, he set out to fashion a small replica, a working model that he could call his own. From the lid of an old and heavy wooden chest, Tommy carved the hull of his yacht with his pocketknife. He labored for weeks until its shape was something similar to what he'd seen at the Broomielaw, adding a bowsprit, mast, and heavy paper sails. When finished, he carried his carving to one of the small, muddy ponds at the High Green and launched his first yacht, a model christened *Shamrock*. His friends soon followed suit, and Tommy, emulating what he saw as the protocol, founded the Crown Street Yacht Club, of which he was the commodore.

Though wielding a keen mind and quick wit, Tommy was irascible. Once faced with handing over some of his marbles, or "bools," to the town bully, a hulking older boy named Wullie Ross, the butcher's son, Tommy refused and challenged Ross to a fight. In a dirt courtyard behind a stand of buildings, Tommy recalled that he and his opponent stripped to their waists and then went at it. With spectators chanting and jeering, the boys pounded each other until one of Tommy's mates, concerned, interceded. Swollen and bloody, Tommy had received a brutal beating but had put up enough of fight that Ross no longer antagonized his gang, the Crown Street Clan.

At age fifteen, Tommy left school and took a job at A. & W. Kennedy lithographers, printers, and stationers and soon after, lured by the promise of an increase, left for Tillie and Henderson shirt makers. Within a year, he left that job, too, shipping out as cabin boy on a Burns steamliner, which made daily runs between Glasgow and Belfast. His ability to scrap on the streets of Glasgow didn't carry much weight on the ship: after just a short time he was made the scapegoat when an oil lamp discolored a cabin ceiling. He was given a week's wage and fired. With a small savings and his shipmates' stories fresh in his mind, Tommy made plans for America. He was smart, and at eighteen had grown tall and strong. And on a raw, early spring day in 1866, he boarded one of five steamers that made weekly service to New York. He carried only a suitcase with a few clothes, a sack filled with food, and his steerage class ticket. The ship belched a long, low horn blast as it backed away from the dock.

According to Lipton's memoir, he lived like a vagabond in war-torn America, hopping a train south to a tobacco plantation in Virginia where he worked for a year. He then moved to a rice plantation in South Carolina where a crazed, knife-toting Spaniard slashed him across the face. Lipton claimed he was a stowaway on a ship to Charleston and then traveled south to New Orleans where he worked as a bookkeeper for a tramcar company. After two years on the road, he returned to New York and secured a clerk's job at a food emporium. It was at this job that he learned how Americans used advertising and customer service to sell groceries. In New York he saw the storeowners paste advertisements in their windows and hand circulars to passersby. He noticed how they stacked their wares neatly on display and learned to appreciate the importance of friendly exchange with customers. With this newfound knowledge and some money saved, in 1870 Lipton sailed for home.

In Glasgow Lipton parlayed his savings into his own business, and on his twenty-third birthday,[1] he opened his own shop at 101 Stobcross Street. The shop was small like his parents' shop and sold many of the same things, specializing in hams, bacon, butter, and eggs. But Lipton employed his American approach to business. Every day he dressed all in white, and he arranged the hams, hanging, so they could be easily seen. He greeted his customers as if they were royalty, gossiping with housewives and handing out treats to their children. He also began his version of an advertising campaign by hanging a wooden ham, painted to look real, above the shop's entrance, which drew curious looks and inquisitive shoppers. At night, he kept glass globes lit with gas jets in the windows, to give the shop a warm, inviting feel—like an enchanted fairy cave, some said—even when he was closed. In addition, Lipton hired illustrator Willy Lockhart to create a weekly cartoon to post in the shop window. These cartoons were simple and to the point, designed to catch the neighborhood's amused eye. One cartoon depicted a line of thin, gaunt patrons walking into Lipton's shop, and then showed them fat and full on their way out. In another a crying pig was slung over an Irishman's shoulder. The man is explaining that the pig is an orphan; its family has gone to Lipton's—and out of pity the Irishman is taking this pig there, too. The cartoons were a success, but Lipton always tried to outdo himself. For his next stunt, he bought two giant pigs, washed them, and tied pink and blue ribbons around their necks. "I'm going to Lipton's, the best shop in town for Irish bacon," read the slogan he'd painted on their sides, visible to all as they were paraded through crowded city streets. Sometimes blocking traffic, the pigs became known as Lipton's Orphans and quickly became the talk of the town.

Lipton's shop expanded at a rapid clip, and to keep up with demand he worked tirelessly, spending long hours there, sometimes sleeping under the counter so he wouldn't have to walk home. "I worked late and early," wrote Lipton. "I was manager, shopman, buyer, cashier, and message-boy all in one. If I had provisions to collect off the Irish boats, I went down to the quay myself with a hand-cart early in the mornings; if my customers wanted anything sent to their homes, I shut up the shop temporarily and delivered them in person."[2]

After six weeks Lipton hired an assistant and then another. Soon he was winning small catering contracts for local businesses. His method was to underbid his competition and make only a small profit. He knew he could work harder than anyone. All it took was time, and the more contracts he earned the bigger the chance his business would grow. Lipton was a stickler for not jeopardizing quality, but he lowered costs by eliminating the middleman, buying all of his meat and dairy products directly from farmers. To obtain the best price possible he always paid cash up front. If he didn't have the cash, he wouldn't buy the product. Lipton frequently traveled to Ireland on purchasing trips and personally negotiated prices. He had an ear for learning dialects and would speak to farmers in their native brogue, so that as far as they knew he was one of their countrymen.

As his success grew so did his zest for advertising. He had purpose-built mirrors fashioned for his storefronts. One, labeled *Before Lipton's,* showed one's reflection as skinny with a frowning face. The other, labeled *After Lipton's,* showed one's reflection as fat with a smiling face. During the holiday season, he commissioned large wheels of cheese into which he inserted gold sovereigns; like the Christmas pudding tradition, a coin turned up in the winning slice. In the early 1870s Lipton dedicated every waking moment to running his business. But this single-minded determination clouded his personal life. Except for his mother and a few business acquaintances he had no friends. His aspirations for fame and fortune consumed him. For the rapacious, young upstart the lure of competition was incredibly seductive.

While Lipton worked unremittingly in Glasgow, in America Nathanael did the same. But while Lipton maneuvered with savvy ease, attuned to the vicissitudes of commerce, the feverish political and business climate of early 1870s America and the acrimonious Cup dealings of

1871 had all but brushed by engrossed Nat. Through colleagues in Rhode Island and Boston he had been privy to gossip, but from Bristol it all seemed far away. Saddled with stress, Nat's world slowly crumbled around him. Overworked and too tired to face each day, he had fallen deathly ill. "Nat had been ailing since Thursday night in Providence and was quite sick with cold and fever," his mother wrote to her oldest son, James. "He was at Corliss's the next afternoon and Saturday morning at his work, and felt quite improved; but when he found himself late for the cars to Bristol, he hurried so very much that in getting into them he felt he had surfeited his blood and, after a while, he felt chilled through."[3] In her letter, Julia Ann suspected small pox and perhaps measles and indicated the Board of Health ordered the family to douse the house and property with carbolic acid.

Nat soon recovered, but was mentally frail. Concerned, James, his older brother by fourteen years and the most financially successful of the family, arranged for him to visit Nat's blind older brother Lewis, the fifth Herreshoff child, who was studying in France. Much to Nat's protest, on February 10, 1874, he set sail aboard the German steamship *Goethe*, leaving from New York, bound for Cherbourg. The trip was intended to help him wind down, to lift the burdens of workaday life. Though harried and fed up, recovering from illness brought about by acute stress, the twenty-six-year-old had become set in his ways, a product of a childhood defined by structured time and imposed focus. Even at six and seven years old, he'd spent his days operating John Brown's ropewalk or when allowed leave from John Brown, his incredible talent was used building windmill blades for James. At eight, prodded to learn complex math, he drew blueprint-quality, three-dimensional scale images while other children his age fumbled with caricatures and awkward animals. Work had consumed his life. It was all he knew. His voyage on the *Goethe* was his first transatlantic passage, his first trip abroad, and his first respite. His journal entries, however, indicate that his work had been indelibly seared into his personality. On February 13, three days from New York, he wrote:

> The "Goethe" is a Clyde built vessel of 3600 tons burthen belonging to the Eagle Line steamer between Hamburg and New York. Is 375 feet long, 40 ft. beam, 32 ft. deep. Engines of 3000 effective horse power and 600 nominal. Compound engine, cylinders one of 60"

and one of 104" diam. with 4 ft. stroke. Are inverted direct acting with cranks at right angles. Have reservoir between cylinders which the high pressure exhausts into. Plain slide valves worked by link motion with cut off valves to each. Air pumps and circulating pumps worked by beams off one side. The engineer drove me out of the engine room the first day and they pretend not to understand English, so I cannot get much information.

Still clinging to his analytic way of viewing the world, the next day he wrote in his journal:

The propeller is 19 f. diameter and 27 f. pitch, making 52 rev. per minute; without slip it would go ahead 27x52 = 1404 ft. per min. Taking her speed at 12.8 knots or 1281 ft. per minute the slip 1-1281/1404=.088. The distance run today is 308 miles. Latt. 44° 6' N. Long. 47° 29' W.

This afternoon the weather is quite fine; the wind is directly aft but not enough to render any assistance by setting sails. The sun shows himself once in a while. There is quite a heavy swell from the N which makes the vessel roll consider able. I have a clear space of about 330 ft. on deck to walk. This afternoon I walked it 32 times. 330/5280 = 1/16. 32x1/16 = 2 miles. The time of walking sixteen times was 19 1/2 min. I make about 121 steps in the distance. In the evening the wind is a little fresher and nearly dead aft. Have set foresail and fore and main topsails.[4]

After landing in Cherbourg on February 20, 1874, he visited Paris with Lewis and then traveled to Nice, arriving on the 23rd and staying with their cousins, Charles and Helen Eaton. After a few days of settling in, Nat noticed their small sloop *Helen* was in disrepair; with his brother, he set out to fix it—sanding, varnishing, and rebuilding the rig and sails. His prescribed break from boats was evidently short-lived, for at the same time he and his brother had begun building a small double-ended sailing canoe named *L'Onda* in a carpenter's shop on the Rue St. Phillipe. They finished *L'Onda* on April 6. Sailing both boats to Cannes, they entered *Helen* in a regatta and, with Nat at the wheel, finished first, sailing "three times around the course to finish when the native boats had gone but twice around, so easily won."[5]

L'Onda, tippy and difficult to sail, was only a temporary diversion, their most memorable voyage shooting the rapids of the River Var to the ocean, whereupon Nat, in his own words, "got a dunking."[6] The brothers began a third project, building *Riviera,* a sixteen-foot open sloop made of mulberry wood in the same shop on Rue St. Phillipe. Especially designed and built with light construction and large rig to accommodate Mediterranean sailing conditions, *Riviera* would transform their Grand Tour into a Grand Cruise.

Following Nat's directions, blind Lewis worked alongside his brother. Building almost every piece by hand with limited resources, *Riviera* was no small undertaking. Nat later wrote:

> There was no saw or planning mill . . . only a yard having "deals" [rough, uncut lumber] from Norway & the north countries—and there I selected suitable ones and hired two whip-saw men to cut them up into boards of required thickness. There was no wood available that could be steamed and bent, so the boats were built with a "chine." There was no good fastening to be had, only copper wire nail, and crude brass screws. The cousin I was staying with could speak French and was the greatest assistance in finding where things could be had, and bargaining for them. . . . I had to make the pulley blocks having shells of sheet brass. I cannot recollect how I obtained the brass sheaves? There was no lathe . . . There were 14 pully blocks in the outfit.[7]

After cutting *Riviera's* canvas sails, Nat instructed Mrs. Eaton's seamstress how to stitch the panels. The ropes and spars were specially made. In an orange orchard near the Eaton's home, Nat painted his boat set upside down on two sawhorses. On Tuesday, July 14, 1874, after stowing baggage and supplies, the brothers and Charles Eaton sailed *Riviera* and *L'Onda* from Nice "for the westward in a light south wind with all sail set and bunting flying."[8] They tried to sell *L'Onda* on the night of the 14th and again on the 15th, but unable to find a buyer, shipped her to Marseille by train. On the same day Eaton returned home, leaving the two boys to their own devices.

That Nat gravitated toward boats, the objects of his failing health, was a testament to his deep-seated love of sailing. Building boats was what he knew. Without family obligation and the pressures of the working world, without exhaustion, he could bask in his skills. He had a gift for building fast boats and a penchant for hard work, the reward for which was found on the water. With tiller in hand and a blind brother holding the sheets, he felt the same satisfaction he'd had with *Meteor,* his first boat built with John Brown. Like *L'Onda* and the re-vamped *Helen,* this new boat was fast, and in their first day together Nat and Lewis logged forty miles, rounding Cape Benat at sunset, and then rowing along the shore until they found a small, sandy beach to camp for the night.

By Saturday, July 18, they arrived in La Ciotat at 2 P.M., ate, and then visited the machine shops of the Maritime Company, one of the largest marine engineering firms in France at the time. "We saw large boiler and engine work," wrote Nat in his passage log. "[There were] five large steamers and one on her beam ends in the dry dock where she had fallen over a few hours before we arrived—a bad accident killing several men and injuring the ship."[9] On the 19th they arrived in Marseilles and then traveled on to Basin Jolliete, Bois, and by July 21, with the assistance of a tow from a small steamer, arrived in Arles at 4:30 P.M. On Wednesday, July 22, having a difficult time of sailing the canals, the brothers shipped *Riviera* via rail to Belfort in northeast-ern France. They stopped in Valence, spending the night in a hotel, and then traveled on to Lyon on the 23rd, where they roomed at the Hotel Collet and visited a silk making factory. Early the next morning they traveled up the Saône River to Chalon via steamer, which Nat, fastid-iously described as "a very droll steamer, 230 ft. long and 14 ft. wide of iron."[10] By Saturday, July 25 the boys arrived in Belfort at 12:30 and found "the place was not on the canal as we expected—through an error in reading the map."[11] They in turn, shipped *Riviera* twelve kilo-meters up river to Montreaux Veaux, the highest point on the canal.

Spending the next five days navigating the locks, they arrived in Kehl on July 30 and left there on August 2 after having traveled by rail to see the sites at Strasbourg. On Tuesday, August 4, they entered the Rhine River, but on the next day in a strong west wind broke their mast, Nat noting it was *Riviera*'s "first flaw." Stopping at a sawmill, they "got a stick for a new mast,"[12] and then continued on under a double-reefed, or heavily shortened, mainsail. They traveled forty-eight miles to Bonn where the next day they refitted the new spar and then trav-eled eighteen miles to Köln.

After visiting the cathedral and museums in Köln, they continued on past Düsseldorf to Emmerich, cleared Dutch customs and in heavy headwinds and rain, with a double reef and then only the mainsail peak, they sailed to Nijmegen, a distance of seventy miles. For the next three days, they bucked wind and rain, stopping in Druten, Gorinchem, and finally arriving into Rotterdam on Tuesday, August 11. They quickly made arrangements for passage to London, traveling with *Riviera* aboard the *Aurora,* a 250-foot iron steamer "laden with cheese and hogs."[13]

Having made friends with two brothers named Fischell on their passage to London, Nat and Lewis boarded with the Fischell brothers' aunt in northern London. Spending three weeks there, the Herreshoffs toured the city, Nat purchasing "three great volumes of Scott-Russell on Naval Architecture, and some drawing instruments." He also, "had made a pocket rule having logarithmic slides."[14] After shipping *Riviera* to Liverpool, Nat and Lewis followed by train, and then rowed their boat and belongings to the steamship *City of Brussels,* whereupon they boarded and *Riviera* was hauled on deck and lashed upside down over one of the deckhouses. On September 10, 1874, the *City of Brussels* pulled out of Liverpool. Later in life, Nat made a special addition "from memory" to his *Riviera* log, noting the *City of Brussels* "had a two cylinder horizontal engine of large diameter and short stroke, and I have forgotten if with oscillating cylinders or trunk pistons. However, they pounded terribly during the latter part of the voyage, which I was informed was usual."[15]

Arriving in New York eight and half days later on September 22, the brothers quickly lowered *Riviera* from the deck, loaded their belongings and hoisted their sails "just as a customs officer saw us from the dock and called for us to come back but we did not."[16] They had decided to leave *L'Onda* in France because of the prohibitively expensive import tariffs. Now on *Riviera,* the brothers made their escape, Nat with tiller in hand, Lewis holding the sheet. "With light airs and fair tide in the East River," Nat recalled, "we passed our line to tow bound east." On September 23 with "light westerly wind and very fine weather" he said, they "sailed all day, most of the time 'wing and wing,' and arrived at Clinton, Connecticut, at dark. Went to the hotel and had a good sleep."[17]

The next day, the brothers proceeded eastward and seeing "several little puffs of smoke on the horizon," sailed toward the 40-foot steamer

Vision, clearly identifiable by her narrow, 4½-foot beam. Both John Brown and James were on board, a fitting welcome, for John Brown had built the boat, James had designed her engine's coil boiler, the first of its type, and Nat had designed her single-cylinder engine. They took *Riviera* in tow, the two older, domineering brothers having collected their younger siblings. And it was no doubt a warm welcome. Heading east into Fishers Island Sound, they spotted *Julia* with their father and a friend, Henry Brownell, on board. Lewis boarded *Julia* and sailed with his father toward Bristol. Nat remained with his brothers. James and John Brown asked many questions. They spent the next few hours steaming east, Nat regaling them with his adventures. Nat, their intense younger brother, had returned. His skin was weathered and tanned and looked healthy, in fact. The three brothers stood next to one another, rolling with the whitecaps of Rhode Island Sound. After several hours, they turned north at Point Judith, passed Beavertail Point, and, marking an end to Nat's hiatus, *Vision* steamed briskly into Narragansett Bay.

Nat soon returned to the Corliss Steam Engine Company in Providence, again helping his brother on nights and weekends. Since 1871 John had looked primarily to Nat for his designs, which consisted mostly of moderate-size sailboats and several steamers. That blind John Brown had kept his fledgling shop afloat was a testament to his business savvy. Struggling desperately to rebound from its Civil War slump, America was sliding into a fiscal quagmire. Ulysses S. Grant, then in his second term, was struggling to control the inflated economy, which to help finance the Civil War Lincoln had inundated with $450 million in greenbacks, paper money without the backing of gold or silver. Grant mandated a return to the gold standard, but in 1873 the Northern Pacific Railroad went bankrupt, plunging the country into a depression known as the Panic of 1873. John Brown, having already stumbled once with Dexter Stone, now had a safety net, his older brother James. Still earning a healthy income from his patents, James, flush with capital, had wisely invested in United States Gold Bonds. With the gold standard reinstated he'd made a killing and was netting roughly $500,000 annually. James, ever the avid boat tinkerer, was funneling money into his brother's business and even volunteered his time to help new owners of John Brown's yachts become acquainted with their handling and maintenance.

James was intent on playing a role in his brother's business. He, like John Brown, assumed an air of entitlement when it came to his younger siblings. Although James's influence and money was a boon, John Brown was indeed a gifted foreman, who had also honed a management style underscored by his gift for calculating precise cost estimates. "It is a well-known fact that the blind have wonderful memories," wrote L. Francis Herreshoff, describing his uncle.

> [A]nd perhaps J. B. could remember the cost of several hundred yachts. When an estimate of the cost of a new yacht was needed, and Captain Nat had explained her to J. B. in a very few words, J. B. would go home and think about it all night. The next morning when he came to the office he would say what the yacht would cost and, after she was built, his estimate was remarkably accurate.[18]

His prescient business sense was bolstered by a keen attention to detail. One day an antique connoisseur boasted to him that he'd acquired an old chair for which he'd paid a high price. When John Brown ran his fingers over it he noticed the inside faces of the seat frame were cut with a buzz plane, thereby identifying the antique a fraud. By fashioning his cane with measured notches, he'd acquired a scrupulous sense of proportion. On more than one occasion his sense of acuity led others to believe he feigned blindness. One local legend recalls an incident when John Brown, having ordered a new horse harness with ten stitches per inch, ran his fingers over the finished product and protested, for the harness had only eight and a half stitches per inch. In disbelief and visibly disgruntled, the harness maker measured and found John Brown was correct.

This diligence and his brother's bankroll had delivered some success, but the yacht market was quickly shifting from sail to steam. Forced to follow, John Brown expanded his shops, despite the squally financial climate. "John was trying to compete in prices with those doing inferior work," wrote Nat, "and [that] got in the way of . . . attending closely to his own shop and workmen, and so got in debt."[19] Nevertheless, John Brown and his crew of workmen pressed on and although working full-time designing pumping engines for Corliss, Nat took several long leaves to help in the shop and sail his brother's boats in various races. Nat's designs had proven invaluable, but his ability to win with his boats provided the marketing John Brown needed to secure more orders.

Having steered countless boats from a very young age, Nat was becoming an incredibly skilled helmsman. Through his brother, he'd acquired an intuitive feel. Through years of practice, he'd developed confidence and style. "Even when in my early teens," he wrote, "I had the knack of sailing boats & yachts to win, and was in demand in every available race."[20] He had an eye for detail and had developed the same subtle touch, balance, and hearing as his blind brother. He felt how a yacht tracked through water, the way its rig cut the air. With just one hand on the tiller, he could feel proper sail trim and mast alignment. He knew precisely where on the deck the crew should center its weight. With one glance ahead he could see the wind on the water, anticipating it, steering his boat ever so slightly to windward in the puffs and footing—steering ever so slightly downwind—for speed in the lulls. He had, after all, designed the hull and rig with these characteristics in mind. These traits had funneled through his fingers as he chiseled, planed, and sanded his models, yielding smooth, fluid motions on the tiller. Nat glided around racecourses, steering his designs to decisive victories. He and John Brown knew that fast boats sold well. Nat's prowess at the helm was the best advertising they could possibly ask for.

Although working hard, Nat seemed to have rolled into a period of intellectual freedom. He had established himself as a worthy designer so valued that he was granted a number of holiday leaves from the Corliss factory. He had also established a leading role in his brother's company. Although John Brown was never afraid to voice his opinions to his brother—on the contrary, he still hounded him as if he were a boy—Nat had developed a newfound sense of excitement in his designs. Perhaps his adventures on *Riviera* had rekindled his fascination with the sea. Perhaps, he felt having ventured out on his own, he was finally independent. The end result was a young designer of twenty-seven years who began to challenge the paradigms of naval architecture and engineering.

During the winter of 1875 he began experimenting with new designs, mounting *Riviera*'s jib and mainsail rig on an iceboat, which he sailed religiously on Bristol Harbor throughout January and February. During his voyage through Europe, he had envisioned a two-hulled boat with high stability, low weight, and a large sail plan. This idea complemented his experiments with the iceboat. If a craft mounted on multiple thin, metal runners could reach breakneck speeds, why couldn't a soft-water vessel achieve the same on thin, wooden hulls? Having carved hull models and sketched ideas for rigging, Nat, in a corner of his brother's shop and with the help of the shop's workers, built the puzzling design. It had two twenty-five-foot, deep and narrow hulls. They were connected by two cross braces. At centerline on the aft brace he mounted a rudder. At first he designed the rig with two masts mounted on the center of each hull, but finding the rig weak and the boat difficult to steer, he substituted them with a single mast mounted to the forward cross brace, supporting a main-and-jib sail plan. He experimented with his new design through 1875 and into 1876. That winter, again, the iceboats were rigged for further testing. "But O, the times they have on the ice, for the harbor is frozen over," wrote Nat's Aunt Anna to James Herreshoff's wife, Jane. "Charley made a large ice boat, and Nat put his French sails on his, and did they not fly! All day long, without their dinner they rushed to and fro like mad creatures from another planet."[21] Although Nat finally honed his new creation in 1876, his work at Corliss took center stage.

Though still mired in post–Civil War reconstruction, America, in its 100 years, was eager to celebrate all it had accomplished. To highlight the country's myriad technological achievements, Philadelphia had planned a grand Centennial Exposition. Despite heavy spring rains that had turned Philadelphia and the fair grounds into a muddy swamp, thousands flocked to the city. On May 10, 1876, the Exposition opened to blasts of steam whistles, a hundred-gun salute, and a choir singing Handel's "Hallelujah Chorus." Over 30,000 exhibits were displayed, filling 167 buildings. Alexander Graham Bell unveiled his new electric telephone. Thomas Edison demonstrated his recent automatic telegraph machine.[22] Having assisted on the design of one of the Exposition's most awe-inspiring entries, Nat was sent by the Corliss Company to oversee the installation and running of the colossal Corliss engine, the largest steam engine in the world. Rising more than forty feet, the engine generated 2,500 horsepower and drove over 8,000 parts simultaneously.[23] Nat later wrote:

[I] had charge of starting [the engine] up at time of opening of the Exposition. When steam was turned on by Pres. Grant and Dom Pedro by two little gold plated cranks . . . Mr. Corliss, very prettily slipped [them] off and presented one to each. My position was below the platform with the engineer who was to take charge after I left, and where all duplicate controls were.[24]

John and a few guests had attended the exposition aboard his self-made, forty-seven-foot steamer *Viola*. Nat's father Charles and his brother Lewis attended in their twenty-two-foot catboat *Julia*. Although the Exposition ran through November, attracting over 10 million visitors, Nat left shortly after the opening-day demonstration, obtaining a furlough from Corliss and returning to Bristol, where he began his final catamaran trials.

After christening his new boat *Amaryllis,* Nat entered the Open Centennial Regatta on Long Island Sound on June 23, 1876. Although considerably less auspicious than the Philadelphia Exposition, the Centennial regatta had absorbed the former's celebratory energy and was touted as a grand celebration of sail, with yachts of all shapes and sizes—from extreme sandbaggers (centerboarders with such enormous sail areas they required moveable sandbags for ballast) to large cabin yachts—registered. At deck level *Amaryllis* was thirty-three feet long and each hull twenty-seven inches wide; at the waterline she was thirty feet long and twenty-four inches wide. The hulls were sixteen feet apart and planked with half-inch cedar. The two rudders connected to a tiller in the cockpit by wooden bars calibrated so that the inner rudder rotated at a greater angle than the outer, allowing the boat to turn smoothly on her axis. Nat's son, A. Griswold Herreshoff, later described *Amaryllis:*

The hulls are connected together by two crossbraces and supported the cockpit and framework somewhat similar to an iceboat on 16 ball and socket joints so arranged that when the hulls are allowed to pitch freely longitudinally, but are restrained from rocking sideways except through a small angle and are so connected that one hull cannot move ahead of the other. The mast is tyed to the framework in such a manner that the movement of the hulls does not move the mast and shake the wind out of the sails. She is rigged with a jib and mainsail of 900 square feet, 300 in the jib and 600 in the mainsail. Her total weight is 3,500 lbs or about ⅙ that of a normal boat of the same area. She is fitted with a marine speedometer which has indicated a speed of 19½ miles an hour without being tuned up.[25]

The race began in light wind. With her high-wetted surface compared to the monohulls and her inability to heel, which prevented her sails from falling naturally (by gravity) into an efficient light-air shape, *Amaryllis* was painfully slow. L. Francis Herreshoff recounts, "the sand-baggers sailed by her. As they did they hailed the *Amaryllis* with ridicule and abuse for the sandbaggers were notorious for their tough crews."[26] But as the wind built *Amaryllis,* lacking the heavy ballast of the keel yachts, took off. With her narrow hulls producing little wave-making resistance, *Amaryllis* shot ahead. Nat found the boat was difficult to tack in a breeze and the leeward hull had a tendency to plunge deep into the water, which slowed the boat, but he made fine headway. *Amaryllis*, now sailing at roughly twenty knots, quickly charged past the fleet. For a boat of this size, the speed was shocking. The average 150-foot American clipper topped out at fifteen knots in a gale. Now tripling the speeds of her competitors, this 33-foot catamaran left everyone dumbfounded.

Though considered a capricious oddity in U.S. waters, the catamaran had for hundreds of years intrigued designers. Originating in the South Pacific, proas were championed for their light weight and high stability. That these swift craft had transported islanders across oceans seduced numerous designers to attempt their own models. On July 31, 1662, the renowned English diarist Samuel Pepys, noted that Sir William Petty had "won a wager of £50 in sailing between Dublin and Holyhead with the pacquett-boat, the best ship or vessel the King hath here." In an investigation of multihull designs, the Royal Society organized a race against three traditional sailing vessels. He continued:

> In their coming back from Holyhead they started together, and this vessel [catamaran] came to Dublin by five at night, and the pacquett-boat not before eight the next morning; and when they come they did believe this vessel had been drowned, or at least left behind, not thinking she could have lived in that sea. Strange things are told of this vessel.[27]

Almost 170 years later, Scottish yachtsmen gathered on July 29, 1831, to watch George Packer and the first William Fife launch the twenty-two-foot multihulled *Flying Fish* into the Clyde. Although plagued with breakdowns, *Flying Fish* was fast and had piqued her designers' curiosity. A year later in 1832 Fife built the sixty-foot *Ruby Queen* proa, which reached speeds of ten knots.[28] But without paying customers, experimentation tapered. That catamarans were not as conducive to hauling the same bulky loads as monohulls most likely relegated them to obscurity.

Ever willing to challenge the status quo, Nat had reintroduced the multihull concept and even secured a U.S. patent. He had tried a rather eccentric design with *L'Onda,* his French sailing canoe. But *Amaryllis,* skimming across Long Island Sound, went further. He had intentionally built the yacht using ultra-light materials, knowing any excess weight would counteract the design's advantages. His weight and shape calculations paid off, for Nat and *Amaryllis* crossed the Centennial Regatta finish line with a substantial lead. But the shocking performance prompted some competitors to protest, and the prize was ultimately handed to the second-place boat. So alarming was the speed of Nat's catamaran that most clubs voted to exclude the type from future races. "There is no doubt the catamaran outclasses the ordinary craft as to speed," wrote Nat, still disgruntled later in life, "but it is deplorable the clubs did not recognize them and arrange for special classes."[29]

Despite the race committee's rebuff, Nat's catamaran generated inquiry from the yachting fraternity. Returning to Bristol that summer and eager to experiment further, he hashed out plans to build more. But his brother's yard had taken numerous orders for steamers. Using James Herreshoff's 1873 coil boiler design, the same used in John Brown's *Vision,* Nat designed and built a number of launches designed to transport people to and from larger vessels at anchor. Using steam-bent frames, the launches were light and could be easily hauled using davits, a difficult and even dangerous process with heavier sawed-framed launches, especially in a rolling sea when they sometimes slammed perilously into the hull of the mother ship. The coil boilers were light, weighing about 70 pounds per horsepower; used relatively little fuel (about 2.21 pounds of coal per horsepower hour); and lacking large-diameter tubes or drums, were less likely to explode than other designs.[30] The boiler, consisting of a long snaking piece of tapered iron tubing, maintained high pressure quickly even after the steam had traveled a distance from the firebox. Whereas conventional boilers of the day took up to an hour to build sufficient steam, the coil boiler took less than five minutes. The downside of the coil boiler was its expense: the tubes, made from several hundred-foot-long strips of sheet iron, had to be carefully rolled, bent into shape, and the long continuous seam welded. Because the tubing was one continuous piece, when deposits built up, the entire unit had to be replaced.

Despite its downfalls, the coil boiler had revolutionized the marine steam engine. And although James Herreshoff had designed it, Nat's ability to integrate the boiler with its engine and then meld the other components of a boat—hull, steering, and finish work—into one unified concept had allowed their relatively small, fledgling shop to compete with large, industrial yards. Although still working only nights and Sundays for his brother, Nat filled the role of ten designers. The integration of complex engines and hull shapes normally accomplished by a team of architects at larger yards fell solely on his shoulders. The responsibility was overwhelming and the workload oppressive. To his benefit, however, he was unhampered by office politics, waffling opinions, and the challenge of fusing disparate work styles. Nat Herreshoff did it all. He was a veritable one-man show. While his brother honed his gift for management, Nat asserted his fluency in the language of design.

It was the Herreshoff brothers' streamlined approach and budding reputation that attracted the U.S. Navy. Mired in bureaucracy and ever conscious of public opinion, the Navy was naturally drawn to this forthright, hard-working yard, and in 1876 they ordered the Herreshoff brothers to build the country's first torpedo boat. Fifty-eight feet long with a narrow, double-ended hull and 50½-inch-diameter coil boiler mounted at midships, a swept-back smokestack rising at centerline, Nat's torpedo boat attained speeds of twenty miles per hour, the fastest for her size in the world. Carrying a "spar torpedo," a bomb attached to the end of a long wooden pole, *Lightning*, with her low profile and stealthy engine, was designed to approach quietly, deposit a lit bomb below the waterline of the enemy ship, and then quickly reverse, speeding away. With the success of *Lightning*, torpedo boat orders from England, Russia, Chile, Peru, and Spain flooded the Herreshoff offices. With the workload increasing, Nat worked longer hours. A formal photo portrait from 1876 shows a man twenty-eight years old—his hair parted neatly on the left with a full brown beard, bordering on unruly. He wears a dark suit, white shirt, and bowtie. His eyes, avoiding the camera, look tired.

With the busy work schedule in Bristol, Nat was again granted leave from Corliss. In the preceding years he had patented two valuable breakthroughs, the variable valve gear and the "dash pot," a device accelerating the rate valves opened and closed. Nat had handed these patents over to Corliss, and they rewarded him with ample time off, no doubt with the knowledge that their driven young employee was spending this time honing his trade. With another sabbatical, Nat spent long hours on his brother's designs, but he also took the time to tinker, building four thirty-one-foot catamarans. He had such faith in these designs that he planned to start a business of his own, securing a patent in 1877.

He built three boats that year (and one more in 1879) and although they sold, they were more expensive and time consuming than he'd anticipated, and the venture proved unsuccessful. In the spirit of their European cruise, Nat and Lewis sailed the catamaran *Tarantella* from Bristol to New York, up the Hudson River, and back. But later that year, unbeknownst and using Nat's name, Lewis wrote a letter to the *Spirit of the Times* magazine, dated November 10, 1877, recounting the brothers' voyage. His letter discussed the cruising potential and speed of the catamarans and was very much a sales pitch. When the article ran on Saturday, November 14, 1877, Nat was outraged. He couldn't even cut his losses without being saddled by an older sibling. James, the successful entrepreneur, still inundated him with endless "advice," constantly judging his design work; John Brown worked him to the point of physical breakdown; and now Lewis, his brother closest in age (four years older), the blind companion with whom he partnered on multiple extended voyages, had penned what Nat saw as a self-aggrandizing letter. Lewis had betrayed him. With few options, Nat returned that fall to the Corliss Company.

Once again, Nat reached a low point. He was overworked, tired, and his attempt to strike out on his own had failed. John Brown and his small work crew had successfully delivered not only *Lightning* and a number of small steam launches, but they had also recently completed sea trials for *Estelle,* a 120-foot steamship—by far the biggest vessel he'd ever made. Because of the scale, he'd farmed out much of the work, with the hull built in nearby Fall River, Massachusetts, to Nat's model and plans. The engine was built at the Rhode Island Locomotive Works in Providence, and the boiler was built in his yard in Bristol. The boat was designed with such precision that she easily achieved her contracted sixteen knots. When the bronze rudder fell off and was lost near Goat Island off Newport, *Estelle* tracked through the water perfectly true. The sea trials resumed, the crew simply dragging an anchor to change course. Because of alleged ties with Cuban insurgents, *Estelle* was confiscated by the U.S. government. But the success of the project prompted an order for an identical boat, *Clara,* from the Spanish Navy. The grand scale of *Estelle* had officially put John Brown on the map and he knew he needed help. Nat wrote:

> I had made models and designs for both craft and it was apparent John needed my full service, so I reluctantly resigned from the Corliss Steam Engine Company on December 31, 1877, and took up designing and draftsmanship for John. I gave up a salary of $1,400 per year, and took one of $1,000 with John, but I had decided the business could be built up and there was prospect of better times in John's business if certain rules were adhered to.[31]

On January 1, 1878, Nathanael Herreshoff teamed with his brother. They called their new joint enterprise the Herreshoff Manufacturing Company.

5

THE STEAM ENGINE

January 1878–April 1890

As partners, the brothers overhauled the business. But unlike John Brown, Nat had a lot to lose. He held a well-paying job at a highly reputable firm, at which he had a lot of autonomy. To strike out into a vacillating business, Nat felt he needed to lay down rules.

> I therefore made a verbal agreement with John that if I joined him, our entire efforts would be given to business, that John's indebtedness . . . should be settled [as] soon as possible, that we should borrow *no* money, and that any capital needed must come from earnings, and new tools or expansion of [the] plant should also be from earnings. Our object [was] to be to turn out the very best work possible and deal only with those who appreciated and could pay for good, honest work.[1]

John Brown agreed to Nat's stipulations. As partners, one of their first moves was to improve the old tannery. During the previous five years John Brown had steadily enlarged it, so that by 1878 the structure was more than a hundred feet long. Still, the shop was unheated and poorly lit. Nat bought the shore lot next to the tannery from his mother and loaned it to his new company. On the property he designed and built a 65- by 36-foot shed "well lighted by windows and by gas, and steam heated,"[2] the heat being a luxury for the workers at the time. Fully committed to their joint venture, the brothers pooled the rest of the business assets, although John Brown never relinquished control, maintaining the title of president. Although they'd likely allotted shares proportionate to their investments, the agreements were most likely verbal, hashed out by the dictates of their longstanding, complex, and often contentious relationship.

With a new sense of focus, Nat and John transformed their small firm into a working company with clearly defined goals and job descriptions: Nat would design and oversee the yard, John Brown would run the business side. And John ran it well. Admired and well respected, he established a congenial rapport with the workers. He was quick-witted with a sharp tongue and enjoyed the yard's spirited banter. Nat, serious and forbidding, kept his distance from the men. Each morning and afternoon he made his rounds of the workshops, overseeing the day's progress. If he saw a problem, he addressed it through the shop foreman, who would in turn relay Nat's criticisms. He avoided speaking to his workers directly. For one reason, he couldn't keep their names straight and often complained of being unable to pronounce them. But with the brothers' roles clearly defined and complementing their abilities and dispositions, the yard hummed along. John Brown charmed clients and made the workers feel a part of a family. He learned all their names and those of their wives and children. John maintained morale; Nat designed and built boats at a blazing clip.

Now high on the Navy's list of contractors, the brothers took more orders. Nat carved the models, drew the plans, and saw each boat to completion. John Brown kept the books, managed personnel, and stroked the customers. As still more steamship orders flooded the shops, Nat shifted his designs to iron and steel construction. He had used these metals before and was still using wood on his smaller designs, but suitable lumber had grown increasingly scarce in the United States. By the 1870s and early 1880s commercial shipbuilding from wood had become localized to Maine and the lumber areas of the West Coast. After the Civil War, New York and Boston began building commercial ships almost exclusively from steel. But busy supplying railroad and bridge construction, steel mills struggled to keep up with the demand. In addition, high tariffs left shipbuilders arguing with policy makers that they couldn't compete with foreign firms who bought steel for significantly less.[3] Nevertheless, the Herreshoff brothers outbid their competitors and even continued to supply steamships to foreign navies.

It had been a hundred years since the first steamers plied U.S. waters and in that time they'd become ubiquitous. And although Nat and John Brown had cut their teeth on small sailboats, they'd honed a recipe for light construction without sacrificing strength and applied that to steam. And although they didn't build the largest steamers, they built the fastest—and the Navy and private yachtsmen, for whom speed was a priority, were eager to pay.

In five years, the brothers produced forty-three steamyachts and a number of smaller launches. With mounting profits, they continued to update the shops with the latest tools and equipment. What was once a wooden shed across the street from the Herreshoff home was now a working waterfront. A photo from 1882 shows a long pier aside the old tannery, which had exploded into three buildings and a network of pilings and floats. The once tiny beach was littered with lumber and boats on stands, bits of line, saw horses, and wheelbarrows. An additional shed was added to the old tannery. Next to these buildings was Nat's larger shop, built on the property purchased from his mother in 1880. With wide sliding doors that opened to the bay, it too hung out over the water. Next to the shed was a wooden crane mounted on a stone pier.

While the Herreshoff brothers expanded their boatbuilding operation in Bristol, Thomas Lipton expanded his grocery chain across the British Isles. By 1880, Lipton had opened twenty stores throughout Scotland, each turning a hefty profit. He was personally at every opening, wearing his starched white overalls and pressed white apron. The shops were all built to the same pattern—a horseshoe-shaped counter, with hams hanging from the ceilings, gleaming counters piled high with stacks of butter. Lipton sought to hire only intelligent, hardworking assistants and store managers, whom he judged with a critical eye, and each night, following his Stobcross Street example, they left their storefront windows lit with glowing gas globe lamps.

In nine years of business he had forged new supply channels, securing the lowest prices, which he passed on to his customers, and transforming the working class diet in western Scotland. Families that had once subsisted on bread and potatoes could now afford dairy products and ham. His ability to control market share allowed him to dictate how eggs, cheese, and butter were produced and stored so that he received only the highest quality. When Irish farmers and crofters were unable to meet his demands, he started buying in Russia and Scandinavia. When there weren't sufficient resources there, he moved farther abroad and bought his own stockyards in Chicago, Illinois, and later Omaha, Nebraska. At full capacity his Johnstone Packing Company processed 2,500 pigs a day, enabling him to drastically undercut his competitors by selling ham at threepence a pound.[4] By the mid-1880s his shops covered all of Scotland, England, Ireland, and Wales. Lipton, by then in his mid-thirties, had become a millionaire.

But as his business grew and his name achieved greater notoriety, his flair for self-promotion consumed him and he began doctoring the details of his life. Although much of Lipton's past (including that recounted in this volume) has been cross-referenced and substantiated, Lipton worked hard to market an industrious, estimable image. And his efforts paid off. His autobiography, *Leaves from the Lipton Logs,* published in 1930, the year he died, is largely a fairy-tale, rags-to-riches story riddled with vagaries. The 1950 biography *The Lipton Story* by Alec Waugh provides a detailed chronicle of his life, but largely perpetuates many of the same myths. And through the years countless newspaper and magazine articles and yachting histories have canonized Lipton's careful embroidery. But in 1998, Glasgow-based writer James Mackay released a new analysis, *The Man Who Invented Himself: A Life of Sir Thomas Lipton,* a meticulously researched volume debunking many of Lipton's embellishments. Mackay scoured census and immigration records, birth, death, and stock certificates, and among countless other records, the eighty-five bound volumes of newspaper clippings Lipton amassed during his lifetime. His analysis concludes that vainglorious Lipton heavily padded his life story. Although he embellished mostly picayune facts, such as his age (he was two years older than he claimed) and dates and locations of certain events, he also carefully guarded others. For the most part Lipton's bluffs weren't malicious—but instead carefully crafted to promote a gleaming public persona.

Mackay underscores the extent to which Lipton heavily guarded his private life in his quest for acclaim. Citing Glasgow city records, Mackay asserts that soon after opening his first shop Lipton married nineteen-year-old Margaret McAuslan on May 12, 1871. The city records also show that during the next two years they had two children, Thomas and William, the first succumbing to fever at ten months. After their second was born on September 15, 1873, McAuslan disappeared. Mackay surmises that Lipton likely paid her to relocate to Canada.[5] Lipton never discussed this publicly, instead basking in the notoriety that came with being one of Britain's wealthiest and most eligible bachelors.

Despite his almost pathological mendacity, we can follow Lipton's later rise to wealth and fame with more certainty, for with the addition of each new store in his proliferating chain the press took note. Public scrutiny of Glasgow's grocery king reached its apex when at the end of the 1880s he transformed his business—and all of Britain— with an inquiry about tea.

Surfeited with stardom, Lipton had abandoned his clandestine marriage. Conversely, with his mounting success, Nat, now thirty-five years old in 1883 and freed from traveling to and from the Corliss Company in Providence, overcame his discomfiture and began courting a childhood friend, Clara Ann DeWolf, of the town's notable DeWolf family. They owned half of Bristol and were known by its residents as The Great Ones, their mansions having overshadowed their progenitors' ignoble rise to wealth. Their family estate had bordered the Herreshoff farm on Poppasquash Point, and although there had been an underlying bitterness between the two families, Clara and Nat had played together as children. With pressure from his mother Julia, Nat invited Clara for a sail. They picnicked together and later when Nat showed her the boatyard, she—of a family with seafaring roots—impressed him with her knowledge. Nat continued the courtship and Clara, who was five years older, responded favorably. Ever aloof, Nat habitually left his intentions vague. One could say in these instances he was socially awkward, for most daily verbal exchanges involved giving orders or battling the wills of his older brothers. Eventually Nat proposed and Clara accepted, and the short, wide-eyed architect with a bushy red-brown beard retired to his drawing room and drafted plans for their home.

Nat bought a piece of land called Love Rocks, a small peninsula jutting into Bristol Harbor and overlooking the Herreshoff Manufacturing Company to the north. They were married on December 26, 1883. Although unsubstantiated, it was rumored that on the night of the wedding, his bride Clara waited for him in the second-floor bedroom of their new house. Terrified, Nat slid out the back door into the winter night, rowed out to *Riviera*, the seventeen-foot sloop in which he'd toured Europe, and slept alone in her tiny cabin.[6]

In its early years Nat's marriage to Clara was defined by his busy work life. He maintained his assiduous schedule and saw his wife mostly during meals, which she prepared promptly for him. According to his son L. Francis:

He arose at 6 A.M.—even earlier in the summer—worked in his drafting room or model-making room until 8 A.M. . . . then had breakfast at eight, and sat quietly thereafter for a half hour or so reading the paper or some engineering magazine. At nine or before he went to the boat shop, usually after first visiting the drafting room at the shop where there were three or four draftsmen who inked in his drawings or made working drawings of the various parts taken from his original pencil plans. In this first call at the drafting room he often brought in a drawing that he had made the night before. Next he talked over the day's business with his brother J. B., who by that time had had the morning's mail read. Perhaps then by 10 A.M. he started on a walk over the whole boat plant to inspect every piece of work that was being made. . . . Captain Nat could usually tell at a glance if everything was going as it should . . .

Often by eleven-thirty he would return home, about a two-minute walk from the works, where he set to work at his designing or model making again until one o'clock, when he had his noonday meal. Then perhaps from one-thirty to two he sat quietly reading before he went back to the works to spend perhaps an hour or so in the office and drafting room before making another complete inspection of the works. This inspection lasted until 6 P.M. in the old days [later changing to 5 P.M.], he returned home and set to work again at his designing until 6:30 when he had supper. From seven to about seven thirty he read again and then went to his drafting room where he did either designing or model making until ten o'clock when he retired.[7]

Nat worked seven days a week except during the summer when he would take Clara and extended family members sailing. He designed and had built the twenty-eight-foot, six-inch catyawl Consuelo to better serve these family outings, but with the arrival of their daughter Agnes in 1883 and their son Sidney in 1886 he built a slightly larger catyawl and honored his wife—as his father had done for his mother—by calling her Clara. That Nat was sometimes lacking social grace had become expected, for every aspect of his life was retentive. He ate the same breakfast of Johnny Cakes (a type of cornmeal pancake) every day except Sunday, when Clara served him fish cakes. He never drank, smoked, or took tea or coffee. In line with the etiquette of the day, he wore a hat outdoors and a jacket and tie at all times. He kept to his dutiful schedule and expected those around him to do the same. In the shop, he posted the Herreshoff Manufacturing Company's Rules and Regulations, a stringent guideline for everything from hours of operation to using tools and maintaining secrecy about the company's works. One item mandated: "It is expected that, during working hours, the workmen will give their undivided attention to their work and it must be expressly understood, by each of the employees of this Company, that prolonged conversations and discussions are prohibited." Another stated, "Any workman found guilty of reporting or giving out any information regarding work they are on, or anything regarding shop affairs, will be discharged." Another said, "The regular working hours are from SEVEN A.M. to SIX P.M. with a recess of one hour from twelve to one. The bell will be rung at five minutes of seven and at five minutes of one o'clock as a signal to assemble. At the tolling of the bell, at seven and one, all employees are expected to be in their respective places and commence work. At twelve and six o'clock the bell will be rung as a signal to stop work. No workman must quit work, nor make any preparations to quit work, until the signal is given or until permission is obtained from his foreman."[8]

Captain Nat was particularly disgruntled when labor unions rose up around the country, pressuring business owners to shorten the workday. He later expressed his exasperation in a letter to yachting journalist W. P. Stephens: "Shorter working hours and more for pleasure and with higher prices, are turning our proud country right under. The countries where people are willing to work longer hours are taking the lead."[9]

Despite his obsession with maintaining order, he sometimes displayed a spark of humor, though veiled with severity. Charles Sylvester, a workman in the Herreshoff small boat shop, once told a story of a prank gone wrong. A few workers had strung a board piled with sawdust over the shop's east doorway, hoping to douse an unsuspecting worker. Stationed by the entrance, a lookout man signaled a man holding a trip line. But as the worker approached, the signalman noticed Captain Nat only a few paces behind. He motioned for the man with the trip line to wait but was misunderstood. The line was pulled, and the sawdust crashed down, blanketing the worker. Captain Nat's son, Clarence, recalled: "When Captain Nat entered a few seconds later, he glanced first at the workman covered with sawdust, then up at the trip line and board still dangling overhead. He understood the situation instantly and without a word passed through the shop and out the other door."[10]

That Nat was terse was more a product of his incredible workload than contempt for his employees. During business hours his focus was resolute. By the mid-1880s, except for a few small catboats, they were producing almost exclusively steamyachts and military vessels. The Navy, now emboldened by a federal government playing a more prominent role in international affairs, had pledged to bolster its fleet, which in 1883 consisted of ninety ships, fifty-eight of which were made of wood. Representative John D. Long of Massachusetts described it as "an alphabet of floating washtubs."[11] The Herreshoff brothers worked tirelessly to change that.

With the flood of work came a new level of fiscal security, and so Nat and John Brown built for themselves the ninety-four-foot long *Stiletto,* a dart of a steamship with an eleven-foot, six-inch beam and a boiler representing an improvement on James's coil boiler design. With large valves to facilitate the movement of steam through the cylinders, the compound engine could easily reach speeds of twenty-five knots. The yacht became famous when she faced the steamer *Mary Powell,* thought to be the fastest steamer in the world, on the Hudson River on June 10, 1885. After slowing down to tease the *Mary Powell, Stiletto,* under the command of Captain Nat, powered ahead and beat her by five minutes over a thirty-mile course. "[A] great sweeping streak of silver foam was flung off the Stiletto's sheer," reported the *New York Times,* "and a glistening boiling white mass of spume shot out from under her sharp stern. A moment later two jets of water were shooting three feet into the air behind her, and her bow was cutting through the water like a bullet through the air. She gave a great leap forward and every living soul on board the *Mary Powell,* from the Captain in the wheel house down to the cook in the kitchen, opened his mouth and eyes, held his breath, and stared with concentrated essence of his whole soul."[12] *Stiletto* so impressed the Navy that in 1887 they purchased her and converted the record-breaking yacht into its first warship firing self-propelled torpedoes.

With all this success, the brothers further expanded; having built the large north construction shop and expanded the machine shop in

1884, another large south construction shop was built in 1887. At 165 feet long by 40 feet wide, the south construction shop mirrored the north shop, including matching launching ways and overhead crane systems for moving heavy loads. Their success begot more orders and an ardent following by a wealthy publishing magnate from New York, Norman L. Munroe. Munroe had amassed a fleet of four Herreshoff yachts, including his most recent, the 85-foot *Now Then*. After her launch in 1887, *Now Then* logged runs from Newport to New York averaging twenty-four miles per hour. Munroe had been so confident in his yacht that he even challenged any private yacht to race without time allowance. Although his bet had never been accepted, Munroe had acquired a taste for speed and ordered a new, faster, and larger yacht from Herreshoff in the same year. Mahogany-planked and 138 feet long, the new yacht would be called *Say When* and would surely outpace Herreshoff's previous creations.

On December 7, 1887, Nat logged in his diary (primarily a collection of weather observations) that the Navy had awarded them the contract for a torpedo boat. The newly completed south construction shop housed hull No. 197, to be later named *Ballymena*, a 148-foot steamer ordered from Alexander Brown of Baltimore, their first fully steel-hulled yacht. An air of optimism swept through the yard. As if snapping down their final cards before calling gin, Nat and John Brown saw their concentration and focus come to fruition. But as the winter of 1888 grew increasingly severe, their luck turned.

One night in February at about 2 A.M., Captain Nat was summoned by the yard's night watchman. A southerly storm had whipped into Narragansett Bay, pushing water and sheets of ice into Bristol Harbor. The windswept floes combined with the flooding tide, broke through the doors of the south construction shop and threatened to throw *Ballymena* out of line. Rushing to the shop, wearing hip boots and heavy winter clothes, Nat and the watchman stumbled through the shed by lamplight, attempting to close the shop doors. Water pounded through the floorboards and rushed up the length of the building. With the floor swirling in ink-black water, Nat failed to see that one of the shops removable floor sections had been washed from its place. And with one plunging step he and the light of his lamp slipped through the hole. Raked under the shop, he sank as his hip boots and clothes filled with icy water. Sucked toward the harbor by the drawing waves and trapped by a lattice of barnacle-covered timbers, he struggled against the rush of water. Fortunately, as fast as the wave pulled him toward the harbor, it pushed him back and, no doubt with great luck, he grabbed the edge of the same hole through which he had fallen. Nearly frozen, he hauled himself through the hatchway. Wet and exhausted, through a raging winter storm, he stumbled home. Within a few days he was bedridden with severe pneumonia.

As Munroe's *Say When* neared completion, Nat remained in bed, his wife Clara nursing him back to health. That he designed, built, and installed a significantly more complex engine in *Say When* was inopportune. He had begun toying with his new ideas when they'd received the Navy torpedo boat contract in 1887, but even his older brother James, whose engine contributions had been a great help to the company, was suspicious of Nat's new designs. The engine consisted of five cylinders, using a quadruple expansion system with two low-pressure cylinders. He deviated from his previous designs by mounting the valves at the side of the cylinders and calibrating their timing with a separate crankshaft. Although this setup allowed him to create a more compact engine that could more easily shift into reverse, having five cylinders proved so complex that water often condensed unintentionally, causing the engine to knock and lose power.[13] Captain Nat had worked hard to design something new and bold, an engine that would impress the Navy and outperform *Now Then*. Although his engine worked, it would require precise tuning, a program of slight design modifications, and above all, time. But as *Say When* approached completion he lay incapacitated at Love Rocks.

Captain Nat slowly recovered and the yard made plans to launch *Say When*. As she slid down the rails into Bristol Harbor, Nat knew she was incomplete. Munroe, eager to try his new yacht, was reasonably satisfied, but Nat, unwilling to hand over an inferior product, unwilling to accept that his engine was faulty, kept *Say When* in Bristol, tweaking her engine's settings, making any and all modifications to bolster its steam pressure. That year the shop delivered *Ballymena*, a steamer driven by the same style engine, with success. But Nat continued to work on *Say When*'s engine and even went so far as to install the same overall design into the Navy's vessel. Yet the engine in *Say When* would not produce the results he had anticipated.

He worked through December on the boat with hopes of sea trials in January.

Say When pulled away from the Herreshoff piers on January 5, 1889. On one of the initial runs *Say When* climbed toward her anticipated max speed. It was cold with a rough chop driving down the bay. The weather would certainly hinder a steamer, the cold dampening the steam pressure, the waves jostling the ride. Despite the storm Nat pressed on. But while humming along at just over twenty miles per hour, a boiler safety valve blew open, spilling steam pressure. *Say When* wound down slowly. Frustrated, Nat climbed into the boiler room and screwed down the safety valve—negating the safety feature, the only check if the engine pressure should grow dangerously high. Nat once again put *Say When* to task, slowly building speed. As the steam pressure built, the boiler man added more coal. *Say When* accelerated, her smokestack spewing a stream of white smoke whisked aft by the wind. The engine whined, and the boiler man opened the doors to add more fuel. But just as they passed the Bristol ferry dock there was an explosion. A boiler pipe had burst. The boiler room door had been open. Hot ash, smoke, and steam had blasted the attendant, Charlie Newman, who'd been knocked to the floor and badly burned. He was rushed to the hospital in Providence.

The next day, January 6, 1889, Nat wrote in his diary that there'd been a heavy nor'easter all day. He noted at 7 A.M. the wind blew northeast at thirty knots with rain. He noted at 2 P.M. that it blew northeast at thirty-three knots with heavy rain. He noted at 9 P.M. the wind blew at twenty-five knots with rain. As if the storm raging outside portended difficult times to come, Captain Nat noted in the far right column, "Charles Numan [*sic*] died this morning from injury on *Say When*."[14]

Newman's death cast a distressing pall over the shops. Why had Captain Nat clamped the safety valve? Why had he been so unwavering with his engine design? And how could something so catastrophic happen during a yacht trial? Nat, upset and now plagued with uncertainty, was suddenly embroiled in a heated legal investigation. Though James and John Brown had both expressed their doubts about *Say When*'s engine design, the entire family was united in denying any possibility of Nat's negligence. The steamship authorities pressed on and the legal proceedings stretched throughout the year. Nat's lawyers argued the death had been simply terrible luck. If the boiler door had been closed, *Say When* would have simply lost her head of steam. A bursting boiler tube wasn't unheard of. The incident on *Say When* was an amalgam of worst-case scenarios that had unfortunately resulted in a death.

Nat and John Brown had no other recourse but to continue business as usual, working tirelessly to push the Navy's commission, Seagoing Torpedo Boat No. 1, America's first purpose-built steamer firing self-propelled torpedoes, through the south construction shop. Steel-hulled with two engines providing roughly 2,000 horsepower modeled after those of *Say When* and *Ballymena,* the 138-foot *Cushing* was a vast improvement over her predecessors. The engines, though of the same complex design, were the largest and most powerful ever created at the Herreshoff Manufacturing Company. The *Cushing's* steel structural elements, from the frame to bulkheads, were galvanized to better withstand their salt-water environment. Both the Navy and Nat were eager to assess *Cushing's* performance. And there's no doubt that many hoped a successful *Cushing* could help Captain Nat's *Say When* court case.

Hopes were high as the Herreshoff Manufacturing Company rolled into January 1890. The weather was warm. On January 2 a southwest wind crawled up the bay and Nat noted in his diary that he had picked a dandelion blossom from his lawn. The unseasonably mild weather held, and on January 6 he noted, "The grass is turning green gradually." By the end of January *Cushing* reached completion and was rolled down the ways of the south construction shop on January 23, 1890, at 9:45 A.M., the engines successfully tested that afternoon. Her initial trial run on January 29 was cautiously held at moderate speeds and was deemed a success. Over the next few weeks they continued trials, more than two dozen running into March and filling most of Captain Nat's time. On February 17 Nat noted that *Cushing* logged 23.25 knots (or 26.75 miles per hour) traveling from Bristol to Rose Island, outside of Newport Harbor, and back—a highly successful run. Nat had vindicated his engine design, the Navy was happy, and *Cushing* won ample praise.

Snow fell throughout the night until about 11 A.M. on March 3, 1890, blanketing Bristol in white drifts on the day the *Say When* case went to court. The next morning began with rain and changed over to snow. The court announced its decision: Nat was to pay $4,000 in restitution, a staggering sum in 1890, which he dutifully noted in his diary without additional comment. On April 22, he officially handed *Cushing* to the Navy. Although this much-celebrated battle steamship had firmly established Captain Nat and the Herreshoff Manufacturing Company as virtuosos of the high-speed motor vessel, the court decision had also mandated a penalty far stiffer than any fine. He conspicuously failed to note in his diary that in addition to the settlement, the court had indefinitely revoked his steam license.

THE NEW AGE OF DESIGN

April 1890–May 1898

Herreshoff followed a path that had unfolded before him, as if with each intrepid step a new series of obstacles redefined his life and company. With his license to design and build steamships revoked, he was forced to shift his emphasis to sail. With a series of new shops now lining the waterfront and several hundred workmen on payroll, the Herreshoff brothers had no choice but to adapt. His son, L. Francis, later wrote that there's no doubt the ruling from the steamship authority played an important role in the Herreshoff Manufacturing Company's almost complete focus on sailing yachts after the 1890 *Say When* accident, but it's curious that a company with so much invested in its naval contracts and high-speed steamyachts would not appeal the court's decision. If the *Say When* tragedy had truly been an accident, why not fight it? For one reason, they continued to build steamers, including those for the Navy, despite the alleged interdict. Perhaps Captain Nat made no mention of the ruling because he thought it a hollow reproof. Whatever the reason, he continued building Navy ships, although after 1890 they conspicuously took a backseat to sailboats.

Herreshoff had also endeared himself to America's elite. He had found new benefactors, less demanding than the Navy, with deep pockets and an appreciation of his talents. His new patrons also played by his rules. If you wanted a ninety-foot yacht, you'd get the best in the world. You just didn't ask questions and paid the bill on time. American businessmen liked his style, and as one of the most transformative decades in American history took hold—in business, technology, culture, and naval architecture—these wealthy men were eager to bankroll the next new thing.

With the dawn of the new decade, that same spirit of daring enterprise seized Lipton. During the 1880s, while business boomed, a number of tea brokers from London's Mincing Lane approached him about selling tea in his shops. Because he so disliked the thought of using a middleman, he decided he'd rather not sell tea at all. Lipton had done well by buying directly from the source or becoming his own wholesaler. By the mid-1880s Lipton was making more money than ever, but he still worked tirelessly. He was known to say, "There is no fun like work." He neither smoked nor drank. And other than his mother, he had developed few personal friendships. His mother, however, was almost eighty and her health had been declining for some time; in the autumn of 1889, she died. Lipton had spent his whole life working for her approval. Now she was gone and although his company was prospering, he was tired. During the summer of 1890 he booked passage to Australia for a holiday.

His respite would be more than brief. On a stopover in Ceylon, now the island of Sri Lanka, he discovered a way in which he could altogether forgo the middleman in a tea operation. At the Grand Oriental Hotel in Ceylon's capital, Colombo, he met a representative of his company, Frank Duplock, who had been sent ahead to scout Ceylon's tea growing prospects. Duplock's report was good: because the island's chief crop, coffee, had been hit hard by a case of the blight and tea production was still in its infancy, the island was in dire straights. Duplock told Lipton, "You can buy estates here for a song."[1] In fact, to buy a fully functioning plantation he would only need to spend half of the £75,000 he'd brought with him.[2]

With his newly acquired tea gardens in Ceylon and a staff in Scotland who'd learned the art of blending different varieties of teas, a crucial step in creating a palatable brew, Lipton took the tea business by storm. He had cut out the buyers and importers, the London blenders and salesmen, which allowed him to cut the cost of tea dramatically. Tea that had been selling in Britain for three shillings per pound—too much for the average family that earned two pounds per week—began selling in his shops for one shilling, seven pence and was still generating a profit. He also began to package his tea in smaller units, which kept the leaves fresher and allowed him to sell to customers with less money to spend. His colorful packaging—a smiling Ceylonese woman with a basket of fresh-picked tea balanced on her head—became a trademark image. He maintained a low wholesale cost, a low retail price, and streamlined production: the Lipton Tea slogan, true to his business philosophy, read, "Directly from the Tea Gardens to the Tea Pot."

The Lipton stores were flooded with customers purchasing cheap tea. He continued to advertise in everything from newspapers to train platforms, and his sales shot up dramatically. Because so much business was moving through his small office, Lipton relocated, moving his base of operations from Glasgow to London's City Road. He also transplanted his entire central staff, which had grown to roughly a thousand people. Before Lipton arrived in Ceylon in 1888, the country had exported 24 million pounds of tea per year. Five years later they were exporting 80 million pounds.[3] By the end of 1889 Lipton had 150 stores and was opening another every week. He was making roughly a million pounds sterling per year.[4] As a grocer Lipton had been a millionaire, but with tea his fortune grew exponentially.

Before 1890 Nat and John Brown had built only eight sailboats, four of which were for themselves. *Shadow*, the "compromise type" that melded the deep draft English cutter shape with the beamy American sloop, had won more than 150 prizes between 1872 and 1887.[5] But it was Nat's *Clara*, his small family catyawl, which had caught the eye of Mr. Edwin D. Morgan, the wealthy rear commodore of the New York Yacht Club who kept a summer home overlooking Newport's Brenton Cove. Captain Nat had built him a forty-eight-foot cabin steam launch *Henrietta*, but *Clara* piqued Morgan's interest. In 1890 Herreshoff agreed to build him two similar catyawls—double-masted, galf-rigged sailing yachts. On November 11, Nat and John Brown launched the twenty-nine-foot, six-inch *Gannet* and the twenty-six-foot, six-inch *Pelican*. Both yachts earned glowing praise, and soon Captain Nat was hired by other members to design and build a number of large sail and steamyachts. For the same reason Nat's steamships were coveted, his sailing yachts were prized—blazing speed.

For those who believe everything happens for a reason, the *Say When* tragedy was a hitch that pointed the Herreshoff Manufacturing Company toward its true calling. Although the brothers had worked hard to hone their steamship business, unforeseen calamity had blazed an alternate trail. "Mishaps are like knives," wrote the nineteenth century poet James Russell Lowell, "that either serve us or cut us, as we grasp them by the blade or the handle." Grasping the handle, Captain Nat retired to his drafting room and hashed out plans for a new forty-six-foot waterline, seventy-foot overall cutter for E. D. Morgan. The yacht was designed to compete in the New York Yacht Club forty-six-foot class against designs by naval architect Edward Burgess, who had established his preeminence by designing America's Cup defenders *Puritan, Mayflower,* and *Volunteer.*

After finishing dinner and retiring to his third-floor model room, Nat lit the gas lamps of his study and sketched a rough outline. But unlike an artist whose strokes followed the path of that most aesthetically pleasing, Nat crafted each line according to the dictates of a mathematical formula that handicapped the forty-six-foot class. In 1883 a committee sponsored by the Seawanhaka Corinthian Yacht Club in Long Island Sound set out to create a fair and accurate rating system for handicapping boats. They framed what became known as the Seawanhaka Rule:

$$\text{Rating} = (\text{Waterline Length} + \sqrt{\text{Sail Area}})/2.$$

Although the boats in the forty-six-foot class were all built to roughly the same waterline length, there were discrepancies in their overall shape and sail area, and those differences often played a significant role in their speed around the course. A yacht, however, was only as fast as her "corrected" time around the course. In the same way Nat had devised Boston Yacht Club's table for calculating these corrected times for mismatched yachts (by computing a yacht's rating with her overall elapsed times around the course), he now worked backward. Probing the Seawanhaka Rule, he found loopholes. Using these, he tailored his design to make it appear slower—on paper—than it actually was. Unlike the newly evolving British system of golf handicapping, which reflected a player's skill, the yacht rating system only factored a yacht's theoretical performance, based on design. By designing a yacht that performed better than her rating, he'd have a resounding winner.

Some might argue that placing constraints on an architect can inhibit the creative process, but often it channels it. For instance, when New York introduced zoning codes in 1916 binding skyscraper construction to a setback system determined by street width, architects, unhindered by height restrictions, produced the Chrysler and Empire State buildings.[6] Likewise, the sonnet or haiku is bound by a rigid structure. The fugue or passacaglia, defined by a strict counterpoint, magnify artistic decisions within a known context. As Nat drew his pencil across the page, he hashed out plans to maximize his design for the prescribed rule. Naval architects had done this before, but never with the deft precision of Nat's hand. Each line represented an intuitive sense of geometry, the ability to mesh complex calculus and trigonometry into a definitive shape. At forty-two years old, he had logged roughly the same hours and amassed the same experience as someone in his sixties. He wed his intense study of mechanical engineering with the acute sense of touch he'd learned from blind John Brown. The lines of lead were soon strokes of his knife across a dusty block of pine, and with each sweeping draw, he approached the nexus of personal vision and mathematical precision.

As slivers of wood fell to the floor a curious shape emerged. Under the Seawanhaka Rule, a proportionately short waterline relative to sail area gave a yacht an advantageous time allowance. Nat carved a short waterline with a long overhanging bow and stern. With such vaulting extensions—twenty-five feet total—the bow threatened to dig dangerously deep into a heavy sea. Departing from the paradigm of sharp, concave, clipper bows that had graced the leading edge of yachts since the 1850s, he carved a full, more buoyant, convex-shape, with long, sweeping diagonals. To complement the long overhangs, he increased the sail area. To counteract the heel caused by the large sail plan, he attached a deep, heavily ballasted keel. With her sail area and keel designed in perfect balance, hull No. 411 would lean comfortably to her lines; with her carefully calculated convex or "spoon" bow kissing the water, she would sail with the speed of a longer yacht. The actual sailing waterline dwarfed the load waterline at rest. With a slight of hand, Captain Nat had dramatically increased her speed potential. When heeled in a stiff breeze No. 411 would sail as if she were a faster fifty-six-footer even though her rating had been calculated to a forty-six-foot waterline.

With a cold northwesterly blowing across Bristol Harbor, on May 6, 1891, Captain Nat launched E. D. Morgan's new yacht, christened *Gloriana*. Rumors had been circulating about the design throughout the spring. A month earlier the *New York Times* had sent a reporter to investigate, and Nat offered a rare interview and glimpse of the boat. The *Times* published a detailed description, concluding, "No one can accuse the Herreshoffs of imitating anybody in their design, and if they are right, the others are all wrong."[7] That summer Nat proved he was right. "She made a clean record in the Forty-Six Foot Class," he later wrote, "then supposed to be composed of the most advanced type of yachts known. Mr. Morgan sailed her in his first race and I sailed her for him in the following seven, all of that year, and she won them all."[8]

Gloriana's unprecedented success brought a wave of orders, in particular another forty-six footer, hull No. 414. When Herreshoff began construction Morgan sold his yacht, knowing Captain Nat would improve on *Gloriana's* design and commandeer her winning record. The resultant *Wasp* was another smashing success. Incredibly lightweight and again with large overhangs and a heavily ballasted keel, *Wasp* garnered the full attention of the yachting fraternity. So light was *Wasp* that when she heeled, her hull twisted, sometimes making it impossible to open cabin doors until the boat swung through the next tack. Herreshoff's calculations had paid off, largely because the technology and craftsmanship of his shops could produce structural pieces, particularly in the large rigs and sail plans, which the rule designers had not foreseen. In his 1937 book *Men Against the Rule: A Century of Progress in Yacht Design,* Charles Lane Poor explained that the 1889 Seawanhaka Rule committee had identified their formula's tendency to encourage large spreads of sail in small yacht designs, but presumed it impractical to install proportionately large rigs onto larger yachts. The rule committee believed an unwieldy vessel designed solely to win races would become "more and more an undesirable and expensive thing to possess, and will appear upon regatta courses in a correspondingly diminished number."[9] Their presumptions were wrong.

Captain Nat's *Gloriana, Wasp,* as well as a small yacht named *Dilemma,* equipped with not only the same towering spread of sail and long overhangs but also a thin fin-shaped keel with a large lead bulb at the bottom, the first of its kind, had marked a notable paradigm shift. Designers knew it, the rule makers knew it, and most importantly the rich men who wrote the checks knew it. Captain Nat's pencil dashes began to show larger, more powerful rigs. Overhangs stretched farther. Hulls assumed flatter, wider shapes. When his boats heeled they sailed as if they were longer and faster. And when race committees tallied times and ratings, his boats won.

When Edward Burgess succumbed to typhoid in 1887, divesting America of its foremost designer, all eyes turned to Bristol. The yachts emerging from the Herreshoff shop rivaled that of anything built in the world. And to further amplify the buzz, in *Wasp,* hull No. 414, a lithe, stripped-down racer of the forty-six-foot class, Captain Nat had stumbled upon a captain, a twenty-five-year-old from Scotland with a cool hand on the helm and sharp, tactical mind. Nat realized the young handsome helmsman—with dark brown hair, a mustache, thick brogue, and bulldog stature—could realize his yacht's full potential. That Charlie Barr had been hired to steer and manage a ground-breaking design built of the lightest construction and equipped with the most technologically advanced machinery was a calculated appointment. Herreshoff knew his yacht was only as good as her crew's ability to secure a winning record. He saw in Barr a character not unlike himself, quiet yet demanding, competitive, confident, and driven. And for all the mental dexterity Nat commanded in converting a nest of formulae into a sleek racing vessel, Barr wielded commensurate talents: a percipient feel for wind, water, and the tactical minds of his opponents. He was young, and though in want of experience, he had an eye for excellence. Upon sailing his first Herreshoff yacht, he gained a deep-seated respect for Captain Nat. And when the Wizard first handed the helm to Barr, the sentiment became mutual. Although hiring a captain was the owner's job, Nat's personnel recommendations were accepted with the same deference as his designs.

With *Gloriana* and *Wasp* the Herreshoff Manufacturing Company had made its mark. Though straying from his most ardent professional curiosity, steamships, Captain Nat had reconnected with his lifelong love of sailing. He had learned on John Brown's *Meteor* and had spent countless hours sailing his father's *Julia*s and his own creations, *Consuelo, Clara,* and *Coquina.* Orders for sailing yachts flooded the office. John Brown, dressed in his suit, a watch chain dangling from his pocket, wooed customers, while Captain Nat, ever zealous about his schedule, worked in his third-floor study, ate his meals in silence, and made rounds through the shops like a physician.

Further experimenting with fin keels and corresponding sail plans, Nat employed the concept to bigger boats. Although the fin keel was fast in small boats such as *Dilemma,* they both concluded the design was not effective on larger yachts, citing excessive surface area. Nat, however, had not fully tested his theories. After all he'd only built a handful of sailboats, and all were less than eighty feet. He'd only admired the large racing yachts, most notably the America's Cup defenders, from afar. For almost ten years Burgess had cornered the market for Cup yachts, and he'd done it well, winning with *Genesta* in 1885, *Galatea* in 1886, and *Thistle* in 1887. With Burgess's death, yachtsmen sought the next innovative designer, and with *Gloriana* and *Wasp* shaking the foundation of naval architecture, eyes turned on Bristol.

When the Earl of Dunraven launched a challenge for the America's Cup in 1893, a syndicate headed by *Wasp*'s owner Archibald Rogers, and including William K. Vanderbilt and J. P. Morgan, called on Captain Nat. But in requesting that Nat design a Cup defender, Rogers made a grave mistake, stipulating the new yacht, to be named *Colonia,* must have identical lines to his *Wasp,* and with a full keel of no more than fourteen feet so that the yacht could be moored near his home in Hyde Park on the Hudson. For any other client, Herreshoff would have scoffed, but understanding the financial implications of passing up such an august commission, he accepted, knowing full well that a mere eighty-five-foot imitation with only fourteen feet of draft would fail. The brothers no doubt voiced their discontent, and with a doomed design underway and the threat of losing the Cup becoming increasingly real, E. D. Morgan, still singing Nat's praises for his veritable fleet of Herreshoff yachts—his two catyawls, *Gannet* and *Pelican,* his ninety-eight-foot steamer *Javelin,* his forty-eight-foot launch *Katydid,* and the eminent *Gloriana*—formed a second New York Yacht Club syndicate. And with unmitigated faith, Morgan gave Nat complete autonomy. As *Colonia,* Rogers's distended incarnation of *Wasp,* filled the south construction shop, Morgan's *Vigilant,* the next evolutionary step in Herreshoff's mind, took shape in the shed next door.

Fraught with politics, Captain Nat's entrance into the America's Cup forum had a two-fold impact. First, building two Cup defenders was extremely lucrative. By the early to mid-1890s the Herreshoff Manufacturing Company employed roughly three hundred workers and paid some of the highest wages for skilled labor in Rhode Island. In addition, they continued to maintain well-lit, heated shops. But maintaining a skilled workforce and comfortable working conditions required a high overhead. Filling the shops with boats was imperative, and the more intricate they were the better. Second, Captain Nat had billed himself as a man to reckon with. Even J. P. Morgan, one of the most tenacious competitors and obstinate managers in

America, realized he could not manhandle Nat and his brother. Yes, they were men who worked with their hands from a small seaside village—a far cry from the New York business world—but they established themselves as peers, masters of a game their benefactors believed tantamount to their professional lives.

Though usually aloof, the analytic artist lost in a world of formulae and drawings, Nat could be, surprisingly, socially savvy—especially in the commercial world. He knew where his strengths lay and would steer shop politics and customer gripes to John Brown, who with a clasp of a handshake and the pink of politeness could muffle even the most vociferous cries of discontent. Likewise, John Brown knew when a terse response from Nat could settle a dispute in their favor, the younger brother's piercing green-eyed glare and a simple *no* ending all further discussion. Although their business was modest compared to that of their clientele, Nat and John Brown, with their unflagging confidence, asserted that they stood on equal ground. This was confirmed the following spring.

A month before launching the Cup boats, Captain Nat had finished outfitting his third big project built that winter, the eighty-five-foot waterline yacht *Navahoe,* placed under the command of the rising talent Charlie Barr. With so much work that winter, Nat shared designs for all three yachts. "I had not time . . . to work out complete detail drawings for each yacht," he later wrote, "so both the defenders' rigs were alike, and many of the details were the same as worked out for Navahoe."[10] In sailing *Navahoe* that spring, Nat not only previewed the rigs and sail plans of his two Cup yachts, he also acquired some much-needed practice. Neither he nor Barr had ever sailed anything that big. "I had no experience in sailing large yachts and neither had Charles Barr, her skipper," wrote Nat, "so we had much to learn."[11] Having provided valuable rig tuning data, *Navahoe* became an impromptu trial horse for the Cup defenders. Nat shuffled between boats, lending his expertise to each. But no advice from him would hide the fact that *Vigilant,* sporting a bronze centerboard that when extended drew twenty-four feet of water, outshone *Colonia,* much to the ire of Rogers's syndicate.

Barr and Herreshoff's early-season collaboration on *Navahoe* paid off, for when *Vigilant* was trailing *Colonia* and *Jubilee*—a Boston boat vying for the chance to defend the Cup—*Vigilant's* manager, Charles

Oliver Iselin, called for a change. "It was on this first set of trial races that *Vigilant's* sailing master, Captain Stone, was not doing well and had got back to third place," wrote Nat. "I saw Mr. Iselin, the syndicate manager, having a very animated talk with his friends on the afterdeck; then he told Captain Stone he wanted me to take the wheel, and asked me to. We succeeded in rounding the first mark abreast of *Jubilee* and soon took a good lead, and so ended the race well ahead."[12]

With limited experience sailing a yacht of such size, power, and complexity, Nat won the series and then in the races for the America's Cup steered *Vigilant,* with Morgan as navigator, to a pair of victories against Lord Dunraven and his British challenger *Valkyrie II,* designed by George Lennox Watson. In the final America's Cup race of 1893 off Sandy Hook, the wind built to gale force. Both *Vigilant* and *Valkyrie II* reefed their mainsails, but in the mounting winds, the British boat pulled ahead, establishing a two-minute lead at the windward mark. With no other choice, Nat ordered the reefs cut from the mainsail and every additional canvas piled onto the rig. Nat ordered her spinnaker, her balloon jib topsail, and topsail set. The mast flexed precariously, but *Vigilant* shot ahead. Attempting to regain the lead, *Valykyrie II* set all her sails but her crew watched two spinnakers explode in tatters. On the fifteen-mile run, Herreshoff averaged eleven and a half knots, beating *Valkyrie II* by forty seconds.

Despite unsubstantiated accusations of foul play lodged by Lord Dunraven, Nat had proven himself in one of the most volatile designs America had seen—and in so doing inaugurated a new, extreme standard for racing yachts. They were big and fragile, their decks loaded down with between sixty and seventy crew, and their sails so large and helms so finicky that only the most skilled hand, like that of Herreshoff, could steer them. Above all, they were expensive. *Vigilant* cost approximately $100,000, three times that of *Volunteer,* which had defended the Cup in 1887. But with exaggerated proportions and newspapers reporting ever-mounting bankrolls, public interest boomed. Nineteenth-century yachting, especially competition for the America's Cup, intrigued sports fans. Herreshoff's monstrosities captivated them. Roughly sixty thousand people crowded excursion steamers and private yachts to watch *Vigilant* and *Valkyrie II.* And when Lord Dunraven challenged again in 1895, America waited agog for the short, stooped, introverted man's next contraption.

★　　★　　★

Although Captain Nat, as he was more widely becoming known after the 1893 defense, had skillfully steered *Vigilant* to victory, he saw in young Charlie Barr something special. Nat handed Barr command of *Navahoe,* his first fully metal racing yacht and Barr's first commission on a large racer. Although Barr was good on the helm, he, like Nat, lacked diplomatic tact, perhaps one reason they got along. Soon after *Navahoe* began trials in Narragansett Bay, half of Barr's crew quit. "The men deserted at Bristol," reported the *New York Times,* "and they have determined to do all in their power to induce American sailors not to ship on the Navahoe."[13] The men argued that Barr enforced English rules. Typically English crewmen provided their own sailing uniforms—white boiler suits and deck shoes—and paid their steward for food. In this arrangement they were typically paid well, about $42 per month. Conversely, American crewmen earned about $30 per month with meals and uniforms covered by the boat.[14] Paying the same lower American salaries, Barr tried to push the cost of food and clothing on his men, and they objected. Ultimately, the problem was rectified and the vacant positions filled. His rocky start, however, had just begun.

While en route to England where owner Royal Phelps Carroll planned to race *Navahoe* during the 1893 summer season, Barr, only a few hours from Bristol, smashed the gleaming new yacht square into a pilot boat sailing north near Nantucket Shoal.[15] Limping into Boston for repairs, he spent subsequent days deflecting taunts from yard workers. Although he gathered himself and sailed on, his lackluster performance in British waters led to further discontent. In August the *Westminster Gazette* reported a rumor that *Navahoe* retired from racing in Southampton because of "trouble among the crew over the yacht's failure."[16] Finally, after repeatedly losing, Carroll sacked him and hired Captain Aubrey Crocker to steer his yacht. In Barr's defense, Carroll was known to be hotheaded. At one point during the season he punched a deckhand in the face.[17] Although Barr's inaugural big-boat season had been a disaster, a few notable yachtsmen, including Caroll's friend Philip Schuyler, lobbied for him, attesting that a lack of local currents and tides had hindered *Navahoe* more than her skipper. In addition, Barr had in fact pulled off a handful of wins. He'd also developed a unique sailing style that showed promise.

Born in Gourock, Scotland, a small fishing village where the Clyde River meets the Firth of Clyde, Charlie Barr grew up by the sea. As a boy he apprenticed in a grocery, but losing interest he instead turned to fishing, signing on as a green hand on a local trawler. After one winter of backbreaking work on the North Sea, long-lining flounder from ice-slicked dories and earning little pay, he followed the footsteps of his older half brother, John, who had established himself as one of the Clyde's polished racing skippers. When Mr. J. George Clark, vice commodore of the Clyde Corinthian Yacht Club, sold his William Fife Jr.-designed *Clara,* a fifty-five-foot, twenty-ton cutter, to Mr. Charles Sweet, a barrister at Lincolns Inn, John Barr was hired to deliver the yacht to the United States, where Sweet planned to race during the summer season. Throughout his childhood Charlie had helped on various Scottish yachts as a spare hand, and when a position opened on *Clara,* Charlie, then nineteen, signed on as cook.

Upon arriving in the United States in 1885, John Barr and *Clara,* with Charlie on board, won his first and only race of the season. During the following summer of 1886 they dominated the American fleet. John Barr's success so impressed members of the Royal Clyde Yacht Club that they appointed him skipper of their 1887 America's Cup challenger *Thistle.* During this time, with much practice and no doubt coaching from John, Charlie came into his own as a yacht crew and helmsman. But after losing to Edward Burgess's *Volunteer* in 1887 John Barr fell from grace. The Royal Clyde Yacht Club blamed him for *Thistle's* failure. But although some Scottish yachtsmen had written off John Barr, the American yachting fraternity saw him and his younger brother as skilled sailors and upright gentlemen.

John Barr's yacht *Clara* had also turned eyes on her Scottish designer William Fife Jr., who represented the third generation of yacht designers in his family. A friend of Sweet's, Charles H. Tweed of New York, turned to Fife for his next yacht. He produced the forty-foot cutter *Minerva.* Tweed sent Charlie to manage and captain the delivery. Upon arriving in the United States, Charlie and Fife's new flyer consistently won races. Widely admired and notably superior to her American counterparts, *Minerva* struck a chord, and her captain, young, confident, and competitive, caught Herreshoff's eye. Though relatively new to the game, Charlie Barr embodied all the qualities of a leader. He was intelligent and decisive, handsome, fit, and always maintained a cool composure, even when confronted with a tight situation, which he had an uncanny knack for finding. It was that willingness to drive his boat and crew harder than anyone else that earned him the favor of both owners who wanted to win at all costs and Herreshoff, whose reputation as a designer relied on victories.

Barr studied the rules of yacht racing, which by the end of the nineteenth century had grown into a bound volume with myriad corollaries and countless provisions tailored to individual clubs. In a fraction of a second he could recall with savant-like accuracy any rule that would benefit his boat. Whereas some skippers might steer clear of other yachts during tight mark roundings or pre-start maneuvers, Barr, backed by his utmost confidence in the rules, took advantage of even the slightest hesitation from his opponents. And because he approached every confrontation with such palpable certainty and poise, he wielded the power to even bend the rules in his favor.

Unlike tennis, golf, or football, the rules of yacht racing are less a steadfast infrastructure and more a series of guidelines implemented when situations arise. If a ball is hit, kicked, or thrown out of bounds, play stops and some form of penalty is handed to the offending player or team, whether it is a point to the opponent or the loss of a stroke or down. In yacht racing the rules define which yacht has right-of-way, how yachts will start a race, round marks, and finish. An in-depth understanding of these rules is most valuable when yachts are crossing or in close proximity to one another, for this is when one may most often secure a tactical advantage over the other. The ultimate goal of a yacht race is to sail the prescribed course faster than your competition. But unlike, say, a running race, where your ability to win is based largely on running faster than your opponents, winning yacht races requires an amalgam of speed and tactics and your facility to profit from the rules, the weather, and perhaps your opponents' mistakes.

Although every crewman's work on a racing yacht can make or break a race, it is the captain who assumes ultimate responsibility. He holds the helm and decides where the boat goes. Not only must the captain understand the rules and use them to his advantage, he must have the foresight to inform his crew of upcoming maneuvers. He must have a perfect understanding of his yacht's sail inventory. And above all, he must have a "feel" for the helm and his yacht's movement through wind and water. This "feel" was particularly important on Nat's designs, for his perfectly balanced yachts were extremely responsive.

A sailing yacht is like a giant wing moving through two fluids: air and water. The trimmed canvas wing slices the air, pulling the yacht forward, just as a wing pulls a bird aloft. Below the waterline, a smaller rigid wing comprising a rudder and keel slices the more viscous fluid, also producing lift while providing the lateral resistance needed to maintain headway. If either end of the wing were out of proportion with the other, the yacht would not track true. If either end were twisted—the sails trimmed improperly or the rudder turned too sharply—the yacht, slowed by drag, would slog around the course. When out of trim, the yacht, as helmsmen say, was out of her groove, and this distinction between being in or out, especially on yachts as delicately balanced as Nat's, was perceptible to only the most seasoned hands.

It took a sentient hand to steer a Herreshoff racer. Captain Nat had it. Barr had it. But many struggled. Upon setting sail after assuming ownership of a Herreshoff thirty-footer, one owner promptly returned to the Herreshoff yard complaining his yacht was out of control. Captain Nat boarded and demonstrated, the yacht gliding along seamlessly under his command. Not all his yachts were so reactive. Cruising yachts were designed for comfort with a less finicky helm, a wider steering groove inherent in their designs. Racing yachts, conversely, were designed to win races—and the yachts helmed by strictly professional skippers were extremely sensitive, allowing a deft hand to sail incredibly close to the wind, the wing in perfect trim.

But a helmsman's ability to steer in trim was also dependent on his ability to feel the pull of his sails. A skilled helmsman touched the wheel and felt his staysail sheet a half-inch too slack. He felt the yacht accelerate with a quarter-inch ease on his topsail halyard or an inch of trim on his mainsail. Miniscule adjustments by his crewmembers were channeled through his hands and he felt how each affected the yacht's performance. In every way that Herreshoff's designs balanced every stress and strain, every weight and counterweight throughout the hull and rig, the deft captain, using the sails and rig, maximized that design to his wishes, adjusting the yacht's groove to match the state of the wind and weather ahead. The way the rig bent and sails pulled was adjusted to maintain a balanced wing.

Hundreds of moveable parts and scores of men working in unison channeled through his hands. He kept one eye carefully trained on the telltale pennant at the peak of the club topsail. The other eye quickly glanced ahead, scanning the water for puffs of wind—marked by a patch of dark ripples on the water, or perhaps a set of small waves. With a small puff, the headsail trimmers hauled in their sheets an inch. The mainsail trimmer followed. Barr, maintaining one eye on the pennant, the other monitoring the oncoming puff, felt the boat turn ever so slightly into the wind, the puff washing over the sails, water lapping the yacht's leeward rail as the massive hull heeled. And as the yacht exited the puff, the trimmers eased ever so slightly and the yacht, as if equipped with a mind of her own, fell off the wind a degree or two, assuming her previous course.

Barr held the reins but knew not to overuse them. He used the wheel more as a monitoring device than for steering, feeling the various pressures surging through the lines, the sails, the planks or plates of the hull, allowing the sails to turn the boat. When turning the wheel, he complemented the wishes of the yacht, rather than forcing her to his will. And atop all these minute adjustments, he monitored the progress of the competition. Was the other yacht sailing faster? Was she pointing closer to the wind?

These are the thoughts that passed through the helmsman's head as he steered his yacht around the racecourse. The rules most often came into play when yachts, in close quarters, jockeyed for position. And it was a skipper's ability to recall the myriad rules in a moment's notice that gave him an advantage. A boat to leeward could force a windward yacht to alter course. A boat on starboard tack held right-of-way over a port-tack boat. A yacht clear ahead commanded right-of-way over an overtaking yacht. These basic rules and their corollaries largely dictated how the boats sailed the course. But in those split seconds when the margins of a rule became blurred, when right-of-way was no longer cut and dry, the deft helmsman clinched a tactical advantage. Barr, wielding his 120-foot yacht as if it were a dinghy and aggressively intimidating his opponents with his flamboyant driving style, could bend rules in his favor, skillfully asserting his yacht's right-of-way during those fleeting gray moments, locking in an advantageous position before his opponent could react.

To seize these opportunities, Barr relied on his afterguard—a selected few crewmembers who focused primarily on the mental part of the race—to advise him of tactical situations and timing while he focused on boat speed and maneuvers. Sailing with Barr followed a strict protocol. In a 1948 *Rudder* magazine article L. Francis Herreshoff provides probably the most detailed description of his sailing style:

> He had trained his first mate (who for several years was Chris Christiansen) to keep one eye on him, and when Captain Barr wished to give an order he simply crooked his forefinger slightly, whereupon the mate came close to him. Then Capt. Barr would say very quietly but distinctly something about was [*sic*] follows: "Mr. Christiansen, after rounding the next mark I would like the spinnaker set to starboard. I would like the jib topsail replaced with the ballooner."
>
> The mate would then pace slowly up and down the deck watching the marker they were approaching until he estimated the time and distance right to commence action, when he would roar out, "Take in the yib topsail. Raus mit the spinnaker pole to starboard. Stand by for a yibe." Before this moment everything was quiet, the crew of some twenty men all lying prone in a neat row with their heads near the weather waterways. The second mate crouched in the leeward fore rigging watching the headsails, and the only sound to be heard was the swish and hiss of the waves under the leeward bow, and the low moan of the wind in the rigging. But now the yacht's deck suddenly changed to a scene of intense activity as each man scrambled to his station and stood crouched, ready for action, some at the sheets, others at the upper and lower backstays, while the spinnaker pole was being run out and the man on the bowsprit had muzzled the jib topsail.
>
> Now the mate nods his head at the mastheadsman, and this agile fellow runs up the mast hoops like a monkey climbing a ladder and stands on the fore spreaders in anticipation of changing the main topsail staysail. Now the mark buoy is almost abeam, and the yacht swings like a gigantic turntable as Capt. Barr crouches to leeward of the wheel and pulls the spokes toward him hand over hand. The yacht now rights herself, and the wind, which had seemed quite strong, suddenly becomes very light as the yacht, which before was heading into it at some seven or eight miles an hour, now goes with it, making the difference of some fourteen miles an hour to the wind's apparent velocity. But in the meantime there is the clicking of many winches and the chorus of many orders as the second mate and the tow quartermasters call out in broken English strange words

that are instantly understood and obeyed. Some of the orders are, "Stand by the after spinnaker guy," "Overhaul the leeward backstays," and the whole yacht seems to quiver from the stumping forward and aft of several 200-pound Swedes, when crisp and clear the first mate class out, "Yesus, don't younce de yacht."

The spinnaker and balloon jib are now broken out almost simultaneously and the balloon main topmast staysail is going aloft. Soon everything quiets down again and the only movement is a few hands coiling down sheets and halliards. Capt. Barr has now moved back of the wheel and stands with his eye on the telltale pennant at the peak of the club topsail. He seems perfectly cool and quiet, and no one would have guessed his eye had seen anything but the mark buoy, the compass, and the luff of the topsail. And furthermore, anyone would have thought the maneuver had been perfectly performed, would have thought the crew had performed miracles of sail changing in almost seconds. But now Capt. Barr crooks his forefinger again and the mate approaches him, saying, "Yes, sir," and Capt. Barr says, "Mr. Christiansen, that was done very well, but the next time I would like to see the club sheet slacked simultaneously with the foresheet." "Aye, aye, sir," says the mate as he moves to the weather main rigging with one eye on the luff of the spinnaker.[18]

Barr honed his cool and collected comportment over many years. Aboard *Navahoe,* his management system had not yet coalesced. But despite errors, he'd streamlined his approach, and it was this cogent style of command that affirmed the loyalty of Herreshoff and his New York clients.

When Lord Dunraven challenged for the America's Cup again in 1895, William K. Vanderbilt charged Herreshoff with building a defender. Vanderbilt had helped fund *Colonia,* which had bowed to *Vigilant* in the 1893 trials because he and Archibald Rogers had tried to dictate the design to Captain Nat. This time, however, he teamed with E.D. Morgan and Charles Oliver Iselin and deferred to Herreshoff's better judgment. Their new yacht, aptly named *Defender,* was longer than *Vigilant,* stretching 89 feet on the waterline and 123 feet, 3 inches overall. Captain Nat shortened the keel but added a lead bulb weighing 177,000 pounds. This provided the ballast to build an even loftier rig with larger, more powerful sails. Further experimenting, Herreshoff built the yacht with steel frames, aluminum topside and decking, and a bronze hull that could be finely burnished below the waterline, his first venture into a yacht of composite metal construction. The building proceeded smoothly but as if hinting of the future to come, *Defender* ground to a halt when sliding down the launching ways. The yacht had jammed on her track by an errant lag screw below the tide line. With thousands watching, *Defender* proved unmovable for more than a day until divers could clear the ways and the tug *Right Arm* arrived from Providence to pull her free.

Once *Defender*'s rig was finally stepped and the yacht tested, the New York Yacht Club commenced trials. *Defender* was clearly the faster yacht, sporting a revolutionary nineteen-foot bulb keel and Herreshoff's new cross-cut sails, which minimized stretch, creating a more powerful sail plan. Despite the technological advantages, Charlie Barr, having been commissioned to steer the old *Vigilant,* made racing difficult for *Defender*'s captain, Hank Haff. The New York Yacht Club had decided to defend with an American skipper and crew, excluding Barr—even though, on April 26, 1893, he'd been officially "placed on the roll of American citizenship."[19] Although Barr had garnered a certain cachet in the racing circuit, the position was handed to Haff and hands from Deer Island, Maine. Haff, however, was no slouch. He had been skipper or tactician of three America's Cup winners in fourteen years. Like Barr, he had started as a fisherman; but after proving his skill racing catboats on Long Island Sound, he earned a position as a professional yacht hand and worked his way up to advisor aboard *Mischief* in 1881, *Mayflower* in 1886, and captain and helmsman aboard *Volunteer* in 1887.

Despite Haff's credentials there were those who thought Barr and his polished crew of hand-picked Scandinavian sailors were better suited for the job. Although many believed a race between nations should be conducted with patriots, there were also those whose primary concern was the successful defense of the Cup regardless of the means. Haff, acutely aware of this sentiment, greeted *Defender*'s American recruits with candor.

> I have been told that some of you have been mates and even masters
> of vessels. But you will not be either during the service for which I
> have come to Deer Island to ship you. You will be in the forecastle,

and the work on the yacht will be hard, and there will be plenty of it, night as well as day sometimes. There has been a great deal said about an American crew . . . not wanting to obey orders, of jealousies arising, and that all hands in a short time would want to be the captain. If there are any of you here who have the faintest suspicion that they will feel so in the future, I don't care to go any further with such.

But if you come with me and help me, as you know how, to keep the old Cup, you'll never regret it. You will be treated like men, and next fall, if we are successful, we'll have some fun.[20]

In sea trials *Defender*, the largest yacht to date with aluminum plating, faced a number of hurdles. During the final stages of the yacht's construction, Captain Nat, once again working himself to exhaustion, was stricken with typhoid. Confined to his bedroom, he was unable to oversee final assembly of the yacht's principal structural components, and without his knowledge of the plans a mistake was made. The mast step unit had been installed incomplete and the mast mounted atop it. Because of its improper installation a leak persisted. Once the defender trials began, it didn't help that Barr and his crew on *Vigilant* tested Haff to no ends. Sailing aggressively almost to the point of danger, Barr twice forced *Defender* into shallow water, running the new yacht aground. Despite his attempts to intimidate Haff, *Defender* won the trials and was selected to defend the Cup. Captain Nat recovered and tended to his ailing yacht, but his efforts failed. The mysterious leak persisted and almost ended all future competition for the Cup.[21]

In the first race, with both Haff and Captain Nat at the helm, *Defender* secured a safe lead, beating *Valkyrie III*. But raising the specter of malfeasance, Dunraven accused *Defender's* crew of adding extra ballast the night before to increase her waterline length. *Defender* was remeasured before the second race and found to be in correct trim. As the yachts sailed to the course off Sandy Hook sixty thousand spectators crowded excursion vessels. The course was clogged and as the two yachts vied for position before the start a steamer caused *Valkyrie III* to collide with *Defender*, damaging her rig in the process. *Valkyrie III* beat *Defender* over the finish line but was disqualified. Outraged, Dunraven chose not to sail the third race, claiming the overcrowded course conditions were unsafe. *Defender* retained the Cup but without a proper match.

Upon returning to England, Dunraven published an article claiming the Americans had cheated, sparking a heated inquiry. Dunraven claimed that before the second race, *Defender* sat significantly deeper on her lines, citing that *Defender's* bilge-pump drain had been submerged whereas it had been above the waterline the day before. In his annotation of *Their Last Letters 1930-1938,* a compilation of correspondence between Captain Nat and yachting writer W. P. Stephens, John Streeter argues this waterline discrepancy could have been caused by *Defender's* leaky mast step, an innocuous mistake that roused mistrust and ultimately rancor between not only Dunraven and *Defender's* principal backers, but also England and America. When the inquiry committee dismissed the charges, Dunraven, an honorary member of the New York Yacht Club, tendered his resignation.

In the years following the Dunraven debacle, interest in the America's Cup waned. It was expensive, time consuming, and now litigious. Accusations and wild speculations vaulted the Atlantic. A pamphlet was published accusing *Defender* of using a pump-run internal water ballast system to illegally improve the yacht's performance. As late as 1898, three years after the races, another official inquiry was launched on the matter. Although the accusations were quickly determined false, inspections of *Defender* revealed she was in a declining state of ruin. Captain Nat had not only built the yacht with a leak, but with total disregard for the electrolytic clash of metals. *Defender* was quickly dissolving into a pitted pile of scrap.

Herreshoff had been criticized for his yachts' lack of versatility. He countered that he built yachts to win races, and nothing more. He had, in fact, departed from his strict dictum of functionality, fitting *Defender* with liveaboard accommodations for her crew; but when Dunraven arrived with a stripped-down George Watson design—a veritable shell of a yacht—and a separate steam tender for his crew, Herreshoff reconsidered and had the interior removed. That *Defender* was falling apart did not faze Nat. To those who criticized the yacht's shelf life, he argued she had done her job.

The Herreshoff yard was now operating at full capacity. Both construction shops were full; their on-site sawmill hued rough timber into lumber; their forge, foundry, machine shop, and boiler shop were fully staffed and working six days a week. The Herreshoff Manufacturing

Company's cabinet, joiner, and paint shops outfitted yachts with sumptuous lightweight interiors. A team of draftsmen penned detailed
construction drawings for the builders. To accommodate their
growing fleet of sailing yachts, Nat and John Brown built a sail loft and
secured with each construction contract an agreement to outfit their
yachts with sails.[22]

In addition to their mounting sailboat orders the brothers continued building steamships, likely masking the fact that Nat was drawing
the plans. And as the United States mobilized for war with Spain, the
Herreshoffs accepted orders from the Navy for five torpedo boats, the
largest of which were two 175-footers, hulls No. 184 and No. 185, to
be named the *Porter* and *Dupont*. To accommodate these immense war-
ships the south construction shop was extended, a temporary roof and
floor built over the water. On March 30, 1897, Captain Nat noted in
his diary that *Dupont* was launched at 5:55 P.M. He made no mention
of *Porter* although on preceding days he had carefully noted a wave of
illness that had washed over his family at Love Rocks. On March 14,
his son, Nat, came down with the measles. On March 26, Clarence was
stricken with the mumps. Two days later his son Griswald caught the
measles, and a day later his wife, whom he referred to as Mrs. DeWolf,
caught the mumps. That he noted his wife and children was uncharacteristic, for his diary entries rarely strayed from work and weather.
Clara managed their home and family, and while Nat's children were
young his interactions with them were few. Although he sailed with
them during the summer months, his most conspicuous contribution
to their upbringing was the addition of a workshop/playroom in the
basement of Love Rocks. There he installed a workbench, tools, and an
engine on which they could tinker. This mention of his family's infir-
mity was likely indicative of the disruption it'd had on his already overloaded schedule. Nevertheless, amid this domestic turmoil Nat
launched his latest warship and opened a new chapter with the U.S.
government.

The Navy, again making stipulations, demands, and changes to his
original plans, pushed harder than they'd ever done before. Both
ships were equipped with identical 1,700-horsepower, four-cylinder
engines designed to be light with every component perfectly balanced. According to Captain Nat's son, L. Francis, the Navy demanded Nat change the type of steel for the piston rod guides on

Dupont. Nat, knowing from experience their request was misguided, reluctantly bowed to their wishes. As he had predicted, the new guides overheated, causing *Dupont* to limp around her trial course. Nat, furious, mounted the original guides and completed the trials successfully, breaking thirty knots and surpassing the contract speed—which under the original contract would reward the Herreshoff Manufacturing Company a generous bonus. But the Navy engineers requested still more changes. Obstinate, Nat refused, and in a battle of wills the Navy refused to pay. A flurry of letters passed between Nat and his only Navy ally, a truculent expansionist who sought to build the U.S. fleet, Assistant Secretary of the U.S. Naval Department Theodore Roosevelt.

On June 10, 1897, Roosevelt penned a letter to Nat:

> I have had a long talk with the Secretary. I am not at liberty to tell you all that passed. I think you understand pretty clearly my attitude in the matter, however, at present I think you had better wait a few days. The Secretary has a plan on hand by which he thinks further trouble can be averted, and that will have to be tried first.
>
> I have made a very strong plea that you be given your first payment immediately (but I must request you keep this confidential); I have hopes that my plea will be successful. I will let you know as soon as the Secretary gives me permission to take any further steps . . .[23]

On the back of the letter, as was Captain Nat's method of drafting his replies, he penciled:

> I sincerely hope something can be done to end this very unpleasant state of affairs relative to the inspection of these torpedo boats and that we may be allowed to proceed with the construction according to our specifications and designs unhampered. [There are] those who have shown themselves antagonistic from no other cause that I know of than jealousy.
>
> I am quite sure that if called on to give the opinion of our capability and integrity in doing work connected with these boats there are many men among the yachtsmen who will speak for us. And among them Mr. E.D. M [Edwin D. Morgan], Mr. EM. B [Edward M. Brown], Ex Dect Whitney [William C. Whitney, Secretary of the Navy, 1885–1889], Mr. C Oliver Iselin and Mr. Latham Fish.[24]

Captain Nat's terse response prompted Roosevelt to reply only a few days later on June 16, 1897. Perhaps Nat had struck a chord within the Naval offices, for despite the brash indifference showed him from the Naval engineers, Washington listened. Roosevelt wrote:

> Can you tell me when the [trial] of the Dupont, which you said would take place in July, will occur? I am very anxious for more than one reason to be at that trial; and I am now settling for my tour among the State militia on the Lakes, which will have to be in July . . .
>
> I congratulate you on the Porter. There are two or three points in connection with an alleged change made after she left your hands, concerning which I may wish to consult you later.[25]

Despite Roosevelt's concerned reply, the "alleged changes" to *Dupont* and *Porter* prompted Nat and John Brown to again distance themselves from the Navy. But their decision was inopportune. With McKinley seeking "the eventual withdrawal of the European powers from this hemisphere"[26] and tensions rising with Spain, the U.S. Navy began a flurried period of expansion. By refusing the Navy, thousands of dollars in work shifted to their competitors, including Bath Iron Works, Union Iron Works, Columbian Iron Works, Harlan & Hollingsworth, and the Gas Engine & Power Co.[27]

On February 15, 1898, the U.S. Battleship *Maine* was attacked in Havana Harbor. American tempers flared and while McKinley tried desperately to avoid all-out war with Spain, Roosevelt pushed for mobilization. The yards worked around the clock. On April 22, 1898, American ships surrounded Cuba. Two days later Spain declared war. On May 2, Captain Nat noted in his diary that Commodore George Dewey had defeated the Spanish fleet in Manila. But on May 7, facing the repercussions of his discordant Navy dealings, Nat wrote, "Laid off a number of men on account of lack of work."[28]

THE TEA ENTERPRISE

August 1898–October 1899

By the end of July 1898 the United States controlled Cuba and Puerto Rico. Lionized by the press, Roosevelt and his Rough Riders had become bona fide American heroes. At the Herreshoff yard, Nat and John Brown instructed a reduced staff to finish existing projects. With no big commissions, the small-boat shop built skiffs and small daysailers to keep busy. Bearing the burden of their obstinacy, the Herreshoff brothers watched as America and its burgeoning Navy set out on a bold, new expansionist platform—without them.

But just as business came to a standstill, their luck turned. On August 6, 1898, a cable arrived in New York announcing a challenge for the America's Cup. The typed slip of paper came as a shock. It had been sent from Belfast, Northern Ireland, on behalf of Sir Thomas Lipton and the Royal Ulster Yacht Club. Lipton, the famous tea and grocery baron, was unknown in yachting circles. He seemed an unlikely person to challenge, for he knew nothing about sailing. And the Ulster club seemed an implausible sponsor: American yachtsmen simply presumed any British challenge would hail from the Royal Yacht Squadron.

Although the message seemed strange, when the challenge reached America's Cup Committee Chairman J. Pierpont Morgan, he took it seriously and contacted Captain Nat straight away. Morgan's call was welcomed news: a new Cup defender would keep the shop afloat. The following week America annexed Hawaii, and Morgan purchased *Defender* as a trial horse.

With the announcement, the British yachting fraternity scoffed at Lipton's impertinence. Although Lipton was incredibly rich, when it came to boats he was a hack. In recent years he'd built his business into an empire, but to the British peerage, he was merely a "grocer" attempting yet another shameless display of self-promotion. To an extent they were right. Lipton knew how to bait the press.

A year earlier, while traveling to Ceylon, Lipton ran aground aboard the steamship *Orotava* in the Red Sea. To float the ship off the bar, the captain ordered any excess cargo jettisoned. After persuading one of the engineers to fashion him a stencil, Lipton quickly painted *Drink Lipton Tea* on his tea crates before they were tossed. For weeks, the crates washed up on Arab shores.[1] His stunt was a sensation and covered extensively in papers. Though his audacity gained him recognition, it was a donation that earned him celebrity status.

Later that spring of 1897, the Princess of Wales announced a campaign to raise £30,000 to feed the poor during Queen Victoria's Diamond Jubilee scheduled for the week of June 22. The Princess donated £100 to start the fund. After a month, Lipton, in a casual conversation with London's Lord Mayor, inquired about the fund's progress. They had raised only £5,000. Lipton promptly pulled out his book and wrote a check for £25,000, and the announcement was made that the Jubilee's monetary goal had been reached by means of a generous anonymous donation. Murmurs spread through the London papers, but Lipton kept his secret. And as the country's curiosity escalated and papers speculated, he simply went about his business. Finally, he allowed the Lord Mayor to reveal his identity. The publicity was enormous; Lipton was again featured in every paper in Britain.

After a successful Jubilee celebration he continued his philanthropic streak and donated £100,000 to the Alexandra Trust, another foundation created to feed the poor. Lipton spent the rest of the year traveling in America, where his notoriety had grown to equal that of England. To the celebrity-friendly press, he was a rich, eligible bachelor. He spoke with a London accent dabbed with a hint of Scottish brogue and became known in the United States as "Jubilee Lipton." Back in London at the year's end, his name appeared on the New Year's Honors List as a knight bachelor. On January 18, 1898, he was summoned to the Royal House at Osborne on the Isle of Wight, where in the India Room, kneeling on a silk tasseled cushion, he felt Queen Victoria tap each of his shoulders with her sword before commanding, "Arise, Sir Thomas."

The run of exposure was well timed. Two months after receiving the title, he opened his international chain to outside investors. Lipton—a tall, now stout man with a ruddy complexion, salt-and-pepper mustache, and piercing blue eyes—had earned £2.5 million from the public offering and still owned most of the company. With his business running smoothly and earning a steady profit for his shareholders, he scaled back his time in the office—and hobnobbing in society, firmed his friendship with Edward, Prince of Wales, Victoria's son, who was particularly fond of throwing lavish parties and, as was fashionable within his set, yacht racing. Through his royal friend, Lipton found a hobby that required little beyond monetary investment. And money he had. He took up his new sport with the same fervid investment he'd dedicated to his work. When he began selling tea, Lipton purchased enormous tracts of plantation land outright, cutting out middlemen and quickly climbing to the top of the business. Likewise, when he entered yachting he started at the top—the America's Cup.

But Lipton didn't enter competitive sailing on a whim. He was deliberate and calculating. In every move he'd ever made, he first weighed the financial and political implications. Although his business was paramount, in recent years his social aspirations had become increasingly important to him. Through Edward he had rubbed elbows with the elite—and he now yearned for acceptance. But many British aristocrats felt Lipton had, with his Jubilee donation, bought his knighthood. To the royals, his humble beginnings and lowly vocation were the subjects of ridicule. But Lipton, ever the masterful businessman, had found in yachting not only a path to peerage but also a brassy, new method of advertising.

With his finger on the pulse of public opinion, he sought to capitalize on the 1895 Dunraven debacle. The scandal had been a sensation, commanding headlines for weeks, and he was willing to bet a follow-up challenge would paint his name around the world. A win might also grant the poor boy from Glasgow entrance to one of the most exclusive circles in the world. Lipton had taken a vociferous approach to everything in life. His marketing ploys and effusive donations were legendary, but a challenge for the Cup would top them all.

Upon accepting the order for the 1899 Cup defender, Nat retired to his drawing room on the third floor of his house at Love Rocks, laid down a sketch, and then carved a half model for hull No. 499. To avoid the galvanic oxidation process quickly destroying *Defender,* Nat piled steel topsides on a bronze underbody and stretched the hull to include precipitously longer overhangs. At 131 feet overall (89 feet of waterline), a 24-foot beam, and drawing 19 feet, 9 inches, the new yacht was longer, wider, and deeper than her predecessor. On June 10, 1899, exactly six months after the Treaty of Paris was signed, *Columbia* slid slowly down the ways of the south construction shop. The new yacht, slated to pit expanding America against Old World Britain, became an involuntary symbol of American pride. Nat had never been a political man. He'd been burned by Naval Department politicians enough times to spurn even the most ardent patriotic cries. In building *Columbia* his goal had been only to produce a successful defender.

Lipton, conversely, sought a match for national pride (albeit one that also promoted his business). Wanting to launch an Irish-built boat manned by an Irish crew, he approached Belfast shipbuilders. But lacking experience in building high-performance yachts, they declined. Lipton then approached William Fife III, one of Britain's rising stars who—like Burgess and Herreshoff in America and George Lennox Watson in England—had risen to prominence among yachting circles on both sides of the Atlantic. Among others, he had designed *Minerva,* the yacht on which Barr held his first captain's commission, racking up a notable record. He knew Barr and Herreshoff, their strengths and weaknesses. He knew the American designs rules and how to optimize a yacht to them. And like Lipton, he had grown up on the Clyde. Fife and his famous forefathers hailed from a small seaside village north of Glasgow called Fairlie.

The third generation of yacht designers in his family, William Fife III, or William Jr., as he was known, was born in 1857 and raised across the street from his family's boatyard on the shallow tidal bay known as the Southannan Sands on the North Ayrshire coast. He was the only son of William Fife II, who'd continued the business of his father William Fyfe (original spelling), born in 1785 the son of John Fyfe of Kilbirnie. At fifteen, William Jr. left Brisbane Academy and began his apprenticeship in his father's yard, which, basking in the success of his recent raceboats, was incredibly busy. The yard was small (the boats were built outside) but the Fifes had garnered a reputation for building strong, fast, and beautiful yachts that, like Herreshoff's, didn't leave the yard until every detail was completed to perfection.

In 1865 his father had launched the eighty-ton cutter *Fiona,* which for eight seasons dominated British racing, winning six Queen's Cups and three Albert Cups. *Fiona's* success prompted an order from the Marquis of Ailsa to build the thirty-six-ton *Foxhound.* She won Her Majesty's Cup at Cowes in 1871, prompting an order for the forty-ton cutter *Bloodhound.* Impressed, the Marquis's royal friends responded with even more orders and Fife's yard boomed.

William Jr. entered a busy business with much work to be done. In her detailed history of the Fife dynasty, *Fast and Bonnie,* May Fife Mc-Callum, a Fife descendent, explains that William Jr. lacked the fine woodworking skills of his progenitors—and so shifted his focus to drawing designs. In 1876, at nineteen, he collaborated with his father on a new yacht for the popular five-ton class. In the same year, two new innovative designs from Dan Hatcher of Southampton and a young designer by the name of George Lennox Watson of Glasgow also entered the class. In a series of races between the three off Holyhead Island, Hatcher's *Freda* soundly beat both Fife's *Camellia* and Watson's *Vril,* loosening the Fife family grip on the Clyde. The upset was disheartening, but it sparked a friendly rivalry between Fife Jr. and Watson. Three years later, in 1879, Fife Jr.'s five-tonner *Cyprus* won thirteen of fifteen races she entered, beating Watson's *Nora* in the process.

Under the shadow of his father, who continued to run the family's Fairlie yard and complete the bulk of the designs through the 1880s, Fife Jr. designed and built two smashing successes, *Clara* and *Minerva,* at the nearby Maidens yard where he worked as manager. Under the command of the Barr brothers—John on *Clara* and Charlie on *Minerva*—Fife Jr.'s name resonated in America.

In 1886 he officially joined his sixty-five-year-old father in the family business. He brought to it a penchant for expansion, attempting to set up channels through which he could export yachts to America. But because of transportation costs and import duties he exported only his designs. And he exported a lot of them. In 1890 alone, the Fairlie yard built fourteen boats and William Jr. designed nine others built at various Clyde yards as well as in Southampton, Finland, and the United States.[2] In addition to expanding the company's reach, he also set out to expand the yard itself. Where Fife yachts were once built along the beach, William Jr. erected work sheds. He also saw to the construction of a drafting room and office space. Between 1890 and 1898 he produced over two hundred designs, the majority of which were built at the Fairlie yard and a handful of which were purchased and successfully raced by notable New York Yacht Club members. The performance of a Fife yacht now overshadowed the delivery cost.

While Fife expanded the business and pressed on with his own design work, his childhood rival George Lennox Watson continued producing innovative designs, integrating the latest scientific theories. Watson sought to ground his models in empirical data. Fife McCallum contends that part of Watson's success grew from his access to the early work of physicist William Froude,[3] who, using tank-test models, had pioneered work in the subjects of friction and wave action. Building on this data, at twenty-nine, Watson produced the ten-ton *Madge* in 1880 and then the ninety-ton *Vandura* for Paisley thread manufacturer John Clark. With the success of *Vandura,* Clark, a member of the 1887 Royal Clyde Yacht Club challenger syndicate for the America's Cup, hired Watson to design *Thistle* to challenge for the America's Cup. With such a high-profile commission, Watson's name became ubiquitous.

Though *Thistle* proved an unworthy opponent to Burgess's *Volunteer,* Watson had won the race with Fife Jr. for British preeminence, earning commissions to design *Britannia* for Edward, Prince of Wales and *Valkyries II* and *III* for the next two Cup challenges. The fortuitous run of high-profile jobs earned him celebrity status. But he had failed miserably, plagued by broken gear and unable to win a single race against the Americans. With a mind to shake up the old guard, Lipton, a yachting unknown in his own right, turned to Fife Jr. for the design of his first challenger.

Fife Jr. drew elegant lines for *Shamrock* and oversaw her construction at the Thornycroft shipyard on the Solent. Emulating Herreshoff's *Defender, Shamrock* was of composite construction—steel frames, aluminum topsides, and manganese bronze below the waterline. When *Shamrock* slid into the river, she was 128 feet overall, with 25 feet of beam, and drawing 20 feet, 3 inches. All told, she was three feet shorter than *Columbia* and carried less sail, but with the pundits praising her graceful shape and newspapers announcing that her financial backer had spared no expense, odds shifted in her favor. *Shamrock* was also equipped with a steel mast, one of the first of its kind.

Although *Columbia* had originally been fitted with a wooden spar, Herreshoff immediately built a steel replacement, the first fitted on a Herreshoff yacht. Captain Nat pushed his design a step further and fitted *Columbia*'s mast with a telescoping wooden topmast that could be lowered into the hollow steel lower tube in heavy winds. Stepped on June 30, 1899, the mast, weighing nearly one ton less than its wooden predecessor, was touted as revolutionary. But on August 3, when Barr, at the helm of *Columbia*, lined up with *Defender*, the port spreader buckled and the mast came crashing down.

Herreshoff's first steel mast failed, but the accident was chalked up to learning. In employing new materials and building techniques one always ran the risk of failure. And Captain Nat was known to take special precautions, maintaining a dedicated area of his workshop simply for breaking things. He rigorously tested new materials and fittings, determining breaking strengths, elasticity, ductility, and durability. Although the papers identified the shroud as the culprit, for those who disapproved of Barr, the breakdown vindicated their belief that he shouldn't hold the helm. For them, the toppling mast was another *Navahoe*-pilot boat collision—a red card waved over his wanton racing style, proving once and for all American yachts should be sailed by American crews with American helmsmen. To compound the sentiment Barr was the only foreigner aboard *Columbia*, for as in the last defense, the crew had again been picked from Deer Island, Maine. These men didn't like that he wasn't American-born, and no doubt a catastrophic dismasting helped exacerbate those feelings of discontent. "His crew . . . are expressing the utmost dissatisfaction with their commander," reported the *New York Times*, "and if [the] report is true, they are seriously meditating a strike unless the 'foreigner' is removed from his position and a native American placed in it."[4] As in the last two defenses, Charles Oliver Iselin had signed on as managing owner and with J. Pierpont Morgan paying the bills and Herreshoff building the boat—a formidable trio lobbying for the young Scottish helmsman— no nationalistic grumbling would unseat Barr from his position.

Also helping Barr was the fact that he was one of only a handful of people who could actually steer such a large and unwieldy yacht. *Columbia* represented the next generation in design under the Seawanhaka Rule, and Herreshoff had pushed the limits further. With even longer overhangs, larger rigs, and deeper keels, these "ninety-footers," as they were called— referring to their waterline length—transformed the nature of yacht racing. Because the rule designers had placed the square root of sail area and the waterline length on an equal proportional footing, Captain Nat maintained the prescribed ninety-foot waterline but increased the over-hangs and consequently the sailing length, and then dramatically in-creased the sail area. For the same waterline he'd packed on even more sail power, like mounting a hundred-foot torpedo boat steam engine onto a twenty-foot launch. During Herreshoff's tenure the ratio of sail area to waterline length climbed steadily: *Vigilant* had a ratio of 131:1; *Defender* was 142.5:1; and now *Columbia* was 146.5:1.

A helmsman's skill had always made a yacht sail faster, but as the de-signs became more extreme, steering a ninety-footer in a blow or in close quarters could be downright frightening. Like slalom skiing, one needed perfect control and an eye for what lay ahead. With one lapse in concentration—a misstep or caught edge—the skier runs amok. Likewise, even the slightest miscalculation of the oncoming breeze could cause the boat to heel excessively and round up out of control. So touchy were the ninety-footers that only a handful of helmsmen could steer them safely; Barr, though often accused of being impetu-ous, could steer them like no one else.

Due to a concession made to the America's Cup Deed of Gift, *Sham-rock* arrived in tow to New York Harbor, for previously yachts had been required to sail. Lipton, aboard his motoryacht *Erin,* wined and dined throngs of friends, New York Yacht Club members, and American dig-nitaries, including Admiral Dewey who, aboard the battleship *Olympia* arrived in New York Harbor from his victory in Manila Bay. Lipton's generosity had preceded their meeting in New York Harbor, for upon stopping in Ceylon, Dewey and every member of his crew were given a chest of tea, compliments of the knight.

The celebration of America's victory in its war with Spain com-bined with the upcoming races had charged New York with excite-ment. The harbor teemed with ships and sailors. The upcoming races commanded headlines. And with the anticipated media sensation, the twenty-five-year-old Italian inventor Guglielmo Marconi announced he would transmit news of the races aboard the steamship *Ponce* via his newly invented wireless apparatus. But with fickle winds off Sandy Hook the sailors and throngs of spectators waited for two weeks. Fi-nally, on October 16, 1899, *Shamrock* and *Columbia* sailed the first race of the best-of-five series. And with Barr at the helm and Captain Nat and Charles Oliver Iselin filling out *Columbia's* afterguard, *Columbia* trounced *Shamrock* by ten minutes and fourteen seconds. In the second race, held on October 17, *Shamrock*'s topmast toppled, forcing the yacht to race without her topsail; again, Lipton's challenger bowed to the Americans.

Despite Barr's winning performance, yachting authorities—likely swayed by the Scottish helmsman's xenophobic detractors—were petulant. After winning, *Columbia*—the boat—earned praise. But when shifty, unstable winds had hindered *Columbia*'s performance earlier in the month, critics lambasted Barr. "Captain Barr failed to bring out the good points of the *Columbia*," reported the *New York Times*, following the first failed race attempt. "Many expert racing yachtsmen declared that he handled the yacht like the veriest amateur, and one prominent member of the New York Yacht Club said in reference to Captain Barr's undoubted poor judgment: 'We can do but little against the elements of luck, but we can't forgive absolutely bad management of the yacht.' "[5]

Though Barr and *Columbia* were scrutinized, *Shamrock* had also received her fair share of heat. Lipton had signed on three of Britain's most celebrated sailors, Captain Archie Hogarth as helmsman, Captain Robert Wringe, as second in command, and Captain Ben Parker, a consultant in the afterguard. William Fife Jr., the yacht's designer, was also slated for the afterguard but had fallen ill and was unable to participate in the races. There was talk of infighting among the captains, none of whom were used to taking orders. And without Fife's in-depth knowledge of the yacht, the bickering trio stumbled around the course in *Columbia*'s wake.

In the final heat, Barr was late to the starting line. Sailing downwind, *Shamrock* shot ahead at thirteen knots, water crashing onto her deck. With an icy north wind gusting to thirty knots, both yachts drag raced downwind flying only their three lower sails. Barr, with Captain Nat at his side, ordered the topsail and spinnaker set. *Columbia*'s crew, struggling through the driving spray and whipping wind as the yacht skidded through the surf, set up the sails and prepared the halyards. With the topsail set and straining, Barr ordered the spinnaker hoisted. The sail snaked up the mast, the halyard was secured, and then the sheet was pulled aft, the sail filling with a deafening womp. The pole shot skyward, and the sail twisted in the wind. Hauling rapidly, the sheet trimmers filled the sail. The boat, with a new burst of wind, shot ahead toward *Shamrock,* spray bursting from the bow like a fountain.

Barr maneuvered *Columbia* behind *Shamrock,* using his yacht's mountain of canvas to blanket the leader. As they reached the far end of the course, *Columbia* slipped past *Shamrock,* whose crew, in an attempt to recoup, hoisted its club topsail, but to no avail. Overpowered in the breeze, *Shamrock* heeled out of control, and *Columbia* rounded the turning mark seventeen seconds ahead. The crew hauled the sheets. Barr and a crewmember strained against the wheel, levering the giant rudder, turning the yacht to windward. Now beating upwind, pounding through the waves, feathering the giant wing through the puffs and footing for speed in the lulls, Barr covered—matching *Shamrock* tack-for-tack upwind, maintaining a windward advantage—and he crossed the finish line six minutes, eighteen seconds ahead.

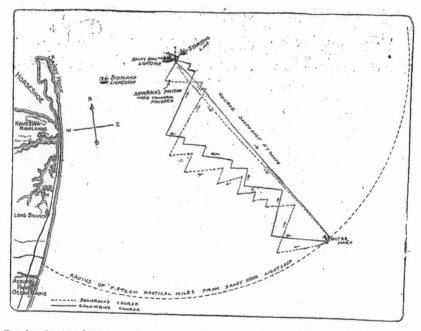

October 21, 1899: Diagram showing the courses sailed by *Columbia* and *Shamrock* in the final race of the 1899 America's Cup series. (Courtesy of the *New York Times.*)

Throughout the series, Barr and Nat had swapped *Columbia*'s helm, Barr steering in tight situations, Nat steering for straight-line speed. The two observed each other keenly; by now, they had solidified a mutual respect. A third, Charles Oliver Iselin, *Columbia*'s managing owner, had proven himself an apt manager yet again. He wore a fine suit and had never worked for a living. It was a guarded relationship he held with the other two, for he managed the money; but the respect he shared for Barr and Captain Nat transcended their business dealings.

In tow, *Columbia,* surrounded by hundreds of spectator boats holding thousands of spectators, glided toward New York Harbor. Below decks Barr and Iselin offered Captain Nat a celebratory whisky. He accepted and downed the first and only drink of his life.

THE FLOP

October 1899–October 1901

As if overwhelmed by obsession, Lipton diverted his attention from his business to chasing the Cup. For the first time since his boyhood fight with the butcher's son, he experienced the frustration of defeat. And although Lipton played up his new role as Britain's amiable sportsman, behind close doors he could be downright callous, a fixated businessman who instilled fear in his employees. He was known to visit his American offices, methodically interviewing his managers and combing through their accounts. After he left, they waited apprehensively. Once in London, he simply cabled back a list of people to be fired.

Lipton was used to having things his way. And with his last yacht's disappointing finish, he sacked Fife and commissioned the designer's longtime rival, George Lennox Watson. With his ongoing relationship with the physicist Froude and a string of winning designs, Watson had infused British naval architecture with modern precision. No longer was he simply carving models like his competition—including Herreshoff. In his intransigent quest to hone his methodology, Watson, with each new design, produced a series of wax models that he tested in an indoor towing tank. Each design was studied for drag and displacement and was tweaked and recast until the optimum shape was determined. Naval architects had long been using formulas to dictate hull shapes—but their theories remained largely untested until the boat rolled down the ways. Watson, conversely, had figured out a way to test his ideas, thwarting the immense cost of failure. It had been nearly fifty years since *America* had won the One Hundred Sovereign Cup from the Royal Yacht Squadron. For fifty years, the United States had dominated, in Cup competition, a nation whose ethos rested upon the laurels of its naval supremacy. Now Watson had devised a way to bring the Cup home.

Lipton sent a letter announcing his challenge in October 1900. The New York Yacht Club accepted and again charged the Herreshoff brothers with designing and building a defender. The yard, working at full capacity, hummed along. John Brown drafted the work order for hull No. 551. Affixing his signature to the remunerative agreement, Captain Nat retired to his drawing room. There he sketched on his pad a profile slightly longer but in the same spirit as *Columbia*. Again, he stretched the model lengthwise—to 90 feet on the waterline—and increased its overhangs; the yacht measured 132 feet overall.

Watson took his proposed design and went to the William Denny & Brothers shipyard at Dumbarton, roughly fifteen miles north of Glasgow on the north bank of the Clyde. The yard was immense, comprising forty acres of land and employing roughly 2,500 men.[1] Although the Denny yard had garnered a sterling reputation for building fast steamers, it was their towing tank—devised by William Denny III and designed by Froude in 1880—that set them apart. Lipton had given Watson carte blanche to beat Herreshoff, and he was prepared to use every advantage in his power.

After drawing several sets of plans for *Shamrock II*, Watson began the arduous task of building and testing his models. Originally, the first models were made of wood, each carved individually, an expensive and labor-intensive system. To cut costs and save time, Denny's engineers devised a system for building wax models. Though the process was toilsome, the wax could be reused and the model shapes refined to pinpoint accuracy.

Models were built in a large box, six to ten feet long and filled with clay. This clay was then hollowed to the rough shape of the hull's outside dimensions. Using wooden templates as a guide, the clay was scraped away and then carefully pounded into the shape of the hull with mallets. When complete, a wooden inner core roughly the same shape of the hull design was made from a wood frame over which linen was stretched and then coated in a thin layer of liquefied clay to prevent the wax from sticking to it. The purpose of this small, yacht-shaped plug was two-fold: it formed a hollow center for the hull, using less wax and therefore making it lighter. It also increased the wax model's surface area, rendering a small reservoir into which water could be circulated to hasten the cooling process. This was then placed over the female clay mold, suspended by wooden supports. Molten wax was poured into the clay box and then allowed to cool for twelve to eighteen hours.

Once the model had solidified, the central core was removed and the top planed to a smooth surface. Fastened by heated screws so the wax would melt and solidify around them, wooden crossbeams were attached to allow for easier handling. Because these models were usually six to ten feet long, built to one-twentieth scale, they were heavy, weighing hundreds of pounds. To help dislodge them from the clay-lined box, water was pumped in, causing the model to float to the top. The model was then cleaned and dried.

A rough estimate of the hull shape, this wax model was then moved to and mounted in Froude's specialized cutting machine. Steam-driven, this ferocious arching lattice of spinning blades required a very coordinated operator to cut the model accurately to the designer's plans. With the line drawings mounted on a pantograph machine, the operator scrupulously followed the designer's lines with the pantograph stylus—which, calibrated with a series of spinning blades, cut the wax model in accordance with the designer's plans. Turning two wheels, one moving the blades vertically and the other moving them horizontally—as if rubbing his stomach and tapping his head at the same time—the machine operator followed the curved lines of the blueprint while chips of paraffin spat from the model.

Once cut, the wax hull resembled the side of Mayan pyramid—a series of wax steps having been cut by the whirring blades. Transported by chainfalls to the scraping station, the hull was carefully faired, the wax steps chipped away. This operation being extremely delicate, it sometimes took several days to cut, scrape, and polish the wax to a perfectly fair shape that matched the original design plans. Once this step was complete, the model was inscribed with guidelines, so that attributes like the location of the bow and stern waves could be accurately measured. Finally, appendages such as propellers or rudders were attached.

The model was then moved to an area called the trimming dock, an easily accessible portion of the tank in which the designer could make minor adjustments. In the trimming dock, the model was ballasted using lead shot so it matched the designer's intended displacement when equipped with keel, rig, sails, and crew. Before the test, the tank water was skimmed with a piece of canvas and the water temperature taken. Once ready, the model was fastened to a device called a dynamometer, a spring-loaded instrument that measured the resistance force exerted by the model. Those measurements were then recorded on a paper roll. The dynamometer was mounted on a steam catapult-driven carriage set on rails, 100 meters (330 feet) long. The distance was long enough for the carriage to reach a constant speed long enough to record viable data, while allowing the technician, who was strapped into the carriage and traveling at eighteen feet per second (12.3 miles per hour), to safely hit the brakes. Froude's system was so sophisticated that the carriage rails were even bent to match the curvature of the earth. Made of brick and concrete, the tank was 8 feet deep and 23 feet wide, holding 365,000 gallons of water.[2]

After each test, the recorded data was taken to the Denny drawing office on the second floor, above the model-making works and the testing tank. Well lit with large windows providing a view of the shipyard, the office consisted of a number of drawing tables and wooden containers, called Deacon boxes, in which the test results were stored after they'd been evaluated. If a model's tank test showed a fault in the design, Watson drew another set reflecting what he'd learned. After weeks and months of testing, when the designs were finalized, the drawings, hundreds of which comprised the plans for a yacht like *Shamrock II,* were traced onto linen. While designing *Shamrock II,* Watson tested at least eleven models to which he made roughly sixty alterations.[3]

By hiring Watson, who placed unprecedented emphasis on the new challenger, Lipton infused the Cup with a new sense of immediacy. National pride mounted. The New York Yacht Club was fervent, riding the wave of patriotism Iselin had stirred up following his 1899 defense. As if his crew had stormed San Juan Hill, Iselin wrote:

> This is the third time I have successfully defended the America's cup—the blue ribbon of the sea, and each time I have felt the great responsibility placed upon me, and have not only felt responsible for the performance of my boats, but responsible for the work of my crew. Knowing the eyes of all the world were upon you, it has been my greatest ambition in this as in other contests to have the world say you were better than the English crew. . . . But now that the battle has been fought and won, I trust that you and the officers of Columbia will forget any hard words from me, and only remember the glorious victory we have won for our country.[4]

Although Watson, like most successful naval architects, had multiple projects under way, he wasn't overseeing a shipyard with hundreds of employees. Cushioned by Lipton's bankroll, Watson spent hours studying tank-test results, tweaking his line drawings, comparing those with the designs of *Columbia,* optimizing every aspect of his yacht. Conversely, in 1900, while hull No. 551 grew around her frame, the Herreshoff brothers had scores of boats in various stages of production and undergoing routine maintenance. Not only was Captain Nat building the new defender; he was also making plans to outfit *Columbia* as a trial horse—his loft building new sails and the Boston firm of Charles Billman and Sons making adjustments to the rigging.

Letters show *Columbia* received everything from new hardware to careful alignment of the topmast shrouds and spreaders. On December 26, 1900, Herreshoff received a letter from E. D. Morgan, who'd bought out Iselin's share and was now managing *Columbia,* explaining, "I have engaged Barr as skipper and shall leave no stone unturned to turn the boat out in good fighting condition next year, which with your assistance should accomplish what is most needed, that is: make the new boat race for all she's worth, and thereby put her and her crew in a condition suitable to meet Lipton or Lawson or anybody else."[5]

To Herreshoff it must have seemed like Morgan was contradicting himself. In a quest to prepare the new boat for Cup competition why would he tie up Barr with *Columbia*? What did that mean for his new boat? Barr and Herreshoff had worked closely both on and off the water, their tight-knit relationship leading to an open exchange of ideas. Iselin, who had fallen ill, conspicuously dropped out of the running. His meticulously saved letters from each of his Cup defenses abruptly stop with *Columbia*'s yacht inventories at the end of 1899. Nevertheless, William Butler Duncan, a former Navy man and well-known amateur yachtsman, was managing Captain Nat's new yacht. Although Duncan was backed by a syndicate of August Belmont, Oliver H. Payne, F. G. Bourne, James Stillman, and Henry Walters, all New York Yacht Club members with ample funds to support a successful defense, Belmont, the syndicate head, principal backer, and vice commodore of the club, had the year before argued with Herreshoff over the performance of his new eighty-one-foot steamer

Scout, built to serve as a tender to his New York Yacht club seventy-footer *Mineola.* Writing to Belmont on April 16, 1900, Captain Nat defended himself:

> I am to say the least surprised and pained to hear of the dissatisfaction you have expressed for I have been feeling very much pleased with the boats (Scouts and Mirage [*Scout's* sistership]) at what appeared to me to be their fine performances. . . . the speed attained on the trial has to my knowledge never been exceeded by any small vessel using anthricite [*sic*] coal for fuel and having an open fire room.[6]

He had known Belmont for years. The New Yorker was a savvy businessman who'd invested heavily in New York's new electric subway system, which was under construction. And although his mild criticism was not taken personally, it was well noted. Nat replied by letter, written as usual in draft on the back of the received. His words were diplomatic but firm. As far as he was concerned Belmont's rebuke was par for the course: clients would always quibble. But Nat would never fully let it lie.

The bickering aside, construction of the new boat began on schedule. Pressure, however, from *Columbia's* management, lead by E. D. Morgan, the man who'd funded *Gloriana* and had granted Herreshoff his first Cup commission, arrived at the Herreshoff Manufacturing Company in the form of numerous letters. Morgan's biggest gripe had to do with sails. Nat and John Brown typically secured agreements to produce sails for their yachts. For the most part, their customers didn't complain, for although their prices were high, Nat's experimentation with cuts, weave, and sailcloth configurations and his loft's ability to work seamlessly with the Herreshoff rigging shop made their sails some of the best in America. They hadn't, however, considered the need to simultaneously suit multiple Cup defenders with their immense spreads of sail.

Hull No. 551, christened *Constitution,* was slowly lowered down the ways by a new mechanical launching system at the Herreshoff yard on May 6, 1901. The new yacht was a marvel of design, a further refinement of *Columbia.* Whereas *Gloriana* and his first Cup defender *Vigilant* had heralded a paradigm shift in form, *Constitution* marked a shift in construction. "The contest is no longer one of fundamental principles of design," wrote the *New York Times*. "It is now a battle of skill in building."[7] Using a new longitudinal framing system—a skeleton of thin frames or "stringers" running from bow to stern over widely spaced web frames—Herreshoff used thinner bronze plating, ranging from ¼ inch at the keel to ³⁄₁₆ inch at the deck, cutting the weight of *Constitution*'s hull by seven tons. A lighter hull not only cut the construction cost, it also allowed him to shift weight to the keel without changing the displacement. By adding tons, literally, of stability, he increased the sail area and the yacht's overall speed. *Constitution* carried roughly 14,400 square feet of sail, about 1,300 more than *Columbia*. The longitudinal frames also provided an infrastructure around which the plates could be laid up flush with each other. Previously, plates were lapped like giant clapboards. Although the seams were aligned with the flow of water, a seamless yacht would ultimately produce less drag and, with the plates snugly interlocked, greater strength.

"If an egg is held accurately end to end," wrote the British journal *Science Siftings,* "a strong man may strive in vain to break it. The principle of the Herreshoff boat is the same. The hull is a self-sustaining whole, so fragile that one might almost pierce it with a walking stick by an accurate blow, yet so strong in its entirety that tons of waves may assault it and avail nothing." Although *Constitution*'s ¼-inch bronze plates were not likely to succumb to the tap of a staff, the writer calculated her framing system was, for its weight, ten times stronger than that of a railroad bridge. "Ten trains could pass on a structure no heavier than Constitution's hull, yet with the same security that they rumble over the thick iron pillars of the L."[8]

In addition to her final fitting out—including stepping of the mast by Charles Billman and Son and the installation of Nat's custom-designed, two-speed, wire-rope winches—*Constitution* required, naturally, a new set of sails. Concurrently, E. D. Morgan with the backing of his distant cousin J. P. Morgan, pressured Nat to shift his attention to *Columbia*. "I am awfully disappointed that the Columbia's mainsail has not yet been begun," wrote E. D. on May 16, "as I had hoped to spend this leisure time in stretching it into shape."[9] The grumbling quickly became public. Nat wouldn't budge. *Columbia* would simply have to wait. That J. P. Morgan had been strong-armed by a small-town monopoly was sensational. The *Liverpool Echo* recounted:

He ordered a new mainsail from Herreshoff who replied that he could not get the cloth for it until after the Cup races are over. Mr. Morgan sent to the mill for facts, and found that the sail could really be made in less a than a week, but that Herreshoff had formed a sort of sail trust, and put himself at the head of it, and neither the contract nor the sail could be made without his consent. This was a case of Morgan being fought with his own weapons, and it is said that he was very angry.[10]

We don't know if Nat and John Brown maliciously snubbed the Morgans as the *Echo* suggests. We do know that Nat favored *Constitution* and that he was intent on affording his newest yacht every advantage. Although both E. D. and J. P. Morgan had been generous benefactors, Nat had grown increasingly obstinate. Only the year before, in 1900, when one of his seventy-footers, *Virginia,* had warped out of shape, Nat told his longstanding client, William K. Vanderbilt Jr., he'd have to pay for repairs. Vanderbilt didn't agree. In his memoir *Yachting Memories* naval architect Clinton Crane recounts the ensuing battle of wills:

> Herreshoff advised the owners to send [the boat] back to Bristol to have metal straps fitted between planking and frames, the work to be done at cost but the owners to pay the cost. One of our clients, W. K. Vanderbilt Jr., felt it should have been done for nothing by the builder as it was his fault. [Captain Nat] was so annoyed that he commissioned me to have the work done in City Island, though I assured him that even without my fee it would cost more.[11]

Ultimately, John Brown kept a sharp eye—metaphorically speaking—on the bottom line and likely asked his younger brother for some flexibility. They accepted the sail order, but it wouldn't be completed until after the races. With so much work and so little time, Nat spread himself too thin.

Shamrock II was launched from the Denny yard in late April surrounded by optimism. The British journal *The Field* wrote: "The average British Sportsman long ago arrived at the conclusion that our American cousins are one too many for us at the yacht game, and most yachtsmen refuse to accept the hardy annuals offered as apologies for

successive defeats." The article, however, offered an apology, explaining
that Fife was relatively inexperienced at building boats to an American
rule, whereas, "The chances of *Shamrock II* are better, since Mr. Watson
has had considerable [American] design experience."[12] A month after
the article was written, on May 9, *Shamrock II,* while practicing off
Southampton, lost her gaff topsail yard, the sail and rigging raining from
the mast and a large turning block slamming to the deck a foot from
Sir Thomas Lipton. A few weeks later on May 22, while sparring with
Shamrock and *Sybarita* on the Solent, *Shamrock II,* with King Edward
sailing on board, lost her mast, the snarl of lines and canvas crashing to
leeward. Two weeks later, on June 4, while sailing from Narragansett
Pier toward the Brenton Reef Lightship off Newport, *Constitution's* No.
2 club topsail came unlashed. Just after the three crewmen who'd been
sent up the rig to furl the fouled sail stepped onto the deck, the lower
starboard spreader snapped, the topmast buckled, followed by the lower
mast, and the whole mess splashed into Narragansett Bay.

Newspaper editorials in both Britain and America expressed their
outrage: "[Y]acht designers on both sides of the Atlantic are going
ahead a little too fast," announced London's *Daily Graphic.* "Cutters of
the size of the Shamrocks and the Constitution are dangerous mon-
strosities."[13] The *Daily News,* expressing the exasperation of a nation
that had just lost Queen Victoria in January 1901, went so far as to say,
"Over here we nearly lost our King . . . President McKinley ought to
have been onboard the *Constitution.*"[14] The *New York Times* avowed,
"They are not healthy craft . . . They are enormities unfit for ocean
work . . . The accidents that have happened will cause fear that sooner
or later there will be a disaster in which human life will be lost."[15]

In addition to *Constitution* and *Columbia* another yacht had entered
the running. Backed by Thomas W. Lawson of Boston and designed by
Bowdoin Crowninshield, *Independence* was intended to compete with
the Herreshoff yachts for the right to defend the Cup. Built by George
F. Lawley at the Atlantic Works in East Boston, *Independence* was
launched on May 18, 1901, at 11 A.M. Lawson requested, or rather, announced he planned to compete in the official trials with *Columbia* and
Constitution. The America's Cup committee chairman, Lewis Cass Ledyard, a Wall Street lawyer, informed Lawson that because he was not a
member of the New York Yacht Club, he would have to fly the club
burgee, meaning a club member would have to be on board. A flurry

of letters was exchanged; Lawson was outraged that the New York Yacht Club had barred him from competition. Ledyard and his committee insisted that he only needed to at least brandish some symbolic connection with the club. Lawson refused. Still fuming, he publicly protested what he felt was the club's prejudiced policies. Although he and the public saw Cup competition as a race between nations, Lawson failed to understand that the New York Yacht Club *owned* the Cup. Ultimately, he was allowed to compete in a series of exhibition races but barred from the official trials that would determine the defender.

In the first practice sails, *Independence* stumbled—the rudder seizing, the yacht spinning out of control like a bicycle whose handlebars had suddenly locked to one side. With all hands struggling to control the sheets, the yacht skidded within a few feet of a press boat. During the following weeks the rudder was replaced, and the rig and sails shortened. *Independence* again went out to practice on June 18. In fifteen knots of wind, again, the steering system blew and America's Cup veteran Hank Haff, who was steering, wrested the giant yacht from the brink of catastrophe. After effecting repairs, *Independence* left Boston, sailed around Cape Cod to Martha's Vineyard and then on to New London. There, alongside *Constitution* and *Columbia,* John Hyslop, the New York Yacht Club's measurer, carefully assessed her dimensions and formulated a rating number. Hyslop calculated that if all three yachts started at the exact same time over a thirty-mile course *Constitution,* the fastest boat, would have to finish 42.6 seconds ahead of *Independence* and 76.8 seconds ahead of *Columbia.*[16] If all three yachts sailed perfectly around the course, *Constitution* would finish first, *Independence* second, and *Columbia* would take up the rear.

The Boston boat—with long, flat overhangs that were shallow and wide at the bow and stern—exaggerated every breakthrough in yacht design. Although Crowninshield's rudder had been a dismal failure, he'd made the necessary changes. In addition to installing a towering rig emulating those of *Independence*'s rivals, the designer flattened the hull's ends—just as Herreshoff had done with *Gloriana,* except to an even greater degree. When heeled, the yacht's long appendages not only increased the waterline length but also skimmed across the water's surface like a high-speed torpedo boat.

Sailing off Newport, *Independence* started the first exhibition race two minutes behind *Columbia* and *Constitution,* crawling through light winds. She was so far behind when the Herreshoff yachts finished that the race committee didn't wait. Instead they anchored a small catboat to mark the finish line. Lawson later noted in his self-published volume *The Lawson History of the America's Cup*, "At 9 o'clock [P.M.] *Independence* limped into Newport Harbor, anchoring in Brenton Cove."[17] In the second race *Independence* leaked so badly that she sailed with a pump, water pouring overboard from a hose. *Constitution,* finishing twenty-eight minutes and eight seconds ahead of the gurgling tub, had been plagued by crew errors and lost to the slower *Columbia* by fifty minutes.

In the third and final race, in a building twelve-knot breeze, *Independence* was finally vindicated. Rocketing off the line, she sailed boat for boat with the Herreshoff yachts, rounding the windward mark two seconds ahead of *Constitution.* Ultimately, she was overtaken, but her unwieldy design had proven fast. This spark of hope was short-lived. Although she kept pace, her topmast suddenly parted, the flopping rags threatening the rest of the yacht's superstructure. Crewmen climbed aloft, cut the debris away, and *Independence,* having lost ten minutes to her competitors, commenced the chase. "After rounding the mark the Herreshoff boats split tacks and *Independence* took a long starboard tack," wrote Lawson. "The three rounded as follows: Columbia 1.25.32; Constitution 1.26.08; and Independence 1.36.16. Independence with the three lower sails only made the ten miles in 2m 23s faster than Columbia, thus outsailing the Herreshoff champion at the rate of 14 seconds to the mile."[18]

The second set of exhibition races took place on August 1 and 3. *Independence*—again out of control, stumped by crew errors, and leaking like a colander—fell behind. The yacht, however, outpaced her competitors on the individual legs. Lawson wrote that there was so much torque in the yacht that the bow was at one angle of heel while the stern was at another, the yacht twisting so much in the final race that again the rudder head jammed. Because of these design flaws, the yacht was plagued with a nasty case of lee helm, meaning she had a natural tendency to steer downwind. A yacht sails fastest with a neutral helm; with water flowing evenly over both sides of the rudder and sails and keel balanced, even a 130-foot monster can be steered with the light touch of a hand. Through the design, rig tune, and sail trim, a yacht can be calibrated so that she has a slight amount of weather helm, meaning the yacht has the slightest inclination—if the helmsman were to take his hand off the wheel—to turn to windward. This has two advantages: first, it provides the helmsman with a "feel" for the yacht, an ability to gauge the fluidity of her movement through the water, just as a jockey maintains pressure on his reigns to "feel" his horse's disposition. Second, in a puff of wind, the yacht has the tendency to "feather" to windward, gaining distance to weather (toward the windward mark) while simultaneously spilling excess wind off the sails—wind that would otherwise cause the yacht to heel excessively, requiring brash movements of the helm and easing of the sails and ultimately slowing the boat.

A yacht with lee helm, conversely, tends to dive to leeward, losing windward gauge. The helmsman must fight the wheel to maintain the boat's windward track. The more helm used, the slower the boat goes—the rudder acting as a brake, like a giant canoe paddle held perpendicular to the flow of water. Sailing upwind with excessive lee helm is slow; sailing downwind, especially on a massive yacht like *Independence,* is downright frightening. With the giant mountain of sail rocking like a metronome over the problematic hull, the yacht instinctively carves to leeward as if catching the steel edge of a ski. Again, the helmsman must fight the wheel to maintain control, a nail-biting process considering the potential consequences of a mistake. The worse-case scenario is a crash jibe, occurring when the boat carves too far to leeward and the wind, exerting thousands of pounds of pressure—the force of 1,200 large pulling horses—suddenly fills the backside of the sails, sending them and their respective spars crashing across the deck at blinding speed.

On a yacht like *Independence,* the steel boom would slam into the running backstays, snapping them like dental floss. Roaring across the deck and into the water, the mainsail, now pinned and therefore still full and drawing, would cause the yacht to round to windward. As she does, the spinnaker and topsail, now prostrate to the wind, would lever the boat onto her side. Alas, with her severed backstay, the mast would crumble, bringing the rigging and sails crashing into the water. From beginning to end the whole ghastly maneuver might take five seconds.

In the final race, sailed in heavy winds, a puff washed down over the yacht and Captain Haff fought to keep the bow from diving downwind. *Independence* bucked, the puff causing the yacht to heel to her hatches, water rolling down the deck. Spinning out of control, the wind spilled from her sails until finally the Boston boat righted, regaining composure. Behind her competitors, *Independence* proceeded to chase them around the course and evinced her speed potential. Although *Independence* was soundly beaten and sailed the exhibition trials with a pump hemorrhaging bilge water, she exhibited the potential of the extreme shapes Herreshoff had pioneered. She had also piqued Captain Nat's curiosity.

With the field narrowed to two, *Columbia* and *Constitution* sparred throughout the summer, the former beating the latter with superior crew work. *Constitution* ran aground while racing from New London to Newport during the New York Yacht Club annual cruise, requiring repairs at the Herreshoff yard. With low morale, *Constitution's* all-American crew muddled back into that summer's season of opprobrium. They hoisted and trimmed sails slower and with less accuracy. *Constitution's* older Captain Uriah Rhodes—an "unknown quantity," as W. B. Duncan called him in an 1899 letter[19]—was no match for Barr's sharp, younger guard. Once again, both syndicates ordered new sails. Again, Herreshoff chose his new creation. But against Captain Nat's better judgment, obdurate Duncan demanded a mainsail made from extra-heavy cotton duck. *Constitution,* with her new mainsail and Captain Nat serving as advisor, managed to secure a handful of wins, but as August's light winds settled over Rhode Island Sound, the heavy new sail, sagging on its spars like a lead apron, severely handicapped *Constitution.*

By the end of the summer, both yachts had won nine of eighteen completed races, but *Constitution's* capricious crew failed to convince the selection committee. Had Barr been at the helm of *Constitution* the outcome might have been different. Captain Nat truly believed that. At noon on September 5, after an exhaustive discussion among the members of the selection committee on board the New York Yacht Club's flagship *Corona, Columbia* was chosen to defend the Cup.

The races of 1901 saw *Columbia* pitted against Lipton's second challenger, *Shamrock II,* designed by George Lennox Watson. Watson's tank tests had paid off. His yacht was incredibly fast and unarguably stunning. "The beauty of *Shamrock II,*" wrote the *Paul Mall Gazette,* "has been a good deal like a cold bath for the Americans. It is true they delighted in it, but the enjoyment of it was not unaccompanied by shock."[20] The *World's* yachting reporter announced the Cup was in its greatest danger ever of being lost.[21] At 137 feet overall, with a long, extremely deep keel, *Shamrock II,* wrote the marine editor at *Scientific American,* was "the most refined form ever seen in a Cup challenger."[22]

Carrying roughly eight hundred square feet of sail more than *Columbia* and six feet longer overall, *Shamrock II* was formidable. In his hundreds of hours of tank tests Watson had devised a hull shape that could carry an enormous spread of sail, greatly increasing her speed. On paper, however, *Shamrock II* appeared only marginally faster than the older *Columbia.* If both yachts started at the same time around a thirty-mile course, *Shamrock II* need only finish forty-three seconds ahead of *Columbia* to win. Was that possible? Could *Shamrock II* make up the difference? In trials *Shamrock II* was a full ten to twelve minutes faster than *Shamrock I,* which after sail modifications and rig tuning was logging times on par with *Columbia's* 1899 performance.[23] "The deduction," wrote the *Dublin Express,* "is one which he who runs may read."[24] If the trials were any indication, the pundits were prepared for *Shamrock II* to trounce the American boat.

The common perception that Herreshoff had failed with *Constitution* combined with Lipton's staunch determination to back a winner had many Americans bracing themselves for a British sweep. Although Lipton's philanthropic deeds and humble roots had won the hearts of America, the threat of British conquest—even if it was only for a cup—was exasperating. In addition, Lawson had based his campaign against the New York Yacht Club's exclusivity on the argument that if *Independence* proved to be the fastest boat, he held the right to represent the United States. Although his yacht ultimately bungled the exhibition trials, Lawson's public outcry had instilled a fervent patriotic undertone to the event. No longer was this just a race between wealthy tycoons and their clubs. To the public, the America's Cup had become a competition between nations. That America and Great Britain were politically at odds further fueled this sentiment.

Immediately following Lipton's first challenge for the America's Cup in 1899, British forces invaded the Transvaal in South Africa, sparking the Boer War. British forces systematically exterminated thousands of Dutch settlers and black natives, igniting fevered anti-British sentiments in America. Although McKinley, bolstered by William Randolph Hearst's newspapers, backed Great Britain, many Americans thought the conflict an odious act of imperial aggression. Exemplifying congressional opposition to the war, Senator William Allen of Nebraska barked to a sold-out crowd at Washington's Grand Opera House:

> If there is any country on the face of the earth that owes the British Empire nothing, that country is the United States of America. . . . England seeks to rule all people for mercenary ends. . . . Ever since she has grown to be a world power she has been a robber and oppressor. Her armies and navies have carried troops as blood thirsty and rapacious as those of any Spanish conqueror of the sixteenth century. I hope and believe that the God of justice will in time see that the British Empire is overthrown and a republic established in its place.[25]

Although affable Lipton had spared the event from the tenebrous pall clouding Anglo-American relations, the mounting tensions infused the 1901 event with patriotic fervor.

In the first race for the Cup, held on September 26, 1901, *Columbia*, with Barr at the helm and Captain Nat riding shotgun, sparred for position on the starting line against *Shamrock II*'s Captain Edward Sycamore. From the committee boat, a preparatory gun—a cannon blast signaling the countdown to the start—fired at 10:55. With sails drawing, they ran the length of the starting line between the committee boat and the Sandy Hook lightship. The wind had been blowing east-northeast at eighteen knots but had dropped to ten knots with the preparatory signal. Incredibly aggressive, the helmsmen hurdled their boats at each other, the crews working furiously to trim sails and drive the boats at top speed.

Still maneuvering for a tactical advantage prior to the starting gun, Sycamore rounded the lightship and Barr followed closely behind. The two yachts sailed downwind heading southeast. Barr steered *Columbia* upwind, jockeying for the advantageous weather position. Sycamore, too, steered his yacht upwind, and securing enough room, tacked. Barr tacked on top of him, seizing the windward position. Canvas womped and sheets groaned on their winches. Blocks banged on their shackles. The two captains, eyes locked, measured their speed and position in relation to their opponent. With both yachts on port tack, Sycamore to leeward, Barr, in total disregard of the rules (the leeward boat has right-of-way) bore downwind, forcing *Shamrock II* to make room. *Shamrock II's* crew slacked their sheets and Sycamore wrenched the wheel. The yacht spun on her axis like the sweeping hand of a stopwatch. Despite the frightening rule infringement by Barr, Sycamore cleared his yacht from *Columbia*.

With five minutes until the start both yachts luffed—their sails eased so to only partially harness the wind—their bows pointing toward the starting line. The yachts drifted, struggling to maintain a steady position relative to the other. The mates trimmed their sails ever cautiously to provide headway, essential for maintaining the steerage needed to maneuver quickly. The easiest way to win a match race is to maneuver into an advantageous position before the start and maintain that advantage throughout the race. The afterguard of each yacht had studied the wind and the tide and had devised a game plan of where they wanted to start when the final gun sounded. Unlike a foot or horse race where a gun is fired and stationary competitors race toward a fixed end, yachts jockeying for position before the starting gun can acquire a tactical advantage over their opponent even before the starting gun sounds. They can fight for a windward position, blanketing the other yacht. They can also prevent the other yacht from starting on the favored side of the starting line—the side of the line that could potentially be slightly closer to the windward mark or have more wind or favorable current.

The luffing match is the yacht-racing equivalent of a showdown. The crew remains relatively motionless except for the mates trimming the sails. The captains study their opponent. They watch hands, eyes, their movements, as if at any moment they would lunge for the holster. The yachts luff in unison, the right-of-way rules governing their actions. They move slowly, each yacht testing the other's ability to speed up and slow down. Sycamore did just this and ultimately, in this slow tactical waltz, he broke away from Barr. With the wind fading, *Columbia* broke out her baby jib topsail at 11:08. Two minutes later *Shamrock II* did the same. Having gained a slight speed advantage, *Columbia* gained the weather position. The two yachts charged to the line, crossing early. The gun fired.

Because they were on the wrong side of the starting line before the starting gun fired, the penalty was to recross the line and restart.

Columbia bore down toward the starting line and *Shamrock II* followed. The two dipped to leeward of the starting line. The British boat immediately tacked in an attempt to rid herself of Barr. Barr, displaying perfect composure in his tailored suit and yachting cap, tacked his enormous yacht on top. With eased sheets, his yacht gained speed. Barr footed and the trimmers eased more. *Columbia* accelerated. As the boat reached full speed, Barr nodded to his mates. The trimmers wound in, and Barr nudged *Columbia* upwind, securing a solid windward position as the two yachts, sailing on port tack, charged upwind. "It was one of the hardest fought battles for the advantage at the start ever seen in American racing waters," reported the *New York Times,* "and from the beginning of it to the end Capt. Barr had the redoubtable Capt. Sycamore, reputed to be the smartest starting skipper in Great Britain, entirely at his mercy."[26]

In a dying breeze, *Columbia* forged ahead, gaining slowly on *Shamrock II.* The two yachts sailed toward the Long Island shore looking for small zephyrs from the land. Swapping tacks, the yachts slipped farther upwind, Sycamore chasing Barr who'd pulled out a slight lead. Noting a small shift, Sycamore tacked at 12:54. The two yachts bore down on each other, and Sycamore crossed Barr, securing the lead. The two yachts sailed on, *Shamrock II* holding *Columbia* to leeward. Barr footed for speed and gained separation from Sycamore. He then tacked into a favorable shift, a lift allowing him to sail a higher angle. At their next crossing, Barr regained the lead.

As the wind slumped, the two yachts continued their painstaking crawl to windward, *Columbia* inching ahead. At 3:05:32 *Columbia* rounded the windward mark. *Shamrock II* rounded at 3:12:47. *Columbia* continued to stretch her lead, drifting along, piled high with sails toward the finish. But the east-northeasterly wind died and both boats ground to a crawl. At 4:42 P.M. the red R flag was hoisted to the top of the committee boat's mast. Unable to finish under the specified time limit, the race was called and the two yachts were towed to Sandy Hook's Horeshoe Harbor.

Barr wasn't criticized after Sycamore took the lead during the upwind leg like he had been following the first race of 1899. Perhaps he had gained the trust of his employers, and perhaps his earlier success made him less susceptible to public scrutiny. There was also a tacit understanding that perhaps *Columbia* wasn't the best boat America could have put forth. Lipton had come prepared, and that Barr had out-maneuvered Sycamore and regained a lead, despite the fluky conditions, was a credit to his abilities. Nevertheless, his aggressive maneuver–ing and rule infringement at the start prompted a strident rebuke from Sycamore, which appeared in the *New York Times.*

> The next time Captain Barr resorts to the crowding tactics, he must not be surprised if the *Shamrock* refuses to be crowded, and if she holds her course regardless of consequences. I could have struck the *Columbia* in the start of the last race had it not been that by advice of Mr. Watson and Mr. Jameson I yielded the point and gave way rather than cause any unpleasantness by giving the impression that I wanted to be hoggish. Nothing of this kind is permitted in the rac-ing rules abroad. No Captain would think of bearing down on a yacht and taking advantage of the other man's desire to avoid dam-age to his own and his adversary's boat. I am free to say that no more crowding must take place hereafter, as the *Shamrock* will be sailed ac-cording to the letter of the rules.[27]

When asked to respond, Barr had no comment.

On September 28, with a shot of the warning gun, the two captains attacked each other. Vying for advantage behind the starting line, Barr and Sycamore, eyes locked, spun through each other's wakes. Sailing with aggression, Sycamore took the advantage, holding Barr to lee-ward. With the blast of the starting gun, the two yachts bolted upwind, Sycamore comfortably two seconds ahead and to windward, sailing fast and in clear air. Tacking upwind, Barr tried desperately to break away and pass Sycamore to no avail.

By the turning mark, *Shamrock II* had established a lead of forty-one seconds. The two yachts, racing downwind to the finish, piled on their sails. *Shamrock* held the lead until *Columbia,* carrying fresh breeze and spewing sheets of water from her bow, passed the challenger. In a drag race to the finish, *Columbia,* beat the faster challenger by thirty-five seconds or 100 yards. "The race of yesterday," reported the *New York Times,* "showed the Columbia and Shamrock are two beautifully matched yachts in light weather and their sailing masters are experts of the highest order. Those who went out yesterday saw one of the greatest yacht races sailed in any waters and one of the closest in the history of the America's Cup."[28]

On October 1 an attempt was made to race. *Shamrock II* established a solid lead, but the wind died and the race was cancelled. On October 3 in a ten-knot northwesterly, the race committee raised code flag D, indicating a triangular course, each leg ten miles long. *Shamrock II* led at the start and sailed clear of the line.

In 1901 the rules granted yachts a two-minute starting grace period that began with the starting gun and ended two minutes later with the handicap gun. A yacht's racing time was calculated from when she crossed the starting line to when she finished. The yacht, however, must start within that two-minute window. Although it might seem like this time window would negate the need for pre-start maneuvering, it was often in a yacht's best interest to stay close to her opponent. In one scenario, by staying close to her competitor, she could hinder the other's performance. By wresting a tactically advantageous windward position, shunting turbulent air from her sails onto the other yacht, she would not only sail an unobstructed race, but also concurrently slow her opponent. When beating the clock was just as important as beating the other yacht, this could win the race. In another pre-start scenario, the tactically advantaged yacht could start just before the handicap gun, forcing her opponent to start late. The first yacht's time would begin when she crossed the line. The second yacht's time, however, would begin when the handicap gun (marking the end of the starting window) was fired. A yacht fifty yards behind the line when the handicap gun sounded was forced to sail farther (while being timed) than a yacht starting cleanly at the line within the two-minute window. This starting system wasn't perfect. Often, one yacht started while the other waited for clear air. The system's detractors believed it lacked drama. When yachts started separately, it did. Ultimately, though, it provided a tactical tool, which whenever possible, helmsmen used to their advantage.

Seeing that Sycamore had started cleanly on the more advantageous side of the racecourse (with better wind), Barr waited until Sycamore was gone and then started in clean air, sailing fast off the line. *Shamrock II* led *Columbia* on the first reach, rounding the mark at 11:51:10, *Columbia* rounding behind at 11:52:22, having gained twenty-two seconds on the challenger. At the end of the second leg, and with the wind having reached fifteen knots, the two yachts doused their jib topsails. *Shamrock II* rounded the mark first at 12:45:57; having gained thirty seconds on the reach, *Columbia* rounded at 12:46:39. Sailing upwind on the final leg, Barr worked his magic, matching Sycamore tack for tack, sailing higher and faster. At 1:20:35 Sycamore tacked to port. Five seconds later Barr followed, solidifying the windward position. Holding Sycamore to leeward, Barr extended his lead, still sailing higher and faster. "Columbia approached the line at railroad speed," reported the *New York Times,* "and rushed across it at 2:15:05, a glorious winner amid the cheers of the spectators and the wild shrieks of a hundred whistles. Shamrock followed 1 minute and 18 seconds later, a thoroughly beaten boat."[29]

Sparing no time, the third race was scheduled for the next day, October 4. But *Columbia,* up two-nil to *Shamrock II,* was in desperate need of sail repair. Because the American yacht had never received new sails from the Herreshoff loft—the new set having gone to *Constitution*—her mainsail was badly warped, the head, L. Francis Herreshoff observed, was stretched longer than the gaff. According to Captain Nat's son, Barr and A. W. Hathaway, the Herreshoff loft's head sailmaker, spent much of the early morning attempting to fasten a shorter head rope along the existing one. When that failed they sewed small folds into the sail, reshaping the sagging bag into a rough semblance of the sleek wing shape it had once had.[30]

A single mark was set fifteen miles south-southeast of the starting line marked again by the committee boat *Navigator* and the Sandy Hook Lightship. An eight-knot north-northwesterly breeze pushed crisp autumn air over the racecourse. As the preparatory gun sounded at 10:45, the two yachts shot upwind on port tack. Barr tacked to starboard and then bore off; Sycamore followed. Heading back toward the starting line with two minutes to go before the start, Barr again, rounded up onto port tack and luffed. Sycamore followed, but carried *Shamrock II's* momentum a distance to windward. With *Columbia* to port, Sycamore bore away on starboard tack. Barr filled *Columbia's* sails and followed. Running back to the line, Barr held the lead. Sycamore, just behind Barr, raced toward the line, the crew extending the spinnaker boom to starboard, hoisting *Shamrock's* balloon jib topsail and spinnaker. The starting gun fired, *Columbia* crossing ahead of *Shamrock II.*

Upon hitting the line, Barr, to the west of Sycamore, crooked his finger and told the mate to hoist *Columbia's* spinnaker. A fifteen-mile drag race to the outer mark ensued. *Shamrock II*, with her greater sail area, passed the defender at 11:20. During the next half hour, *Shamrock II*, sailing faster, extended her lead to roughly three hundred yards. At noon, with a favorable wind shift, *Columbia* gained. But as the wind shifted back, *Shamrock II* continued on her way, maintaining an advantage into the mark.

Rounding cleanly at 12:48:46, Sycamore, sailing on starboard tack, set a course for the finish line. Barr, in preparing to douse *Columbia's* spinnaker, experienced trouble. One of the balloon jib topsail hanks, a bronze snap shackle holding the sail to its stay, had somehow hooked into the spinnaker and was tearing it. Unable to douse the sail without destroying the spinnaker, a crewmember was hoisted aloft to clear the snare. When he'd finished the job the crew finally doused the balloon jib topsail. But as they started on the spinnaker, it fouled, sliding over the bow and into the water. Thousands of yards of cotton-silk weave skimmed the surface, threatening to sink and wrap around the hull. The crew, working frantically, hauled the soaked mess, like a heavy net, out of the water and onto the deck. *Columbia* rounded the mark at 12:49:35.

Crossing at 1:07 *Shamrock II* held a sound lead. "And now every expert in the fleet expected Shamrock to tack on Columbia's weather bow," reported the *New York Times*, "and having put the defender under her lee, keep her there. But this was precisely what Shamrock did not do. She held her port tack for a good minute, going away from Columbia and out to seaward, while Columbia was rushing in toward the land and toward the better wind."[31] Pouncing on Sycamore's mistake, Barr steered *Columbia* into a fresh, shifting breeze. Barr tacked in the new wind and accelerated. Although Sycamore still held a slight lead, Barr, footing fast to the west, chipped away. As the breeze lightened *Columbia* raised her jib topsail at 1:15:45; *Shamrock II* followed at 1:16:35. On port tack, the two yachts sailed abeam of each other until *Shamrock II*, footing faster, pulled ahead, securing a quarter-mile lead. Barr tacked to starboard at 2:03:30. A minute later *Shamrock II* followed, but *Columbia* led to the left side of the course and was first to enter an oncoming wind shift from the left.

At 2:10, a dark patch of water, slipping past *Shamrock II's* bow, washed over *Columbia*, providing a substantial lift—a wind shift that allowed her to steer closer to the mark, reducing her distance to it. Sailing higher and faster than her opponent, *Columbia* reaped the benefits of the fortuitous puff for roughly ninety seconds. Barr watched his headsails, eying his telltale pennant, while the afterguard provided updates on Sycamore's progress. One eye on the sails, the other scanning the water, Barr saw yet another puff. At 2:14, the patch of wind slipped into place, the headsail trimmers ordering an inch more sheet as the puff hit the bows, the yacht heeling to her rails. The mainsail trimmer, watching his sail, perhaps added a touch of trim. With eight to twelve knots of wind and flat water, Barr and sailmaker Hathaway couldn't have asked for more forgiving conditions for their ailing sails. Too little wind and their overstretched, sagging canvas would prove too inefficient to drive the boat to windward. Too much wind and the sail's draft, its most powerful area deepened excessively by stretching, would make the boat difficult to control.

Having gained a substantial lift, Barr tacked. But as the two yachts approached, it was evident that *Columbia* would not cross ahead of *Shamrock II*. Sycamore tacked to cover at 2:16:15. Almost immediately, Barr tacked away onto starboard. Sycamore, leading the defender to the west, was first to hit a left shift at 2:20. Both yachts footed into the new breeze; *Columbia* tacked to port, and *Shamrock II* followed. Barr, a quarter mile to windward and half mile astern, had established a great deal of leverage—here referring to his tactical ability to capitalize on a westward wind shift. Although he was a half mile astern, a west shifting breeze would rotate the obtainable sailing angles to the left, skewing the playing field to provide a marked advantage to the westward lying yacht.

Between 2:20 and 2:30 *Columbia* and *Shamrock II* swapped tacks. "Barr was working short tacks at this juncture," wrote the *New York Times,* "feeling the wind with great delicacy and skill."[32] The two yachts continued to battle to windward, the breeze lightening and the tide ebbing against them. Every movement of wheel, sail, and crew was critical. Sycamore and Barr stood calmly at their helms, weighing the effect of myriad factors threatening to slow them down: the shifting of wind and tide, sail trim, crew placement, their feel for the helm, cool autumn air, and warm summer water and how it affected the wind strength aloft compared to the wind strength on the deck. After an hour of traversing the course, the two yachts met at 3:20. Again, *Shamrock II* tacked to port, *Columbia* following a minute later.

As *Shamrock II* footed for speed in new wind, *Columbia* steered higher, pinching to windward, sailing toward the finish. Barr's pointing ability was so pronounced that he took the lead. As the two yachts neared the finish line, yachts from the spectator fleet scurried out of the way. *Shamrock II* tacked onto starboard, beating toward *Columbia*. Again, they approached each other at a steady clip. *Shamrock II,* having gained back a few feet, was even with the defender. "At 3:30 exactly," wrote the *New York Times,* "Columbia was seen to luff. Her headsails shook and she had to go about. She had been forced to tack by Shamrock's inalienable rights under the rules of the road."[33] With both yachts on starboard tack and *Columbia* to leeward, they aimed for the finish line. Unable to lay the line—steer high enough to windward to cross it—Barr bore off, footing for speed. *Columbia* burst ahead—inching out from under *Shamrock II*—and gained enough separation to tack. Sycamore, pinching in an attempt to make the line, matched Barr by also tacking. Now Sycamore burst ahead, his sails luffing, momentum carrying him across. The gun sounded. *Shamrock II* crossed the line first at 3:35:38; *Columbia* followed two seconds later. Although Sycamore won the race to the line, Barr won the race against time. *Columbia* won by forty-one seconds corrected time.

"The fault is in the bottom of my boat," Lipton told the *New York Times.* "The model is unquestionably the thing. This was the weather the Shamrock wanted. I have done my best. If the boat doesn't go my men can't make her go. The Columbia beat the Shamrock to-day because she is the better boat. The man most likely to design a better boat than the Shamrock II is Mr. Herreshoff."[34]

Shamrock II, racing the same *Columbia* that had beaten her predecessor, fell in three straight matches in the fall of 1901. Lipton was anything but discouraged, for he had made considerable progress; in the final race *Shamrock II* actually finished ahead of *Columbia*. The result was encouraging. The millionaire had found something he liked to do as much as work. Even though he preferred to watch the Cup matches from his steamyacht *Erin,* he was determined to finance a winner. With the same insatiable drive he had applied to business, Lipton went after the Cup, backing his syndicate with all of his resources. For his next challenge he returned to his first designer, Fife, and told him to pull out the stops. He was willing to go bigger, faster, and more extreme than any sailing yacht ever built. He would spare no expense.

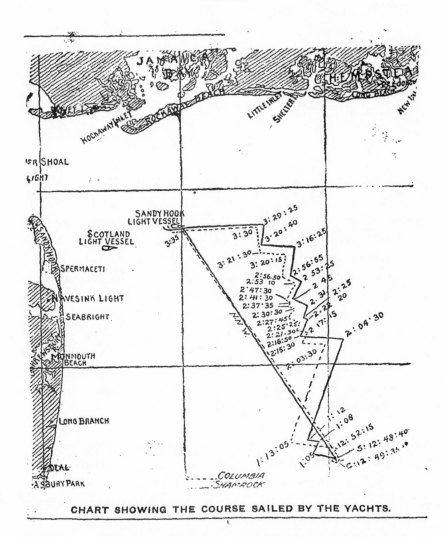

CHART SHOWING THE COURSE SAILED BY THE YACHTS.

October 5, 1901: Diagram showing the courses sailed by *Columbia* and *Shamrock II* in the final race of the 1901 America's Cup series.(Courtesy of the *New York Times*.)

9

THE TEMPLE TO THE WIND

Autumn 1902

On the evening of October 7, 1902, Sir Thomas Lipton wrote a letter. He had just turned fifty-four in May and his two Cup challenges had made him famous. As a businessman he had proven he could overcome any obstacle, and with his company running smoothly and providing a solid 12 percent yearly dividend to its stockholders, he was eager to launch another challenge. So in his office on City Road in London, he sat in his hand-carved mahogany chair, stooped over his roll-top desk, and penned a letter to the New York Yacht Club. He wrote:

> In thus desiring an opportunity of making a third attempt to obtain possession of the America's Cup I hope I may not be deemed importunate or unduly covetous of the precious trophy.[1]

Lipton paused and gazed over the city. From his desk he could see through a large, multipaned factory window an unmitigated view of London's begrimed rooftops. He had no trouble deciding on the rest of the wording; he had written similar letters twice before. When complete, the parchment he sealed into its envelope announced his third challenge for the America's Cup. He had resolved to win at all costs.

In two attempts, Lipton had bowed to Herreshoff despite having hired Britain's top naval architects and most-polished skippers. In his third challenge, Lipton hired them all—Fife and Watson, Wringe and Sycamore. If one designer-captain team couldn't do it, then perhaps both could. Herreshoff, still crestfallen from *Constitution's* failure, wanted nothing to do with the next Cup. In addition to the *Constitution's* poor performance, there were a number of factors exacerbating his hesitancy. His wife, Clara, had been ill for some time, and his chronic rheumatism prevented him from working for days at a time.

But his and his wife's health were less likely to deter him than complications in his professional life. His inability to provide new sails to *Columbia* had spurred the antipathy of her partial owner, J. P. Morgan. Frustrated that he was unable to secure sails even when defending the America's Cup, Morgan had closed a deal with famed English sailmaker Thomas W. Ratsey, whose firm had furnished Lipton with his canvas. Morgan outfitted Ratsey with a new loft at the Jacobs Yard on City Island, northeast of New York City, so that he would never be faced with the inconvenience of waiting for sails. In addition, with Lipton's challenge, the American yachting fraternity had begun speculating about the next defense. In Boston and New York talk circled around boats designed by W. Starling Burgess, Edward Burgess's son, and Bowdoin Crowninshield, the architect of *Independence.* Feeling undermined and moribund, Captain Nat shrunk from the prospect of another massive effort. He told Iselin, who'd signed on as point man for the New York Yacht Club's defense, he was through. Iselin wouldn't listen. The assiduous managing owner cajoled Captain Nat in repeated letters. By September 1902 Nat, diffident, had agreed to pick up his chisels and planes and carve another model.

Iselin, though traveling through Europe during the summer of 1902, had spearheaded a major letter-writing effort to secure personnel contingent on an official challenge from Lipton and the Royal Ulster Yacht Club. He'd witnessed Barr and his precision command of a slower boat sway the New York Yacht Club's America's Cup Committee to forgo *Constitution.* To win, they needed him. If Nat couldn't improve on *Columbia* and *Constitution,* the brash captain was their only hope. He quickly secured Barr's release from August Belmont's employ. Iselin then sent Barr to procure his key officers. "Mr. Christensen did not want to engage on the only terms I could offer him," wrote Barr to Iselin from City Island on October 9, 1902. "I therefore sent him to Commodore Ledyard with a letter and the Commodore engaged him commencing his pay on 1st Oct. As the thing stands at present the Commodore says I may consider myself engaged if a boat is built but only on that condition."[2]

The Cup Committee deliberated over the letter sent from Lipton announcing a forthcoming challenge. With the go-ahead from New York, Herreshoff carved his first model. For Iselin, raised on Long Island Sound in a family for which sailing bordered on religion, any compromise was unacceptable. If a yacht could be made more powerful, it was done. As a boy, sailing in the fickle winds near New Rochelle, he was considered gutless if he did not pile on as much canvas as his boat could hold. Defeat in the Iselin family, one that had amassed great wealth in the shipping trade, was contemptible. As a young man, Charles Oliver Iselin, though not the best sailor in his family, was ardent in his study of sailboat racing, lessons being administered by the family's boatman, a captain hired to privately coach him and his siblings. After graduating from Columbia Law School in 1874 he began working for his father's banking firm; but swayed by his interest in sports—namely sailing, polo, hunting, and quail and pigeon shooting—he left the working world. Although his older cousin William Iselin was touted as the family's best sailor, Charles Oliver's inability, or rather his unwillingness, to pursue a vocation led him to focus his energy on racing.

At age twenty-one, he sailed his sloop *Dare Devil* to a string of victories, but he made a name for himself racing sandbaggers, centerboard yachts ballasted with moveable bags of sand and carrying incredibly large sail plans stretched across overhanging booms and arching bowsprits. Employing the Iselin family's brazen approach to the sport led him to dominate fleets. In 1887 he entered the America's Cup world and sailed as a crewmember aboard Edward Burgess's *Volunteer.* In 1893 he signed on as managing owner of Herreshoff's *Vigilant.* He again managed *Defender* in 1895 and *Columbia* in 1899. Although conspicuously absent due to illness in 1901, he'd earned a name for himself as both a ferocious competitor and punctilious manager. He knew how to raise money and hire the best. His success rested not on juggling every detail, but delegating judiciously and relying on those he trusted. In the world of bigboat racing, Barr was one of them. And Captain Nat was the other.

But after seeing Herreshoff's first model, Iselin asked the architect to push further, to explore the limits of possibility. He wanted a yacht bigger and bolder than ever before. Just as the height of a building is governed by the size of its footprint and construction materials, a racing yacht—one that won't fall to pieces—is constrained by her waterline length and construction materials. Generally, architects design structures that adhere to a sense of proportion so to ensure they are strong and safe. Iselin, conversely, hired Herreshoff to design something fraternizing with collapse.

As early as September 1902 newspapers began speculating on the new vessel. "In the opinion of well informed persons," wrote the *New*

York Herald on September 18, "Herreshoff's next cup boat will be of the extreme type, possibly of the freak order. They say that from both the Shamrock II and the Independence much was learned and that the famous designer will not be caught napping. One or two of the leading yachtsmen of the [New York Yacht] club are very positive that the models of both the Columbia and the Constitution will be laid aside and a new order of things prevails at the Bristol works."[3]

Herreshoff's ability to create a freak would largely depend on funding. A yacht of such monumental proportions demanded not only the most advanced materials, but also trial-and-error testing and a large workforce. This required money—and lots of it. Iselin enlisted a group of ultra-rich backers who could thwart Lipton's bottomless pool of cash. In conversations with members of the New York Yacht Club, Lipton had expressed his desire to scale back the exhaustive proportions of the yachts, instead sailing Cup competition in seventy-foot load waterline yachts. This would cut the cost tremendously, with the yachts requiring less building material, less crew, and smaller sails. But the change wouldn't curb the time investment. Club members would still be responsible for overseeing myriad details: from construction and hiring of crew to organizing trial races, press coverage, the Cup races themselves (requiring the cooperation of the U.S. Navy for crowd control), the printing of regulations for the hundreds of spectator vessels, and countless other tasks. The effort was so great that when Lipton announced he would like to race again in 1902 (the challenge announced immediately after his 1901 defeat), members of the New York Yacht Club denied him, citing the Deed of Gift required two years between matches. Most yachtsmen directly involved sat on boards of large companies and had families and, of course, their own yachts to attend to and were not willing to spend every summer defending the Cup.

In addition, with Roosevelt's ascendance to the presidency after McKinley's assassination, Americans began to question the gluttonous hoarding of wealth that had come to define the end of the nineteenth century. "...TR chose foes who ... wore the diamond stickpins of 'economic man'—the organizers of the great trusts, the stockjobbers, the 'malefactors of great wealth,' and the 'criminal rich,' "[4] wrote Kevin Phillips in *Wealth and Democracy: A Political History of the American Rich*. Phillips pointed out that by 1890 more than half the country's wealth was concentrated in one percent of American families. Midwest farmers were left destitute in the wake of industrial expansion and the resultant concentration of wealth in the East. And as policy began to reflect Roosevelt's progressive agenda, public opinion impugned these captains of industry. Garish displays of wealth such as international yacht races could have made some members reluctant, especially those feeling pressure from newly forming antitrust controls. "The men who would be called upon to defend the Cup were not particularly pleased with the prospect," wrote the *New York Evening Post*, quoting W. Butler Duncan Jr., manager of *Columbia* in her 1901 defense, "but they would defend the cup to the best of their ability."[5]

Members of the New York Yacht Club had soundly rejected the idea of seventy-foot-load waterline yachts for Cup competition because they feared the cycle of organizing races would never end. That Lipton had challenged without blushing for cost or time investment, brandishing at all times an implacable smile, had even roused indignation. "A touch—just a touch—of animosity," wrote the *New York Times*, "adds interest to any contest, and its complete absence from the make-up of one of two combatants imposes a really tiresome strain on the other . . ."[6] Iselin's insistence to push his new defender beyond prudence was largely an attempt to thrash Lipton so severely that he would not challenge again. He charged Herreshoff with exploiting every possible advantage afforded by the rules so that another challenge by Lipton would be futile.

To fund his boat of ambition, Iselin, with the help of Commodore Lewis Cass Ledyard, mobilized a defense syndicate comprising some of the wealthiest men in the world to pledge $300,000 in start-up funds. These contributors included James J. Hill, founder and owner of the Great Northern Railway Company; Henry M. Walters, president of the Atlantic Coast Line Railroad Company and notable art collector; William G. Rockefeller, the New York representative for the Rockefeller interests in the Standard Oil Company; Elbert H. Gary, chairman of the board of U.S. Steel; Clement A. Griscom, president of the International Navigation Company; William B. Leeds, president of the Chicago and Rock Island Railroad; Norman B. Ream, director of the Chicago and Northwestern Railroad, the Erie Railroad, and the International Harvester Company; Peter Arrell Brown Widener, director of the Traction [Cable Car] Company of Philadelphia and the Metropolitan Street Railway Company; and Cornelius Vanderbilt III, the young scion of the Vanderbilt fortune, working for the New York Central Railroad Company and a partner with August Belmont in forming the Interborough Rapid Transit Company, which was busy building the first New York City subway system.

The syndicate exemplified American aristocracy, a group of men as close to royalty as the United States could muster. Their public role was a tricky one, for their power and wealth was both venerated and scorned. Reports of elegant society functions—balls and luncheons, horse shows, and yachting events—dotted newspaper headlines. A few pages later, however, the same celebrities were cast as greedy devils, indifferent to the plight of the poor. Blushing at their own improprieties, the gilded set atoned by funding public projects and monuments to their good names, such as museums, universities, and libraries. Some sought to "clean" their filthy lucre by funding things of beauty. Syndicate member Henry Walters varnished the proceeds of his father's liquor business with a priceless art collection. Others, like the Rockefellers, took a more direct route to salvation, handing over large sums to the church. In his 1934 book *The Robber Barons,* Mathew Josephson describes an instance when John D. Rockefeller donated money to the Euclid Avenue Baptist Church in Cleveland. The pastor noted that some had accused Rockefeller of giving the church stolen money, but then conceded, "he has laid it on the altar and thus sanctified it."[7]

This compulsion to mask one's transgressions with payment was nothing new. Following the rise of Europe's merchant class, many of the giant Gothic cathedrals had been built on guilt. "Traders and others gave alms to cathedral chapters because profit was still synonymous with sin," argues Robert A. Scott in *The Gothic Enterprise: A Guide to Understanding the Medieval Cathedral,* "—some merchants had a bad conscience that bishops helped assuage by securing contribution for building cathedrals."[8] These civic projects not only fulfilled the rich man's need for penitence but also projected his fiscal power on rival merchants, lords, and kings. The edifice and its accoutrements became the medieval platform for self-promotion.

These myriad forms of conspicuous consumption were well catalogued by sociologist Thorstein Veblen in his 1899 book *The Theory of the Leisure Class.* Veblen contended the leisure class—that group of people at the apex of society, excused partially or completely from the conventions of middle- and lower-class life, such as physical work or thrift—brandish their efficacy through elaborate displays of wealth, such as ornate clothing, jewels, villas, and ostentatious gifts. Although the members of the New York Yacht Club syndicate had built their empires on everything from railroads and oil to steel and steamships, they all had yachting in common, channeling their conspicuous consumption into opulent floating palaces, liveried crewmen, and extended summer cruises to Newport and Bar Harbor.

In soliciting his millionaire colleagues, Iselin announced plans to build a yacht like nothing before. Hull No. 605 would be bigger and bolder than anything previously conceived, a gleaming bronze, golden-hulled yacht, with white sails, and white-clad crew. Perhaps building a sailing vessel of such grandiose proportions, of such regal stature, could offset the industrial grime and social inequity upon which they'd built their fortunes. Perhaps through their donations they could atone, like the kings and wealthy merchants who preceded them. Perhaps they could build a great temple to the natural world—a temple to the wind—a vector through which they not only cleared their collective conscience but also buttressed their roles as civic leaders. "It became a sign of one's place in the church and society to claim that the height of the nave of one's cathedral," notes Scott, "the magnificence of its tower or spire and grandeur or beauty of its stained glass, the length of its nave, its overall mass—whatever—was greater, bigger, better, more audacious than any that had preceded it. Indeed, as a practical matter, it would have been impossible to raise the money needed to undertake building a new cathedral unless it was to be more impressive than any already planned, under construction, or completed."[9] For his new boat Iselin demanded a "spire" bigger and bolder than anything ever built before.

One need not read dense volumes on Gothic architecture or social theory to understand that a sporting competition between the wealthiest people in America and Britain would be a test of national character. The country that could design and build the swiftest yacht and train the ablest crew would assume a position of honor. But would that really prompt such a dramatic mobilization of resources? For Lipton, there was no hiding the fact that his Cup challenges were business ventures, his yachts large, lavish advertisements. But would pride alone spur a group of American businessmen, all of whom were carefully skirting the limelight, to embark on such a lofty endeavor? Or was it just the fun of competition? The officious tone of letters and solemnity with which New York Yacht Club members approached the subject suggests otherwise.

The Wright brothers tackled the quest for human flight because of its society-altering utility. If they could build a mechanism for sustained air travel, it would change the world. Building a racing yacht wouldn't change anything. So why expend such resources for a game? Like human flight, did it have far-reaching implications? If we consider yacht racing a form of conspicuous consumption—spending exorbitant sums simply to prove you can—then, status-wise, yacht racing was very effective. As urban centerpieces, the cathedrals played the same conspicuous role, projecting a sense of legitimacy and importance on the community's prominent figures.

In addition, argues Veblen, by participating in sports, like yachting, the leisure class indulges its "predatory habit of life."[10]

[In] the countries of civilized Europe the hereditary leisure class is endowed with this martial spirit in a higher degree than the middle classes. Indeed, the leisure class claims the distinction as a matter of pride . . . The enthusiasm for war, and the predatory temper of which it is the index, prevail in the largest measure among the upper classes, especially among the hereditary leisure class.[11]

For example, Veblen asserts horse racing, like yacht racing, surfeits leisure class combativeness for it "gratifies the owner's sense of aggression and dominance to have his own horse outstrip his neighbour's."[12] One could argue that yacht racing was an outlet to express this "predatory" or "warlike" nature. The robber baron's ferocity in the business world was legendary; this was a way to vent that predisposition through sport, while collaterally asserting social and fiscal power.

Ultimately, we don't know whether hull No. 605 blossomed out visions of grandeur or whether Iselin simply pressed the syndicate into service, arguing it was their duty as club members. Although their contributions would surely have some far-reaching social or business repercussions, it's highly unlikely they had consciously thought of Veblen's ideas—or ever heard of him, for that matter. Every syndicate member had *a lot* of money. And although some club members complained that the Cup defense was a drain, it's likely Iselin targeted those who wouldn't flinch. The checks flowed freely from the syndicate to

Iselin to the Herreshoff yard. The newspapers on both sides of the Atlantic published a handful of stories about the New York Yacht Club syndicate upon the acceptance of Lipton's challenge. These articles identified the millionaire members and their business affiliations, but little else. As the season wore on they were rarely mentioned. The trust was content to lay low. They may have decided to build a temple, but no pastor had "sanctified" their money.

10

THE BUILDING OF
A GIANT

September 1902–March 1903

In stark contrast to the ambivalence expressed by some members of the New York Yacht Club, the American public answered with ardent enthusiasm. Responding to widespread anticipation of the Royal Ulster Yacht Club's official letter, papers followed the story unremittingly. On September 24 the *New York Herald* ran the insipid headline, "No Word of Cup Challenge."[1] By October the expectation had grown imminent. "Members of the NYYC who expected that the challenge for the America's Cup would arrive by the steamer Germanic yesterday," reported the *New York Daily Tribune,* "were disappointed when the foreign mail was delivered to find that the document had not yet arrived.... No cable message has been received at the NYYC Clubhouse up to midnight regarding the challenge."[2]

The official challenge arrived on Wednesday, October 15, on the Star Liner *Oceanic.* The *New York Times* went so far as to announce the 11 A.M. arrival of the ship and that the international mail would be ready for distribution by 2 P.M. The America's Cup Committee—consisting of Vice Commodore Frederick G. Bourne, Secretary George A. Cormack, former Commodore E. D. Morgan, former Commodore Edward M. Brown, former Commodore J. Pierpont Morgan, J. Malcolm Forbes, Archibald Rogers, and W. Butler Duncan Jr.—received the letter that afternoon by special delivery. Feeling ill, Commodore Lewis Cass Ledyard did not attend. The committee deliberated over the letter embossed with the seal of Royal Ulster Yacht Club and agreed to the terms.

The next day, on October 16, 1902, the contract for hull No. 605 was signed, dated, and logged in the Herreshoff Manufacturing Company's construction book. After having seen the extreme model carved by Captain Nat, W. B. Duncan sent a telegram to Iselin, saying "Nat has gone far enough this time."[3]

★   ★   ★

Across the Atlantic Lipton mobilized his personnel. "The new boat will be designed by Fife, assisted by Watson, both of whom are the best talent available and are working together with the greatest harmony," said Lipton in an interview with the *New York Sun*'s London correspondent. Lipton continued:

> As in previous challenges, we will spare no expense. We will do everything possible to attain our objective.
>
> We will expect to make great improvements on Shamrock II. I cannot disclose our intentions to our opponents, but the new challenger will not be clothed in the same material that made Shamrock II shine like gold. The designers would not design a new boat unless they were sure they could improve on the old one. That is all satisfactory.
>
> It does not pay Fife and Watson to design these boats. They are losing money over my small contributions, but it has become a matter of love for the flag with us all, and that is what is in our hearts. We don't know what Herreshoff is going to do. He is a wonderful man and may beat us; but I don't think so.[4]

It's doubtful that Fife and Watson actually lost money on their Cup design, as Lipton suggested. But considering the hundreds of hours of tank testing, the profit margin was likely slim. The two British rivals had been hashing out design plans for months—trading ideas, with Watson giving Fife ample advice on how to proceed. On February 13, 1902, Watson sent Fife a complete set of plans for *Shamrock II* with an accompanying letter that promised to "put rigging plan[s] in hand, detailed lists of weights, details of masts and spars."[5] The letter discussed the internal bracing structure of *Shamrock II* and then the rigging plan. It also confirmed Lipton's statement that they would not build the boat from bronze. "Now as to construction," wrote Watson, "I think we are both very much at one on that point, namely steel hull and aluminum deck. As to form," he continued, "I don't think there was very much wrong with the after end of 'Shamrock II.' I think it is just possible that I unduly narrowed her at the extreme after end, as I noticed she never carried the water right out to the end of the taffrail; but I made this long stern mainly as a platform for getting my mainsheet put on, and for that it was certainly most effective. Our latest boom and gaff were splendid sticks, and stood like gun-barrels, as also did the mast; but there was undoubtedly a lot of stretch in the rigging . . ." Watson went on to suggest changes to the bow shape but suggested Fife use American-made turning blocks for his lines. "They were beautifully made," he wrote, "very light and could justifying being a bit lightened still. . . . Coleman is an exceedingly smart fellow—far and away above our block makers here in England." Finally, Watson gave Fife some advice about working at the Denny test tank: "Get these [data] in hand as early as you possibly can, as it is incredible the amount of time you can take on these. Of course a great deal of the ground is prepared, but I kept running my head up against one stone after another, and although I had more than a year of it, was actually experimenting while she was on the loft."[6]

Although Lipton had compensated Watson for consulting, Fife was in charge. One can speculate as to why Lipton had waffled between designers, flopping from Fife in 1899 to Watson in 1901 and now back to Fife for 1903. Was this just another example of his pernicious hiring and firing habits? Wouldn't a designer capitalize on his previous mistakes? Possibly. He likely thought Fife with Watson consulting a reasonable compromise. At the time Lipton was under incredible pressure. When in 1900 the Prince of Wales had nominated him for membership to the Royal Yacht Squadron, Lipton was blackballed. In 1902 Yacht Squadron members again affirmed their ardent disapproval of Lipton. "Should the King, exercising his royal prerogative, force the matter to an issue," reported the *New York Herald,* "many members of the squadron contemplate withdrawing and forming another organization."[7]

Despite the royal rebuff, that year rumors circulated that Lipton would soon be granted a peerage—to one of the noble titles of baronet, baron, viscount, earl, marquis, or duke. But some also believed that the honor hinged on a victory in New York.[8] As always, Lipton was eager for acceptance. Winning was imperative. Although his decision to shuffle naval architects was questionable, he hired the same builder. After the challenge was accepted, heeding Watson's advice, Fife, without delay, began testing models in Froude's tank at William Denny & Brothers shipyard.

On the juncture of River Leven and the north bank of the Clyde, the Denny yard had been building boats since 1844. But boatbuilding had been a family trade since 1814 when the first William Denny had teamed up with Archibald McLachlan and built the *Marjory*, which became the first steamer running the River Thames. Concurrently, William's brother, Peter Denny, ran two shipbuilding companies, Lang & Denny (1822 to 1839) and Denny & Rankin (1839 to 1867). In 1823 William established William Denny & Sons, working with his first son John and third son William. When their father died in 1833, the yard was passed down to John. He, unfortunately, died five years later. With the death of his older brother and the rapid decline of the town due to Dumbarton's foundering glass industry, William II left for Govan where he took a job managing a shipyard. In his absence, his father's company fell apart.

While Alexander, the fourth son, was working as a naval architect in Paisley, his younger brother Peter worked with William II in Govan. Determined to consolidate their efforts, the three brothers teamed up in 1844 and created Denny Brothers based in Glasgow. Later that year they moved back to their hometown of Dumbarton where they leased a small chunk of land on the north shore of the River Leven's mouth and overlooking Castle Rock, a monolithic crag on top of which was perched an ancient military stronghold of the Scottish kings.

In 1850 Peter Denny forged an alliance with two local engineers, purchasing the defunct glassworks and starting an engine construction plant to outfit ships from the Denny yard. The newly expanded firm built the first compound engines for Cunard, Austrian Lloyd, and the Peninsular & Oriental Steam Navigation Company. So rapidly did William Denny & Brothers fill the void left by the failed glassworks, that the shipyard built housing for its workmen, the district garnering the name Dennystown. But just as the yard began to realize its full potential, William II died. A few years later Alexander and then James retired from the business. Peter Denny, the fifth of six brothers, kept the company alive, building, among other ships, high-speed blockade runners for the American Civil War.

Requiring more room, Peter purchased land on the opposite bank of the river, a peninsula joining the Leven with the Clyde, and in 1868 took his eldest son, William III, as a partner. Like his uncle and grandfather, William III was a smart businessman and hard worker devoted to the technological improvement of the firm. He purchased more property in 1881, expanding to the yard to the castle walls, and introduced the use of milled steel and, most significantly, the construction of a model towing tank designed by Dr. Froude. The strength of the firm had also been bolstered by adding additional partners, including Walter Brock (1873) and William III's brothers, John (1881), Peter III (1881), and Archibald (1883). But in 1887 William III, the company's catalyst, died at age thirty-nine. Despite the tragic loss, the brothers kept the business afloat.

In 1894, William Denny & Brothers celebrated fifty years in business. In that time they'd built exactly five hundred hulls and earned a reputation for the ability to build anything, having turned out barges, sailing vessels, steamyachts, paddle steamers, cargo and passenger ships, dredgers, tugs, sternwheelers, oil flats, and—according to a 1932 history of the firm—"even an 'electric launch.' "[9]

With Peter Denny's youngest son, Leslie, and Walter Brock's son, Henry, having joined as partners in 1895, the firm ramped up production and their capabilities. Between 1891 and 1895 they produced 81 vessels comprising 109,024 gross tons. During the next five years they produced 116 vessels comprising 156,043 gross tons, including the *Bavaria,* built for the Allan Lines Atlantic service in 1899, their first steamer over 500 feet long and 10,000 gross tons. In contrast to hulking mountains of iron and steel, in 1901 they built the comparatively gossamer *Shamrock II* for Sir Thomas Lipton. Watson had toiled over the resistance graphs logged during the tank test. The final draft melded Watson's vision with raw empiricism. For every hunch, a mathematical solution was sought until the design reached fruition.

The Denny yard, a sprawling compound enveloping Dumbarton's waterfront, defined shipbuilding on the Clyde, and the workers, many of whom lived in Denny-owned housing, defined themselves by their jobs. Cloaked by a specially built shed over berth No. 1, *Shamrock II*'s builders fomented such patriotism that they vied to outstrip each other's abilities. They forged the bronze and aluminum yacht around her frames, riveting each seam with exquisite care. That *Shamrock II* had lost in 1901 was a letdown, but the races had been closer than ever and the entire town of Dumbarton had become devoted to their new yacht's success. "At the time of the Shamrock II contests," wrote the *Dumbarton Herald,* paraphrasing Archibald Denny, "the townspeople had their screen on the Common, reporting the progress of the races, and their spirits went up or down as the news was favourable or the reverse, and it was something to say in these days of stress and strain in competition that they had a little town with a little people in it who displayed that kind of interest in the work they were doing."[10] By 1903 the Denny yard employed roughly 2,200 workers. And with the same fervent drive for perfection, the yard, managers, and designers—Fife with Watson consulting—looked to the Denny tank like a crystal ball, confident they would divine a yacht to beat the Americans.

The flurry of building preparations vivified patriotism on both sides. There was some talk that Lipton would man his trial horses, *Shamrock I* and *II,* with Americans. After a brief outcry, British papers refuted the claim. There had also been an offer from yachtsman C.W. Post of Battle Creek, Michigan, to charter *Shamrock II* from Sir Thomas Lipton for $10,000 during the 1902 season, proposing that with an all-American crew (the best in the world, he claimed) Lipton's yacht would easily beat *Columbia* manned with a British crew. The letter and Lipton's deferential reply ran in every major newspaper. Lipton argued a race of Americans on *Shamrock II* vs. *Columbia* and her original crew would be more cogent. "If you wish to do this," he replied, "I will not accept a charter of SII, as you so kindly offer, but I will let you have the use of her during the coming season without charge . . . I do no not wish to discourage you, but I feel certain that the *Columbia* would lick you."[11] Post turned him down, insisting that only using crews from both countries would the experiment prove conclusive. The New York Yacht Club ignored the exchange.

Lipton's yacht was well underway, and his name commanded headlines across Europe and North America. On June 25, 1902, King Edward conferred the title of Baronet upon his friend Lipton. In the same widely syndicated announcement, the mystery novelist Dr. Arthur Conan Doyle was granted his knighthood and the new honorific Sir.[12]

Just before dawn on November 26, 1902, the Herreshoff yard prepared to cast the keel of Captain's Nat's newest creation. At 5 A.M. the shop's boiler department, under the direction of foreman Benjamin Wood, stoked the furnace fire under the lead melting pots in the south construction shop. By 7 A.M. when the first shift arrived, the pots were fully heated, most of the lead having been melted. Meticulously shaped to Captain Nat's design specifications, the keel mold, a reinforced wooden frame lined with clay, was thirty feet long, seven feet at its deepest point, and three feet wide tapering to a trim bottom edge. Into the giant clay mold, workers piled five tons of lead pigs. Concurrently, workmen fed the melting pots, and furnaces, and still others, wielding fire hoses, stood by in case of flare-ups. One worker kept a detailed tally of every pig used. Once the lead pigs had filled the bottom of the mold, workers poured molten lead from a moveable spout into the gaps. A series of pipes leading to the shop windows helped ventilate the furnaces and rising smoke and steam. The *New York Times* noted most of the lead had been poured before noon and "the remainder added gradually to fill in cracks and depressions in the cast through shrinkage, by cooling on contact with the mold."[13] With the 102.3-ton keel slowly cooling, the largest ever for a single-masted vessel,[14] Captain Nat left the south construction shop at five o'clock and walked the short stretch of Hope Street to Love Rocks.

The design for hull No. 605 called for a lead keel bolted externally to its frame, the rest of the yacht being constructed on top of the massive brick of ballast. Four days later with the lead sufficiently cooled, Captain Nat ordered the mold removed. Upon inspection, the casting was deemed perfect. The next day, on December 1, workmen sliced away a four-inch groove twelve to thirty inches wide and spanning the full length of the keel. Inside this they drilled holes for mounting the lag bolts used to fasten the keel to the yacht's frame. Supported with wooden blocks, its deepest section facing aft, the keel formed a leaden shoe on top of which Herreshoff would build his defender.

Having honed his design according to the dictates of the tank tests, making sequent modifications to numerous wax plugs, and having climbed the stairs hundreds of times from the Denny tank to the drafting rooms, where four women carefully copied his drawings onto linen with ink, Fife began the building process. He decided not to cast a giant lead ingot to be bolted to a heavily reinforced frame (as Herreshoff had), opting instead to mold ballast directly into a lighter-weight frame. To avoid warping the steel frames, the likely outcome if he tried to pour the lead in its entirety, he began the process of smelting one ton per day, pouring thin layer upon layer as the builders continued construction on the rest of the yacht.

As inchoate skeletons of the two yachts sat in their respective sheds, newspapermen, barred from inspecting the yachts, speculated. The frames and hull materials were of particular interest. The strong and light construction that had contributed to Captain Nat's success was largely due to his fastidious attention to building materials. While Fife spent countless hours testing his hull designs, Herreshoff tested his metals. Using a machine comprising two giant screws and a pressure gauge, he tested the breaking strengths of square-inch swatches of Tobin bronze and nickel steel. Upon completing the tests, the steel demonstrated a strength advantage—the *New York Herald* reporting that nickel steel exhibited a tensile strength of between 105 and 110 thousand pounds. Tobin bronze had a tensile strength of only 70 to 80 thousand pounds. In addition to its strength advantage, the nickel steel was considerably lighter. Despite the advantages, however, the report announced that Captain Nat would likely plate the new defender in bronze, for it could be burnished to a golden shine, the advantage of a smooth bronze hull outweighing the weight savings with steel.[15] Other papers, including the *Commercial Advisor* loudly denounced the Tobin bronze hypothesis, arguing that "[with] nickel steel there will be saving in weight of hull of 12 percent, or something more than one eighth of the whole. If we take that the bronze hull weighed forty tons, this would give us a nickel-steel hull of thirty-five tons. The five tons saved will be used to better advantage in securing greater stability."[16] Captain Nat's furtive relationship with the media left a trail of unanswered questions and he was content leaving it that way. On his orders, reporters with prying eyes would be chased from the shop grounds. When *Defender* was under construction and two reporters were seen in a rowboat sketching the profile, Nat ordered his workmen to blast them with hot rivets. In another instance, a man caught poking a camera lens into the shop was lassoed by a workman in the sail loft and dragged from his boat into the harbor.[17]

Despite Captain Nat's lockdown, information leaked. By the first week in December the *Evening Sun* reported workmen were fairing the lead casting and the shops were still waiting for a large consignment of nickel steel bulb angles for the frame.[18] These frames would be bent into the shapes of Captain Nat's plan and then fastened to the keel plate. The new yacht, the papers announced, would also be braced with longitudinal frames, a design configuration pioneered on *Constitution,* requiring fewer web (rib) frames and lightening the hull. Once perfectly smoothed, the keel was shod in thick plates of Tobin bronze while along the previously cut ridge of the keel's top edge, four hundred nine-inch lag bolts were sunk into predrilled holes. Three bronze plates were fastened tightly into the groove, forming the keel plate, the plinth of hull No. 605.

While the Herreshoff yard waited for its shipment of framing steel, a fire raged through the Denny yard, destroying the fitter's shop. Only through a harrowing effort were the firefighters and members of the yard able to save *Shamrock III* in her shed. The yard, however, had been socked with $100,000 in damage, forcing the management to lay off over seven hundred workers. "I am thankful that the new challenger has escaped," said Lipton to the *New York Times*. "But I fear that the damage done to the shipyard may seriously retard the work on her. If her models, which were not in the shed, are destroyed, it will be a very serious matter."[19] Ultimately, the models were found and the building of *Shamrock III* resumed, the best made of the unfortunate contretemps.

But as the world scrutinized the builders and designers to uncover an advantage, Nat's original trepidation came back to haunt him. "In the opinion of most yachtsmen the relative merits of the Constitution and the Columbia and the possibility that Captain Nat Herreshoff has reached the limit of his skill as a designer are questions that have not yet been decisively decided," wrote the *New York Times*. "J. Pierpont Morgan, owner of the Columbia, believes that his boat is the best that Herreshoff ever had built or ever will build." Herreshoff's fear that perhaps he was simply too old and erstwhile percolated into pubic discourse. An extravagantly expensive albatross, *Constitution* haunted Nat's new defender, which not yet in frame, had already been stripped of her efficacy. "There will be no trial boats for a new defender next summer," continued the *Times*. "Each one of the three boats that is entered is a possible defender, and she will be commissioned, fitted out, and sailed as such."[20]

On December 11, the first consignment of framing steel arrived from the Pennsylvania Steel Company in Steelton. One hundred nickel steel angle bars between seventeen and twenty-eight feet long arrived at noon via express train, along with a car of steel plates to build the mast and steel billets used for bracing irons in the yacht's interior. The lot was trucked to the Herreshoff yard, whereupon the blacksmith shop, with its fires at full capacity, immediately began the process of heating and shaping the bars according to the lines of the hull. While the finished blackened lengths of steel piled up in long, wine-glass arcs, workmen spent days engrossed in the painstaking process of attaching the fore and aft joints to which the stem, sternpost, and longitudinal framing would be secured. Because of the structural importance of these pieces, workmen proceeded methodically.

Her frame far ahead of the American yacht, *Shamrock III* filled her Denny yard shed. When Britain's *Yachting World* asked Lipton if the collaboration between Fife and Watson "embod[ied] the ideas and experience of both our leading designers . . ." Lipton replied, "Absolutely accurate; and I feel confident that the work will be justified in the result."[21] Spewing patriotic treacle, Lipton wrangled a public relations advantage, intimating Britain's finest designers, having pooled their knowledge, would finally prevail over the feckless Americans. "I never saw a more smartly modeled boat," he told the *New York Sun*. "I do not like to rhapsodize, but when completed she will be one of the most perfect vessels of the kind ever launched. If money and skill can beget success it will be ours next fall. I am confident she is a Cup lifter."[22] No one had ever challenged for the America's Cup three times. And no one had sunk so much money into it. In addition to his design team, Lipton had also hired Captain Bob Wringe, the champion helmsman who'd dominated the American circuit at the helm of August Belmont's Herreshoff-designed *Mineola*. Wringe had also served as mate aboard Lipton's first challenge under Captain Hogarth and had been sailing advisor in *Shamrock II*'s afterguard during the races of 1901.

Implacable, Nat maintained his quotidian schedule. After working in his home office, he descended to the dining room where he ate his breakfast in silence. Donning his hat and coat, he walked up Hope Street and toured the shops where, with his customary perspicacious stare, he surveyed every detail. By the end of the first week in December the blacksmith shop had cast pieces for both the stem and stern posts; the sail loft, having received a large shipment of cotton duck from the looms in Lawrence, Massachusetts, was working at full capacity. With the new Ratsey loft now in place and producing sails at City Island, Captain Nat and John Brown made a special point to begin sail production early. The loft was already a third of the way finished with a new mainsail for *Constitution* and the patterns for her new forestaysail were already underway. But with the Cup frenzy having taken hold,

Captain Nat still had numerous other orders underway, including three thirty-foot sailing yachts[23] and a new steamyacht for Selah R. Van Duzer of New York.[24] By the end of the year, the lower section of the bronze stem was secured to the keel while the blacksmiths continued shaping the upper section. They had also begun bending and riveting the steel plates for two masts, one for the new boat and another for *Constitution*. At the same time, the Herreshoff sail loft had started on No. 605's headsails.

By January 11, the first five steel web or belt frames had been erected and attached to the keel plate. These eight-inch-wide steel-plate frames—spaced six feet, eight inches apart—would form the rib cage of the yacht's midsection. Captain Nat's longitudinal webbing system would brace these frames fore and aft, requiring fewer heavy ribs with the same overall strength. With the New Year having come and gone and spring only a few months off, the south construction shop bustled with activity. "When the doors of the shop were opened today," wrote the *New York Herald* on January 11, "an opportunity was given to note the large force of men at work about the keel and the frames. . . . there are a thousand and one small things that are in hand for the boat and will be ready as soon as the men who are shaping the craft want them."[25] In addition to his job as shop overseer, Nat, in consult with John, their supplier liaison, doled out tasks to his foreman who in turn doled them out to work crews. Walking through the shops, he monitored their progress, anticipating the next steps, and like an orchestral conductor, timed the work of each team so to converge in synchronicity.

With the sternpost still incomplete, the framers worked from the midsection toward the stem. By the end of January fourteen web frames alternating with sixteen intermediate frames—lighter-weight frames attached to the keel plate but not extending to deck level—arched upward. On January 25, after shaping two twenty-foot by four-foot wide by ⅝-inch thick Tobin bronze plates to the dimensions of the hull, workmen bolted them to the frames, one on port and the other on starboard and both hemming the top of the keel.[26] A thin layer of lead was shaved from the keel to allow the hull plate to lay flush with the keel shoe, the idea being that the overlap hull plates would distribute some of the strain normally confined to the keel plate.[27]

During the next few weeks workers from the blacksmith shop piled Tobin bronze plating next to their respective sections or stations, the yacht being divided into carefully measured vertical planes corresponding with the lines pulled from Captain Nat's original model. Precisely cut, the plates were lifted into place—thicker toward the keel and progressively thinner toward the deck—and the slow task of tiling the hull in bronze matched the sail loft's equally painstaking task of aligning and sewing No. 605's enormous panels of cotton duck. The boat shed, sail loft, and rigging shop worked at full capacity. When the plating along the sheer line was completed, the riveters fastened the shear strake, comprising lengths of two-inch by two-inch steel angles. When completed, the ³⁄₁₆-inch aluminum plate decking was laid, riveted, and reinforced with three-inch diameter pipe trusses running from the bilges of each web frame to the deck.[28] With the hull taking form, word spread that the new yacht would be named *Eagle*.

Shamrock III was at a similar stage of construction, not including Fife's slow method of pouring the lead, ton by ton, into the keel's shell plating. Captain Wringe had spent a month in Dumbarton during the early building stages but had left to Southampton to rest before the season began in earnest. Conversely, in Bristol Barr had not yet shown at the Herreshoff shops. By the second week in February, as an incentive to hurry, the Herreshoffs announced a fifteen-cent-per-day pay raise for metal workers.

The push to finish the yachts was on—and with the energized atmosphere came more speculation from the press. "If this report is correct," proposed the *New York Sun* on February 15, "the new defender will have a mast thirty feet longer than that of the Constitution and she will carry more sail on a single stick than was ever put on vessel." The same report announced, "[Fife] has been impressed with the ability of low-powered yachts to beat those that spread large sail areas . . . a vessel of easy form with moderate sail spread could more than hold her own with more powerful craft in any kind of weather."[29] These statements presaged a reversal in the design trends of the last thirteen years. Was Fife onto something? The smaller and less-powerful *Columbia* had beaten the towering rigs and sail plans of *Constitution* and *Shamrock II*. Herreshoff was in fact building big, but was that the answer? Had Iselin, in his demand to stretch the yacht to extreme proportions beyond Nat's first model, been rash? Had Nat erred by capitulating? He had knowingly produced a flop when he heeded Archibald Rogers's wishes to model *Colonia* after *Wasp* in 1893. Could that happen again? Could a less powerful yacht profiting from a poignant application of the design

rule produce such an advantageous rating to render an excessively powerful yacht impotent? All of these questions quickly led some to believe
that ninety-footers had reached their speed limit. Despite the insoluble
barrier between Nat and the press, he publicly refuted the proposition.
"He is of the opinion," reported the *New York Herald*, "that there is still
room for improvements, and hopes that the new boat will assist him in
convincing the 'yachting experts,' who are constantly talking of cup
challengers and cup defenders as being practically reduced to a one-
design class, that they are mistaken and have long been on the wrong
track."[30] The same yachting "experts" who'd harkened the end of development in the ninety-footers announced hull No. 605 would not be
called *Eagle,* but rather the *Republic.*

With a third of the hull plates bolted in place and awaiting rivets,
workmen laid the steel keelson—a load-baring hunk of metal braced
on the centerline and designed to bear and disperse the weight and
strains of the mast. In the north construction shop, workmen built the
boom, bending steel plates into shape and riveting them to the growing tube. The hoop-like rings used to hold the sails to the spars were
also being fashioned, piles of them mounting in the shop's corners. In
addition, workmen lathed and sanded the hollow wooden bowsprit
and topmast.

By the beginning of March the John A. Roebling's Sons Company
in Trenton, New Jersey, had completed building hull No. 605's 24,000
feet of galvanized wire rigging rope. "This rope ranges from one half
inch to one and three-eighths inches in diameter," reported the *New
York Herald,* in its indefatigable desire to dole out every minute detail
to the public, "and is composed of six strands, each strand, for most of
the rope, consisting of nineteen wires twisted together. The rope used
for standing rigging all contains a wire center, while the running rope
has the strands twisted around a hemp center in order to give greater
pliability."[31] Upon receiving the consignment, the Herreshoff shops
ran each diameter rope through their rigorous tests, stretching them
until they popped. The following day, Tuesday, March 3, *Constitution*
was launched at the Thames Towboat Company in New London. Captain Uriah Rhodes, the same man who'd succumbed to Barr in the
1901 trials, packed the yacht's spars onto a barge and the two vessels
were towed around Point Judith into Narragansett Bay and north to a

mooring at the Herreshoff yard. With No. 605 and his 1901 design now demanding his full attention, Nat fell under considerable pressure. On March 12 the *Bristol Phoenix* noted that Captain Nat had chased a photographer down Hope Street who'd taken a photo of him. Nat demanded he hand over the negative. "The plate was thrown into the street," wrote the local paper, "and Mr. Herreshoff broke the plate with his feet."[32]

During the second week of March Herreshoff workmen began construction of the steering gear, referencing and modifying the patterns from *Columbia* and *Constitution*. The Herreshoff drafting room organized its thousands of drawings according to application, for a successful type of block, winch, or steering system was often used on multiple boats. When Captain Nat identified a problem it was rectified and redrafted for future use, affording later models an evolutionary advantage. Only designs unique to a particular vessel were stored together. In its immense proportions hull No. 605 had many one-off parts, but the most vital components had already been thoroughly tested. In *Skene's Elements of Yacht Design*—a seminal volume on naval architecture first published in 1904 and since resurfacing in eight editions— the author, Norman L. Skene, quotes the maxim, "Good design makes use of that which has gone before."[33] In many of her principal parts, Nat's new defender was the offspring of her predecessors, but in many ways he'd gone off on a limb. *Constitution* had followed the lines of *Columbia* but his new yacht was different. "[Herreshoff] has departed from the two older boats," wrote W. P. Stephens. "At best we can only conjecture whether he selected this extreme form from the conviction that it represents a distinct advance in speed . . . or whether he merely availed himself of an opportunity to experiment."[34] In fact, Nat *had* commenced a grand experiment. The yacht taking shape in the south construction shop hurdled generations. Stephens believed that Captain Nat could afford such a leap of faith, for he could rely on *Columbia* and *Constitution* in case of failure.

On March 5 the *New York Times* announced *Shamrock III*'s new mast was "the most remarkable achievement in yacht construction in the United Kingdom,"[35] pointing out that the new spar weighed 1,500 pounds less than the mast of *Shamrock II*, an enormous advantage, for every pound removed aloft can also be removed from the keel without affecting balance. With the same sail area and a lighter displacement, the yacht will sail faster. Denny's workmen, explained the article, expressed some concern over the spar's flimsy appearance, but reassured that Fife was so confident in the design he'd decided not to build a spare. Watson, likewise, was so confident that he wagered the first bet of the upcoming races. With an anonymous New York Yacht Club member, Watson anteed five pounds to the New Yorker's ten, not willing to accept the American's three-to-one wager because, as the *New York Herald* wrote, "[Watson] said it would be highway robbery because he had great faith in the challenger."[36]

In Bristol, by mid-March, the lower staging around the defender had been removed. The hull, filling the shop to capacity, loomed over the workmen. Twenty riveters continued the laborious process of fastening Tobin bronze plates to their frames, while eighty more worked furiously on the yacht's myriad other components. The Herreshoffs had announced a launch date of April 11. The bigger Denny yard, despite the fire having impeded work for some weeks, planned to launch *Shamrock III* on St. Patrick's Day, March 17, 1903. Denny yard workers completed the aluminum decking on Fife's challenger, covering it with thin wood fiber sheathing. With launch dates looming, tensions were high and the press fought for information. So coveted was every word that a former employee of the Herreshoff Manufacturing Company, who had allegedly stolen plans for *Columbia,* was caught applying for a job and seeking entry to the shops. Because the yard would often take on extra help when it had particularly heavy workloads, not every builder was local. Another worker identified him and told the filcher to leave. When he returned to a local Bristol hotel, he received a note from Captain Nat, ordering him to get out of town. In its account the *Mail and Express* said the man sent a reply reading, "I'll stay in this town as long as I please. The Herreshoffs don't own it." With this, the hotel manager advised him to leave, brandishing the dark swagger of Bristol's waterfront: "You are unwelcome here," he warned. "March is an unhealthy month in Rhode Island."[37] The man left that day.

As launch day approached, *Shamrock III* was hoisted onto a set of pontoons, from which she would be lowered into the water, for the River Leven was too shallow to accommodate the yacht's nineteen-foot draft. But on the morning of March 17 a southwesterly gale with heavy rain pelted the Firth of Clyde. In expectation of the launch the town had shut down for the day. Even the Denny yard workers were granted leave after 9 A.M. A series of platforms had been erected and decorated with garlands and shamrocks. Painted white with a wide green band hemming her waterline, the yacht was festooned with decorative greenery. By noon, the wind dissipated and the sun broke through the clouds. As the Denny yard gates opened thousands flooded the waterfront. Some, the *Glasgow Evening News* reported, used ladders to climb to the workshop shed roofs.[38] "[A]ll around the shed was black with sightseers," reported the *Dumbarton Herald*.[39] Thousands more lined the opposite bank of the Leven. Some took to the river in rowboats, and others scaled Castle Rock to catch a glimpse. At 1:00 P.M. a special train from Glasgow delivered the launching party to Dumbarton along the Caledonian rail system. Once in town, Denny's yard superintendent, running a shamrock-garlanded locomotive, pulled the passenger car to the yard gates where it was met with music from the band of the 1st Dumbartonshire Rifles. Lipton greeted his guests, amongst whom was the Countess of Shaftesbury, the christener, whose husband, the Earl, was a former commodore of the Royal Ulster Yacht Club. "The Countess was very quietly gowned in black," noted the *Glasgow Citizen,* "with dark furs, open at the throat, showing some creamy tinted lace. Her hat, with broad turn-up brim at the left side, was of black lace and chiffon, worn with chenille-spotted fine black veil." The paper also noted, "Most of the guests of both sexes had shamrock buttonholes."[40]

With Lipton's royal guests and knighted gentry in attendance, the launching of *Shamrock III* became a celebration of Scottish craftsmanship and national pride. "The new challenger perched up on the pontoons looked fit to race for a kingdom much less a cup," wrote the *London Evening News* on the day of launching. "She presented a perfect picture of strength, lightness, and shipbuilding skill."[41] At 1:15, the yard whistle blew, the blocks were hammered from the ways, and as *Shamrock* rumbled into motion, the Countess swung a bottle of wine against the bow, saying, "'I christen you Shamrock III; may God bless you, and may you bring back the cup.' The cheering which started inside the shed as the yacht began to move," wrote the *Glasgow Evening News,* "swelled into a hoarse roar. . . . steam whistles of the ships lying near, and the yard engines, and the explosion of fog signals, added volume to the greeting."[42]

The yacht was taken in tow and dragged to the Garvel Graving Dock, where the launching pontoons were removed. The 170 invited guests retired for lunch in the Denny yard model hall. Toasting the future endeavors of *Shamrock III*, Lord Provost Primose rallied the crowd with nationalistic fervor. The Boer War, which the United States strongly opposed, had taken a toll on Anglo-American relations. Lipton's biographer, James Mackay, argues Lipton's quest for the Cup maintained an amiable rapport between the two countries.[43] Though most likely concerned with cementing transatlantic trade relations, in 1899, after losing the Cup, Lipton arranged a series of conciliatory telegrams between President McKinley and Edward, Prince of Wales. As a token of his commitment to both nations Lipton had flagged *Shamrock III* with both the Union Jack and Stars and Stripes. "It was a pleasant thought that this effort to wrest the sovereignty of the seas provoked no rancour," wrote the *Dumbarton Herald* paraphrasing Primrose's toast. "[If] the cup came over on the *Erin*, he could not conceive that the President of the United States would demand an addition to their navy of thirty cruisers. He would rather that some great diplomatic Pierpont Morgan organized a vast international combine which would relegate to the scrap heaps their ironclads, and leave to the Columbias, Defenders, Vigilants, and Shamrocks the settlements of all international difficulties."[44] That evening, at a dinner held at the Union Club in New York, Iselin announced to the New York Yacht Club's officers and Cup Committee that the defender being built in Bristol would be named *Reliance*.

With descriptions of *Shamrock III* flooding the papers, the *Mail and Express* prodded Captain Nat for his opinion. "Cabled reports are not always accurate, I have found," he said tersely. "Besides, I never criticize another man's work unless I am paying his wages."[45] The reports on the challenger varied, some arguing the yacht was radically different from her predecessors, others arguing she followed a natural progression. All reports, however, lauded the yacht for her sleek beauty. "In general design she resembles Shamrock I," wrote the *Dumbarton Herald*. "Her lines are stronger, and she is fuller bodied than Shamrock II, altogether presenting a strikingly handsome model, and favourably impressing the experts as a speedy boat, and probable cup-lifter."[46]

Shamrock III was 89.78 feet on the waterline, 23 feet wide, with a 21.3-foot forward overhang, a 23.34-foot aft overhang, and a 134-foot, 4-inch length overall. The *Glasgow Evening News* said the hull was deeper and fuller than anything seen in a recent Cup yacht. "Instead of the shallow body and flat-floored type which was adapted from the American centerboard boats," the analysis continued, "she shows a hull which is a decided and welcome return in the direction of the purely British type of racing cutter."[47] The British cutter—narrow-hulled, single-mast vessels with multiple headsails, a retractable bowsprit, mainsail set on a gaff, and topmast on which topsails were set—had become the paradigm in Cup racing. First developed prior to 1800 for French and British revenue ships, the cutter had become the hallmark of British yacht design. L. Francis Herreshoff points out that it was G.L. Watson's ten-ton cutter *Madge* that had convinced American yachtsmen sailing sloops—at the time referring to beamy, single-mast centerboard vessels usually with fewer headsails, without a gaff, bowsprit, or topsails—of the efficacy of the British type.[48] Under the reigning design rules, the cutter allowed one to better match sail plans with wind velocity. L. Francis states that it wasn't until Watson's boat succumbed to Herreshoff's *Shadow* in 1879 that designers began to meld the best features of the beamy sloop and narrow cutter into what became known as the "compromise model."

With myriad design rule changes and advances in materials and building techniques, by 1903 Cup yachts had developed into exaggerated cutter-sloop hybrids, with long, sweeping overhangs, flatter bottoms, and deeper keels placing them in a class of their own. That Fife had modeled a design resembling the tried-and-true English type connoted a sense of balance and proportion that some said had been lacking in previous designs, spurring critics to brand them unwholesome. By the turn of the century there was an imminent feeling that designers had realized the full scope of the Seawanhaka Rule, forcing them to retrace their steps. In 1901 both Herreshoff's *Constitution* and Watson's *Shamrock II* had failed to wring an advantage from the rule's seemingly saturated fringes. In his willingness to revisit a more traditional form, had Fife found the key? Or was his new yacht in fact a compromise type? Though touted as the prototypical English cutter, *Shamrock III* borrowed heavily from her competition, sporting American-made blocks and hollow spars. The design also specified a wire-core mainsheet, a cordage weave until then endemic to the United States. Emboldened by Captain Wringe's experience racing the American *Mineola,* Fife even abandoned the archetypal British steering system, equipping the new yacht with a wheel instead of a tiller, the first challenger to do so.

11

THE FINAL PREPARATIONS

March 1903–June 1903

On Monday, March 30, 1903, twenty-five crewmembers under the command of Second Mate George Peterson arrived in Bristol by the early train and were shown their crew cottage on Burnside Street across from the Herreshoff offices. Barr, his officers, and thirty-three more crewmembers were scheduled to arrive later that week. "They are mostly Scandinavians," announced the *New York Times,* "rugged, active-looking men who have had years of experience in racing on the coast."[1] Mostly hailing from Sweden and Norway, the crew had been handpicked by Barr, and although vociferous protests from those who insisted upon an all-American crew rattled through the New York Yacht Club, Barr, with the support of Iselin and Herreshoff, remained implacable. That he and his crack crew had manhandled an arguably faster *Constitution* in 1901 affirmed the preponderance of expert personnel.

A yacht was only as good as the crew who guided her around the course. An architect's ability to squeeze a tenth of a knot from his conceptual plan will only reach fruition if the crew performs perfectly. Any gain attributed to a flatter floor or a lighter mast or new type of sailcloth is lost as soon as an improperly tended jib sheet slips off its winch drum or a negligent foredeck crew tangles his halyards. On such enormous yachts with so many moving parts and a macramé of rigging woven high above the deck, only the most percipient sailors could keep it straight.

Despite the crew's invaluable contribution, the bulk of the credit for a yacht's performance typically went to the captain and the designer. When the going got tough, however, they also took the heat. And even in cases of gratuitous crew error, the onus fell on them, sometimes bypassing the captain and falling solely on designer. That Captain Nat was frustrated over *Constitution's* failure was understandable.

A photo housed in Mystic Seaport's Rosenfeld Collection captures *Columbia* and *Constitution* during their 1901 trials. *Columbia's* sails are trimmed, the yacht charging ahead at full speed, while two boatlengths behind, *Constitution's* jib topsail luffs uncontrolled, a clear result of trimmer negligence.[2] When the New York Yacht Club America's Cup committee deemed the new yacht inadequate, Captain Nat bore the brunt of the blame.

By the turn of the century most professional crewmen were between twenty and thirty years old and worked full-time as yacht hands. Most had worked as hands on smaller boats, and having proved their skills, worked their way onto larger, higher-paying yachts. Having risen to prominence in both Britain and America in the mid–1800s, big-boat racing originally attracted crew primarily from seaside fishing communities, the men fishing in winter and signing on as crew for the summer yachting season. John Leather, a British yachting historian, naval architect, and descendent of several generations of yacht captains, notes in a detailed essay on crewmen that British big-boat yachting season began typically with the Thames matches in May, competing for prize money along the south coast to the Solent, west to Land's End, up the Irish Sea to Liverpool, Barrow, and then on to the Clyde and then south again for Cowes Week on the Solent and later regattas at Bournemouth, Weymouth, Torbay, and Dartmouth. The season ended in early September, the yachts typically hauled at the skipper's homeport.[3] Big-boat racing in America took place primarily between New Jersey and Maine, the most-prominent regattas being Larchmont Race Week and the New York Yacht Club yearly cruise, which normally began in New York, stopped in New London, Newport, Martha's Vineyard and the Elizabeth Islands, Provincetown, Marblehead, and then on to Maine, the largest yachts competing for the Astor and King's cups in Newport. As larger yachts became more plentiful in the 1880s and 1890s so too did the demand for professional crew. The best were plucked for the top boats, their onboard duties assigned according to skill level. The savviest men were given the most demanding jobs.

Leather notes the two most taxing jobs were bowsprit-end and masthead man. The first position demanded the crewman manage multiple sizes of jibs, jib topsails, and balloon jibs and their halyards at the outboard end of the bowsprit, which was often thirty feet or longer on the biggest yachts. When setting these sails, the bowsprit-end man, balancing on a footrope (a thin line slung below the bowsprit) shimmied to the end of the plunging sprit, bent (attached) the sail onto the forestay, and secured the halyard. When dousing, he gathered hundreds of pounds of heavy and often wet cotton, and either furled and tied it down or removed it, sending it inboard to the deck crew, and bending on another sail appropriate to the wind strength.

The masthead man held the most dangerous position. His job required him to clear tangled sails and lines at the topmast, working quickly, balancing with one hand, his leg hooked around a halyard, at the tip of a wildly swaying spar more than 160 feet above the water. On yachts of the newest generation, he was also responsible for fine-tuning the jackyard topsail trim and securing pins that held the topmasts in position. "A masthead man combined the ability of a racing seaman with the head of a steeplejack," wrote Leather, "quick wits and a sharp knife were his best friends. . . ." For taking these positions masthead men and bowsprit-enders earned a small pay increase and a chance to become mate. The only obstacle was death.[4]

On April 4, Iselin, Barr, and the rest of the *Reliance* crew arrived in Bristol via *Sunbeam,* the 132-foot, 6-inch, 547-ton wooden steamer Iselin chartered as tender to the new yacht. A former fruit carrier between Boston and the Caribbean, *Sunbeam* had been painted and remodeled at Shelter Island, her deckhouse raised, and berths for more than sixty crew and officers installed.[5] Captain Nat and Barr set the crew to burnishing the bronze hull plates of *Reliance.* Only two plates were omitted at the stern, so workers could climb into the hull via ladder from the shop floor. By the first week in April, the *New York Times* reported the "capstan, winches, ringbolts, and hatches are all in place." Although most of the other deck fittings were in the process of being fastened, the *Times* reporter noted the hatch coamings and prismatic skylights had not yet been installed.[6] With the highest tide of the month scheduled for the April 11 launch day, the workman pressed on, not only securing *Reliance's* hull but also finishing the rigging and bending on *Constitution's* sails.

At City Island where *Columbia* had spent the winter, the yacht received an initial fitting out. The famed British sailmaker Thomas W. Ratsey, with J. P. Morgan's blessing, had set up shop at the Jacobs Yard on City Island. "It can be truthfully said of Ratsey," wrote the *New York Journal* upon his arrival in America, "that had Watson and Fife done their work half as well as he did there might have been a different story to write of the Cup races."[7] Herreshoff's sail monopoly had crumbled at the hands of J. P. and E. D. Morgan, two of his biggest benefactors. And although business in Bristol was moving along at a frantic pace, the Herreshoff brothers were miffed. To add fuel to the fire, Herreshoff received two letters from E. D. Morgan. The first identified a problem in *Columbia's* steering system, which had jammed during the previous season in the trials off Newport. The letter was terse and demanding. He wanted someone from the Herreshoff yard to inspect it at City Island. Also noting *Columbia's* topmast was in good condition, he finished the letter admonishing Captain Nat. "My idea was to have an extra one," he wrote, "and I am very much disappointed that you are not able to provide it."[8] The second letter dated April 4, one week before *Reliance's* scheduled launch, was about paint. On his new steamer *Vanish,* Morgan wanted Captain Nat to use the same paint used on his *Daisy.* Bold and patronizing, he wrote, "Of course you understand that the bottom should be quite dry and the salt from the salt water entirely removed from it, and that the paint itself should be constantly and thoroughly stirred while being put on."[9] Captain Nat sent two steel workers from the yard to effect repairs on *Columbia's* rudder.[10] He did not pencil replies on the backs of Morgan's letters.

As Captain Nat received Morgan's second letter newspapers broke the story that someone had tried to sabotage the *Reliance.* Upon seeing a dim light from the south construction shop window, the night watchman investigated, finding a "bit of lighted candle near several overalls and bits of rubbish saturated with grease," wrote the *New York Herald.*[11] The next night, papers reported that the watchman found another similar incendiary heap. Extinguishing the candle on both occasions, no harm was done. Although the papers said the Herreshoffs adamantly denied any impropriety, they also said they posted a second night watchman.

On April 11, 1903, after four months and nineteen days, workers at the Herreshoff yard prepared *Reliance* for launching. They removed the staging and additional supports, so that the yacht rested solely on her cradle, which was mounted on a moveable car atop the railways. The whole system was tethered by steel cable to a winch. Filling the 165-foot long shop, *Reliance* had just enough room to clear the doors, her aluminum deck within inches of the top sill. "How the workmen, in manipulating the aluminum plating on the deck," wrote the *New York*

Herald, "did so without constant contact of hammers with the roof is an enigma."[12] Like Dumbarton, the town shut down for the launch, men sporting suits and hats and women wearing formal dresses. "[T]he invited and uninvited gathered until the shore was a dark mass of hopeful humanity," wrote the *Herald,* "and the bay the colors of the rainbow."[13]

Captain Nat, having forgone his workaday rumpled suit and scuffed shoes, donned a tailored and pressed suit, tie, and hat. Though finely dressed he still busied himself with finishing details, ambulating from the shops to the office to the launching ways and then retracing his steps, most likely his way of avoiding unnecessary small talk as much as tying up loose ends. As the highest tide approached, the Herreshoff family ascended the launching platform. "All the Hereshoffs were visible," wrote the *New York Herald.* "It is family of not merely naval architects, but of professors, chemists, musicians, and linguists, and all flocked to the scene of 'N. G.'s' latest triumph. Blind John [Brown], blind Lewis, blind Julian and blind Sarah wanted to 'see' as well as Charles and Francis, clear-visioned giants, and Mrs. Chesebrough, the widowed sister, whose eyes have done so much service for her sightless brother, all 'saw the great event.' "[14] In addition to a number of local politicians and New York Yacht Club Cup Committee members, Charles Oliver Iselin and his daughters Nora and Fannie were also present. At 5:28 P.M. Captain Nat signaled with a nod, and the yacht rolled from the shed. Swinging a mahogany-handled silver hammer engraved with the yacht's name, Nora Iselin smashed a bottle of American sparkling wine wrapped with ribbons. "With this I christen you the Reliance! And may heaven guide you to victory."[15]

Garlands of holly leaves and roses lined *Reliance*'s rails. At the bow perched a stuffed bald eagle with its wings outstretched. As the yacht immerged from the shed, a band struck up the "Star Spangled Banner" and crewmembers, dressed in sailor berets and dark-colored jerseys with *Reliance* emblazoned across the chest, raised the American yacht ensign at the stern, Charles Oliver Iselin's private signal at midships, and the New York Yacht Club burgee at the bow. *Reliance* rolled down the ways for twelve minutes before floating free of her cradle. Yachtsmen applauded the monstrous defender. With a polished bronze underbody—"glisten[ing] like the back of a new watch," wrote the *New York Herald*—the yacht stunned her inaugural audience. So enamored was the *Herald*'s reporter that he surmised, "The

Reliance's power is likely to kill her opponent."[16] Seven days later this grandiloquent prediction proved sublime.

Having been launched in mid-March, *Shamrock III* and her crew were already practicing, sparring with *Shamrock* off Weymouth on the south coast of England. On April 4, while sailing downwind in a heavy breeze, *Shamrock* collided with a 300-ton steamer, which had approached the racers to snap a photo. "Captain Beavis, on Shamrock I, saw the danger, and bore away as far as he could without gibing his vessel," wrote the Sunday *Times of London*. "It was impossible to clear the steamyacht, however, and the stern of the latter struck the Shamrock spinnaker boom near the end, and, forcing it back on to the main rigging, splintered it in two."[17] Although no one was hurt, the collision had shaken up the crew. But with the broken spar and rigging replaced, the yachts resumed trials.

Exactly one month after *Shamrock III*'s launch, on April 17, 1903, the two yachts vied for position at the start of their eighth trial race. Although sunny, the northeast wind blew cold and blustery. Sir Thomas Lipton, sailmaker Thomas Ratsey, and Colonel Sharman Crawford, vice commodore of the Royal Ulster Yacht Club and chairman of the Royal Ulster Cup Committee, were on board *Shamrock III*. Just before 11 A.M., the yacht, blasting from the starting line toward Weymouth Bay, tacked onto starboard, the sails pulling fiercely. *Shamrock* flew only her jib while *Shamrock III* flew her jib and foresail. With green water cascading over the bow, *Shamrock III*'s leeward rail dove into the wash. Lipton asked the steward William "Billie" Collier, Captain Wringe's brother-in-law, to fetch his binoculars. Collier slid from the windward rail, descended the hatch, and emerged a minute later with binoculars in hand. He gave them to Lipton and climbed, low to the deck, to his station on the rail. With wind screaming through the rigging, the yacht shot into another black patch of water. Just as he resumed a crouched position, a thundering clap rang out. *Shamrock III*'s towering mast detonated, and like an ancient felled tree, there was a pause while the hollow steel tube, lines, wires, and sails rained down. Then with a rush of air and metallic roar the gear slammed into the deck and surrounding water.

The masthead man had been on deck but had been hit with a piece of wreckage, mauling his knee. One sailor sustained a deep scalp wound and another an injurious blow to the thigh. Then someone screamed,

"Man overboard." One account says two crewmen dove in; another attested that they lowered a small rowboat in an attempt to wrest their comrade from the wreckage. In either case the tangled mass of line, wire, and gnarled metal proved too difficult to navigate, and before they could reach him, Billie, the steward, slipped below the surface.

Lipton and his guests were taken to *Erin* while the crew and that of *Shamrock* under Wringe's command cleaned up the mess on *Shamrock III.* "The deck of the yacht presented a sorry spectacle," wrote the *Standard,* "with the broken sail hanging over the side and blood sprinkled about everywhere."[18] On large yachts a mast is typically held in place by a number of stays centering the mast over the hull. On *Shamrock III,* the mast was held upright by a forestay, connecting the top of the mast to the end of the bowsprit; an inner forestay, connecting the midsection of the mast to the bow stem; and two sets of running backstays, adjustable stays that connect three quarters of the way up the mast and dead-end at winches near the stern. Because the boom extended far beyond the stern, a permanent backstay could not be used, so running backstays trimmed to the windward side and slackened on the leeward side provided aft support to the mast. Finally and most importantly, the mast was held laterally by a series of side stays or shrouds, the longest called cap shrouds, which ran from either side of the mast through spreaders—winglike metal levers propping the shrouds outboard—and to the chain plates, reinforced steel straps running down the inside of the hull and emerging at the edge of the deck as a steel eye. Made of wire, the cap shrouds dead-ended in a massive spliced wire loop around a steel thimble. The steel eye of the chain plate and loop of the cap shroud connected via a giant adjustable bolt. This bolt allowed riggers to add or subtract turns to center the mast and tighten it in place. When the puff hit *Shamrock III* that afternoon, the starboard cap shroud splice burst from its thimble. Without lateral support, the mast simply crumbled.

A tug and two barges from Messrs. Cosens's repair yard arrived and a diver secured the masthead. The base was sawed free of the hull and the mast towed to shore. Once on board *Erin,* Lipton cabled the New York Yacht Club, Fife, and the Denny yard. Lipton knew word would spread fast and he wanted to tell all those involved, including the Americans, what had happened. Ratsey, who was on board, cabled his Cowes sail loft. Replacements and repairs began immediately.

Both the *Morning Post* and *Daily Chronicle* reported the crew of both *Shamrock*s and *Erin* had taken up a collection for Billie's wife and child, raising fifty pounds sterling. Lipton was devastated. The loss of a crewman, and his captain's in-law no less, was a heavy blow. Recovering from bruises incurred during the accident, he "was visibly grieving over the loss of the steward Collier," reported the *Daily Chronicle,* "to whom he was constantly making reference."[19] After having been docked at Portland Roads for several days, *Shamrock III* was towed by the *Black Cock* of the Liverpool Screw Towage and Lighterage Company,[20] up the west coast of England and Wales and north to Scotland, east through the Firth of Clyde to the Denny yard.

Immediately after the launch, more rigging work on *Reliance* began, the Charles Billman and Sons workmen installing the bowsprit and stepping the prodigious mast on April 13. At the Herreshoff yard north pier, the riggers attached slings to the metal tube and using the yard's largest lifting shear, hoisted the mainmast (with its telescoping topmast pinned snugly inside) above the hull and then, under Captain Nat's direction, carefully lowered it through the mast gate to the keelson where riggers bolted the foot in place. A bevy of riggers were hauled aloft to attach the standing rigging and spreaders. On April 16, the day before the *Shamrock III* disaster, the *New York Sun* reported, ironically, that Herreshoff's riggers were paying special attention to the shroud splices, pointing out that the wire strands were being hammered into place "to prevent [them] from drawing."[21] Within three days the boom and gaff and their fittings had been installed and Barr's crew was adding a coat of white paint to the topsides and Oregon pine-colored paint to the mast and boom. Those steel workers whose contracts had not expired on the launch day were busy building a spare set of spars. Carpenters covered the deck with a layer of ⅛-inch cork linoleum. And as each new part was mounted, *Reliance,* floating high, sank toward Captain Nat's intended waterline. "The boat looks high in the water because it doesn't yet have the weight of the sails," wrote the *Providence Journal.* In fact, *Reliance* floated three inches above her waterline.

On Saturday, April 25, *Reliance* took her first spin. Leaving the Herreshoff docks, she heeled to her rails in eight knots of wind, barely enough to fly a kite. With Barr and Captain Nat taking turns at the helm, they sailed south, beating upwind to Brenton Reef Lightship. New York Yacht Club Cup Committee members, including Iselin,

Woodbury Kane, Newberry Thorne, Lewis Cass Ledyard, and E. D. Morgan, were present, as well as John Brown Herreshoff and Captain Nat's three eldest sons, Sidney, Nathanael II, and Griswold. "She pointed very high and footed fast," wrote the *New York Sun,* "and at times when designer Herreshoff or Capt. Barr was pinching her so that her head sails fluttered she still sailed fast."[22]

With her full spread of sails hoisted, *Reliance* was immense. From afar she looked like an iceberg teetering atop a canoe. The yacht had performed well, but Barr and Herreshoff said little. The next day with A. W. Hathaway, Herreshoff's chief sailmaker on board, *Reliance* took her second trial run. In the two-hour sail, Hathaway determined the leech—the sail edge running from gaff end to boom end—was too tight on the massive mainsail and that it would have to be altered—no small project considering the eighth-inch-thick four-O duck (the heaviest weight canvas available) sail was the size of a baseball diamond and weighed roughly two thousand pounds. Each panel of the mainsail was twenty-two inches wide and bound to the next by double-stitched, heavy-duty cotton twine. The panels were so thick they felt like cardboard. As Captain Nat and Charlie Barr steered upwind, Hathaway ordered adjustments to sail trim—more outhaul to tighten the lower section of the sail or throat halyard to shift the draft forward. They adjusted the running backstays and sighting up the mast, Hathaway jotted in his notebook adjustments to be made by the riggers and sailmakers. The task was daunting, for the mainsail on *Reliance* was the largest single piece of heavyweight, hand-stitched canvas ever spread on any vessel.

On the second day, Captain Nat steered most of the time, weeding out gaps or inconsistencies in his design. Feeling the helm on both tacks and with Hathaway's feedback, he felt discordance in the rig tune. Every so often, he handed the helm to Barr, walked forward and eyed the sails from a different angle, perhaps conferring with the mates in charge of their trim. As always he spoke little. He relayed ideas to Iselin, Barr, and Hathaway, but mostly compiled his own list of modifications. A new yacht, especially one of such complexity, would require many changes. Sheets and cleats would be re-led, footholds repositioned. Line diameters would surely be swapped thicker or thinner. Captain Nat had the uncanny ability to foresee the proper application of a yacht's sundry parts, but he knew that in any prototype, unforeseen complications would arise. When the yacht finished her spins, all were in good spirits, the crewmen smiling as they coiled lines and folded sails. Iselin and his guests retired for dinner and drinks, and Captain Nat and his sons returned home. The defender had performed nobly.

Reliance's prodigious overhangs prompted comparisons with Bowdoin Crowninshield's *Independence.* But the reports were inconsistent and swayed by nationalistic overtones. Americans believed he had perfectly melded the promising features of the 1901 Boston boat with those of *Constitution.* "The problem before the Bristol designer," wrote *Scientific American,* "was to produce a yacht with all the best features of the scow type, such as great sailing length when heeled and large sail-carrying power, with as few possible of the scow's drawbacks, such as the flat floor forward and the hard shoulders which helped so greatly the undoing of 'Independence' in a troubled sea. And this Herreshoff has achieved . . ."[23] But others, especially in Britain, jeered Captain Nat's overblown design. "She is a cross between Independence and Constitution," announced a syndicated report by the *Paul Mall Gazette,* "[and] in this mongrel combination of two failures, Herreshoff has endeavoured to produce a thoroughbred, and it remains to be seen if he is to enjoy the occasional success to the florist in opposing the rule that the hybrid is unfruitful."[24]

Despite the gibes, Iselin was happy with his new defender, and on April 28 the New York Yacht Club syndicate signed the paperwork and raised its burgee to the masthead. After being towed by *Sunbeam* from Bristol to a mooring in Newport's Breton Cove, Iselin raised his private signal at 2 P.M., declaring *Reliance* officially in commission. The next morning *Sunbeam* towed *Reliance* to Iselin's home at Premium Point in New Rochelle. From there he planned to continue testing his yacht until the first trial race against *Columbia* and *Constitution* at Glen Cove on May 21.

To cull the best defender of the three, the New York Yacht Club planned a series of trials for the summer of 1903. These trials would not only identify the best boat in various wind and sea conditions, but also provide ample practice for the crews. There was no specific formula for picking the defender—no single winner-take-all regatta or speed test—but rather, the trials provided a systematic format from which the New York Yacht Club's America's Cup Committee could make an informed decision on which yacht was best suited to defend. The final decision was purely subjective. In the eighteen completed trial races preceding the 1901 Cup defense, *Columbia* and *Constitution* had each won nine. But Barr on *Columbia* had sailed faster toward the end of the trial series and had consistently outmatched *Constitution* during pre-start maneuvers, so ultimately the committee chose the former.

For 1903 the New York Yacht Club had scheduled a similar system of assessment. After a series of separate regattas held in locations between New York and Newport, the committee would decide. The first trials were scheduled for May 21, 23, 26, 28, and 30 at Glen Cove on Long Island Sound, with one race sailed per day. The second series was scheduled for June 8, 9, and 10 off Sandy Hook. The third series of trials scheduled for June 15, 17, 19, and 20 on the Sound consisted of four races hosted by four different yacht clubs. Next, the Cup Committee planned a series of trials in Newport to be held June 29 and 30 and July 1 and 2. The three ninety-footers would then compete in three races on July 18, 20, and 22 during the annual New York Yacht Club cruise. Finally, they would return to Newport and commence their last trial series beginning July 27. Upon completing this rigorous summer of sailing, the Cup committee would deliberate. At that meeting they'd weigh the performances of *Reliance, Constitution,* and *Columbia* and their crews and pick the yacht they felt best suited to defend the America's Cup against Lipton.

Although the schedule seemed incredibly busy, the full trial schedule amounted to only about twenty races if the weather cooperated. If there was too much or too little wind, the races were postponed. If inclement weather delayed them too long, the race committee would be forced to skip ahead in the schedule. With such a limited window to prove themselves, the captains and managing owners of *Reliance, Constitution,* and *Columbia* combed over every detail of their yachts. They'd ordered their yachts' underbodies burnished, their rigging tuned, winches oiled, and most importantly, tailored their sails so to fit to perfection. This last detail, however, had become an increasingly heated topic.

The Herreshoffs had built sails for all three yachts, but managers E. D. Morgan of *Columbia* and August Belmont of *Constitution* had also approached Ratsey & Lapthorn at City Island. The loft carried the renown of a family who'd been making sails on the Isle of Wight since 1790. To his newly established City Island loft, Ratsey had not only imported some of the finest sail designers and builders in the world, he'd also brought with him an exclusive line on ultra-fine

Egyptian cotton. With his long-running business associate, Richard Hayward, Ratsey had also perfected a proprietary cotton weave and process of soaking the sailcloth in a solution of sugar, lead, and alum, rendering it highly resistant to both stretch and mold.[25] Although Captain Nat's cross-cut sails were considered some of the best in America, Ratsey & Lapthorn held the title of best in the world.

British yachtsmen, however, reeled when they found out that Ratsey was producing sails for the Americans. Not only did they feel betrayed by one of their own, they also felt the international character of the competition had eroded. The same firm was building sails for both challenger and defender. Design measurements once guarded from the opposition were now in the hands of one sailmaker. "What would American yachtsmen think," wrote London-based *Yachting World,* "if the owner of the Shamrock III, approached Herreshoff to obtain a design for a challenger, which he is at perfect liberty to do?"[26]

No one was more angered at this sail order than Captain Nat. Not only had the syndicate managers broken contracts that reserved the exclusive right of the Herreshoff Manufacturing Company to produce sails for their yachts, but they did it, Captain Nat felt, behind his back. At the same time, Nat and Hathaway were having a terrible time with *Reliance*'s mainsail, which even after initial alterations held a shape only slightly better than a burlap sack. In syndicated reports, Reuter's announced the mainsail leech was rounded outward, hanging loosely to leeward for the length of the battens.[27] "Her sails fitted badly, and on them is thrown the blame for her bad behaviour," wrote the London *Daily Express.* "They are said to be altogether too small, and several will have to be made over again."[28]

The sail loft worked unremittingly to slice and sew the giant panels into shape. New sails often required tailoring. Even the finest cotton stretched. It was, in fact, expected to stretch, woven and sewn so that fibers lengthened evenly. If stretch was aptly predicted, sails could be built to accommodate subsequent change. But after the first week in May, *Reliance*'s mainsail was still a mess, the *New York Sun* reporting that her sails were so mismatched they flapped out of control.[29] This detracted from practice, the trimmers unable to hone their respective sails and Barr unable to ascertain an accurate feel for his yacht. To further exacerbate the problem, on May 6 *Columbia* trounced *Reliance* in an unintended, impromptu match-up on Long Island Sound. "Though the meeting might not be quite as decided as wished," wrote the *New York Herald*, "it would surely show something—show possibly, whether Herreshoff had been on a 'hit or miss' mission when he designed the Reliance, or knew exactly what he was doing."[30] The flagging optimism had fomented rancor among the New York Yacht Club benefactors. "I was somewhat disturbed day before yesterday to find the 'Reliance' a little dull in a light breeze," wrote E. D. Morgan to Captain Nat on May 7. "Of course, her mainsail would account for it to a certain extent, but not sufficiently to make us feel altogether happy in that kind of sailing."[31] Iselin came to the rescue, granting an interview with the *New York Daily Tribune* in which he impugned *Reliance*'s detractors, arguing a fleeting race in fickle winds was inconclusive.[32] Regardless of the scuttlebutt, all involved—Captain Nat included—knew No. 605 needed help. On May 9, *Reliance* returned to Bristol.

While *Reliance* was hauled—her sails again recut, standing rigging tightened, the gaff lengthened by sixteen inches, and a two-foot longer boom installed—mounting criticism combined with the Ratsey & Lapthorn sail orders roused Captain Nat's ire. Although we don't know Nat's exact words, an apologetic letter from August Belmont on May 15, 1903, attempts to mollify him. "I have been very much worried and distressed," wrote Belmont, "over the fact that I have hurt your feelings in having my sails [for *Constitution*], which were made by you, altered and repaired here [at Ratsey & Lapthorn] without your assistance. . . . I hope you won't harbor it against me and am sure you will realize that I am rather doing you a favor in not pestering you with details about my boat while you are so busy with your new creation . . ."[33] E. D. Morgan, however, had grown increasingly irate, insinuating Nat had again neglected *Columbia* in favor of his newer boat. On May 14, he wrote a seething indictment. "I am exceedingly disappointed to find that my feeble attempt to help the 'Columbia' in light airs seems to have gone wrong. The facts are that the wooden No. 1 clubtopsail yard is this year about as I found it last year, and my reasons for wanting a steel yard are identical with those that I had at the time of ordering. You can therefore, very well see how disappointed I am not to have the yard that I ordered so early in the season."[34]

We can only infer that being preoccupied with his new yacht and having been bombarded by demands, Captain Nat proscribed Morgan's wishes as he'd done with other captious clients. Nat didn't, however, write him off. Morgan had introduced Nat and John Brown to the world of big-money benefactors. Without him the brothers from Bristol might have tottered in obscurity, hammering together small boats and skiffs for the local market, or perhaps foundered completely when Nat lost his steam license after *Say When's* boiler explosion. Nat's high-profile designs ushered by Morgan had made the Herreshoff name ubiquitous. But although his 1899 defender had floated Nat's name through the squalls of 1901, *Columbia,* with her fixated owner and manager, had now come back to haunt him.

Shamrock III arrived on the Clyde on April 26, following her ignominious 590-mile tow. Denny yard workers had already been begun building a new mast. Because of the immovable weight of the submerged sails, they'd been cut from their spars and destroyed so the wreckage could be towed ashore. The topsail spars had been so badly dented they had to be replaced. Although the main gaff had been damaged, the Denny yard riggers salvaged them, effecting minor repairs. The mast, of course, was totally destroyed. The boom was also abandoned. With the mix of new and overhauled spars installed, painted, and rigged, and new sails bent on, *Shamrock III* resumed trials the first week of May.

Ratsey's new sails turned heads. The suit fit from the rack. "The new sails of the challenger came in for a great deal of admiration," wrote the *Yachtsman,* "and while nothing was given out as to there having been any alternation in the cut of any of them, it was the opinion of many good judges that, if possible, the sail plan looked smarter than before."[35] Lipton's team of experts pooled their knowledge to perfect *Shamrock III*, and no doubt some began to the question the efficacy of the Herreshoff yard. Had the all-in-one model for a boatyard come and gone?

After 1890 when the Herreshoffs began building larger yachts, they built a small loft for sail alterations and repairs. Unable to find a local loft that could produce the quality they demanded, they began producing their own sails. When in 1894 W. B. Duncan ordered a twenty-one-foot fin-keeled sailboat, Nat tried a new type of sail. He aligned the cotton panels at 90-degree angles with the leech and the seams perpendicular to one another. When Duncan and he trimmed the sails for the first time, they found they held their shape better than longitudinal panels, the yacht pointing higher and sailing faster. The design was a success and later that year Nat built a suit for his own *Alerion II,* a slightly larger fin-keeler at twenty-seven feet, three inches. They worked. The loft built bigger sets for bigger yachts. Having laid claim to the cross-cut breakthrough, the Herreshoff loft stepped up production, expanding its cutting floor and securing a deal with the Lawrence Manufacturing Company to produce a special weave of cotton duck. Twenty-five miles north of Boston, the mill freighted large consignments to Bristol, where rolls of fabric were ordered sometimes a year in advance, allowing the cloth to dry and age, seasoning like firewood. During those nine years the Herreshoff Manufacturing Company had no problems filling sail orders, for in every building contract they secured an agreement to produce the yacht's sails.

With guaranteed orders, the Herreshoff lofts produced a lot of sails. Although we don't know exactly how many, we know the loft was flush with work. Whereas cruising sailboats might own one set of extra heavy cotton sails—having them reconditioned every off season, but using them for four or five seasons if the owner was diligent about protecting them from rot[36]—Herreshoff racing yachts required an inordinate number of sails. The typical racing yacht required multiple suits, some for racing and others for practicing, in various cuts and thickness to be used at different wind strengths. Yachts like *Reliance, Constitution,* or *Constitution* would normally maintain a set of about fifteen to twenty racing sails[37] and another set of practice sails, which had typically been used for racing during the previous season. Because of their enormous weight, only those sails applicable to the day's weather forecast would be stowed on board, the others piled onto the yacht's tender.

Profiting from Captain Nat's intimate knowledge of his boats, the Herreshoff loft made superlative sails. There were other successful lofts throughout New England and New York, but none had the capability of integrating a sail plan with the rig and hull design as seamlessly as Captain Nat. When he retired to his third-floor garret to sketch a hull and carve its model, the weight and placement of a yacht's thousands of pieces whirring in his head, he dovetailed the size, shape, and construction of the sails with his mental schematic for hull and rig. In addition, Captain Nat prescribed to his sails the same sedulous testing regimen with which he'd scoured his hardware. He kept a notebook titled *Tests of Canvas* in a drawer of his model room drawing table. Beginning in January 1899 he tested each new batch of sailcloth, noting the details of weave, manufacture, air tightness, and such attributes as "pounds per inch to cause stretch of ⅟₁₆" or "pounds per inch of cloth at failure."[38] Well-tested proprietary weaves sewn into cross-cut panels, arranged to perfectly complement the rig plan, vaulted Herreshoff sails above their competitors.

But with the backing of J. P. Morgan, Thomas Ratsey's City Island firm changed the American sailmaking business. Under the management of Thomas's nephew, George E. Ratsey, who had apprenticed with his uncle in Cowes for eleven years,[39] the large international firm pooled its design knowledge. They arrived with fine Egyptian cotton and engineers privy to years of design information cultivated at lofts in Cowes, Gosport, Southampton, and Gourock, Scotland. Although Herreshoff had pioneered the cross-cut design, Ratsey held British and American patents for a more stretch-resistant bi-directional panel layout, the lower half having panels arranged perpendicular to the foot, the upper half with panels arranged perpendicular to the leech.[40] Although the design proved more effective on headsails than mainsails, orders flooded the shops. Ratsey & Lapthorn quickly ran away from their competition, including the Herreshoffs.

Although Captain Nat and Hathaway had struggled at first, the alterations to *Reliance*'s sails did the trick. The mainsail leech was as "flat as a board,"[41] wrote the *New York Sun*. Captain Nat, Charlie Barr, and crew took *Reliance* for another spin, tacking south down Narragansett Bay in a moderate southwesterly wind. With Barr at the helm, the yacht fell into her stride. Except for some excess sag in the jib leech, the trimmers had better control of the sail shape. The mainsail showed marked improvement, the trimmers able to shift its draft forward and aft to help Barr balance the helm. Because of the colossal sail plan, Captain Nat designed a double wheel steering system, the first of its kind. With one wheel mounted behind the steering pedestal and the other forward, the helmsman could call for help if the steering grew difficult in a blow. Barr, with two or three helpers could muscle the two wheels and *Reliance* into submission. For particularly long legs, Nat also installed a foot brake, enabling the helmsman to temporarily lock the wheel in position. Finally, Nat devised a hollow, chambered rudder into which water could be pumped or expelled to help counteract excessive weather or lee helm.[42] When plagued with weather helm (which forces a yacht to

swerve to windward) water entered a small hole at the base ⟨
der, increasing its overall weight to help the helmsman st⟨
course. When plagued with lee helm (which forces a yacht to ⟨
leeward) the helmsman, using a foot pump, forced air down th⟨
expelling the water and lightening the load.[43]

On the morning of May 15, *Reliance,* in preparation for her ⟨
als with *Columbia* and *Constitution,* left for City Island, whe⟨
would be hauled and her bottom burnished at the Jacobs Yard.⟨
Reliance arrived, twenty thousand people flooded the narrow, thi⟨
a-square-mile island. Upon seeing her out of the water, Clinton C⟨
a well-respected naval architect, told the *New York Herald,* "She is ⟨
more extreme type than I dreamed of. Nothing that Mr. Herresh⟨
has produced is so extreme . . . In winds of certain strength she m⟨
be a flyer, and if Mr. Herreshoff has succeeded in making her fast ⟨
light weather, why, then it will be time to stop building cup racers, f⟨
she will be unapproachable."[44] Crane's praise emphasized *Reliance*'s ex⟨
treme proportions, but to the untrained eye, the yacht looked similar
to *Columbia* and *Constitution: Reliance* was big and white with a towering mast. But even stacked up against the others, *Reliance* looked
enormous. With a freeboard several inches lower than that of *Constitution* and her lines stretched into longer overhangs levered over the
water at acute angles, *Reliance* looked even more precipitous. Like *Independence, Reliance*'s forward overhang did not plunge at the waterline;
instead, it maintained a shallow angle well aft, sloping downward gradually until it plunged steeply downward at the keel's front edge. This
flat forward floor prompted many to brand it a scow or skimming dish.
Although Thomas F. Day, editor of *The Rudder* wrote, "She is a splendid conception, splendidly carried out," he also asserted, "I have no
hesitation in saying she is an overgrown, ugly brute."[45]

While the crew made final preparations, Iselin had Ratsey measure
Reliance for a new set of sails. He told the *New York Herald,* however,
that he had not decided whether *Reliance* would use them.[46] Iselin had
tried to obtain rig measurements from Captain Nat, but Nat refused to
hand them over.[47] His hesitation was understandable. Ratsey was
building sails for the competition. In addition, any work that went to
the City Island loft was work taken away from Bristol. With mounting
exasperation, Nat protested. Ultimately, Iselin decided *Reliance* would
race with Nat's canvas.[48]

With *Columbia* ready to race and *Reliance* almost complete, *Constitution* prepared to be hauled at the Riverside Yard in New London. But as she crept up the ways, the cradle chains snapped under her weight. *Constitution* slipped backward, floating, undamaged. August Belmont made arrangements for *Constitution* to be hauled at the Jacobs Yard as soon as *Reliance* was launched. As if the seeds of her ill-fated 1901 season had suddenly germinated, when climbing the ways at City Island, that cradle buckled. *Constitution* wrenched hard to port and then again to starboard, the cradle feet gouging the bronze plating. Just when onlookers thought she would fall, smashing to her side, the yacht groaned free, slipping backward into the mud. Attaching a hawser, the tender *Satellite* dragged her into deeper water. After assessing the severity of the dents, *Constitution* was towed to Morse Iron Works in South Brooklyn for repairs.[49]

The first of the trials began on May 21 in Long Island Sound, the course off Matinecock Point. In excruciatingly light wind, *Reliance* and *Columbia* matched up, *Constitution* still being repaired in Brooklyn. The stumble on the ways had bent the stem and dented the plating in front and on the bottom of the keel. Yard workers believed the cradle had been weakened from hauling the immense weight of *Reliance*.[50] After a postponed start, the two yachts started across a glassy Long Island Sound. With cold water and warming air from land in the early season, Long Island Sound often experiences a great deal of wind shear, in which wind velocity and direction change with altitude. With near calm conditions at the water's surface but ample wind aloft, *Reliance*, with her taller rig, shot ahead of *Columbia*. Barr also avoided the strong flooding tide. *Columbia*'s helmsman did not. Throughout the race Barr's nimble crew made smart work of maneuvers, besting a series of mishaps by *Columbia*'s crew, including the parting of the jib topsail tack. Unable to replace the sail quickly, the crew watched the sail luff for several minutes on the third leg. *Reliance* beat *Columbia* around the twenty-five-mile course by fourteen minutes, forty-three seconds.

The second trial was held on May 23 with all three ninety-footers on the line. In a light south-southwesterly wind, the three yachts jockeyed for position. *Columbia,* staying out of the way, allowed Barr on *Reliance* and Captain Rhodes on *Constitution* to joust for an advantage. Miscalculating a wind shift to the east, Rhodes fell behind *Reliance*. Barr ordered his balloon jib on the first leg—a reach—and the yacht shot ahead. The three yachts picked their way through fleeting patches

of wind. After rounding the first mark, *Reliance* gained one minute on each yacht, still coasting from puff to puff. Rounding the third mark, *Reliance,* harnessing wind aloft with her towering rig, ghosted to the finish. The wind dying completely, the race was called off and *Reliance* deemed the unofficial victor.

That *Columbia* had performed so poorly was a surprise to all but Captain Nat. Although adamant about his yacht's preparation for trials, prodding Nat for new hardware and then outfitting *Columbia* with a new suit of Ratsey sails, E. D. Morgan had given the comparatively inexperienced Lem Miller command. "She was helmed by an amateur . . .," wrote Thomas F. Day in *The Rudder,* ". . . no attempt was made to race the boat, she being simply sailed over the course, keeping well out of the way of the real contestants."[51] Morgan's querulous correspondence with Captain Nat quickly subsided. Despite the fluky conditions of the initial trials, *Constitution* asserted herself as *Columbia*'s superior. To further exalt and vindicate the taciturn designer, on May 24 the *New York Herald* ran the headline, "Two Rivals Give Place as Queen to the Reliance."[52]

Between May 26 and 30, the New York Yacht Club Race Committee ran three more races from Glen Cove. The first was the closest, *Reliance* and *Constitution* trading places through moderate conditions dotted with occasional strong puffs. The first leg was a reach, all three yachts piling on sail in the building breeze. As *Columbia* once again fell behind, Rhodes on *Constitution* jockeyed with Barr, who was having trouble controlling *Reliance*. Several times on the leg, Barr ordered the jib topsail sheets slacked to ease the helm, finally ordering the bowsprit man to hoist a smaller sail.[53] The two yachts rounded the first mark off Oyster Bay only seven seconds apart, *Constitution* in the lead. After filling her spinnaker, Rhodes forced Barr to sail high. In the fast maneuvering, *Reliance*'s crew handled their sails cleaner and gained a few seconds. As the two leaders approached the third mark, a tug with barges in tow closed in. Cavalier Barr, with *Reliance* charging, slipped the yacht between the mark and the barges, the *New York Herald* reporting, with only six inches of clearance on either side.[54] Rhodes, deigning to follow, rounded the tug, barge, and mark and lost nearly a minute. Barr extended his lead and ultimately beat Rhodes by more than two minutes and *Columbia* by almost sixteen. Both *Reliance* and *Constitution* sailed brilliantly. "On the other hand," wrote the *New York Herald,* "the yacht which time and again defeated the *Constitution* and twice successfully defended the cup made a showing that a tired mud turtle would have been ashamed to own."[55]

Constitution's good fortune didn't last. In the fourth race, while sailing neck-and-neck with *Reliance* a large puff slammed the two, driving their rails deep into the Sound. A loud crack shot from *Constitution* and her topmast exploded. Although the mainmast remained intact, *Constitution* was forced to retire, *Reliance* rounding the twenty-five-mile triangular course eight and a half minutes ahead of *Columbia*. The crew quickly effected repairs, installing a new topmast and repairing the topsails. Two days later on May 30 the three ninety-footers lined up again for the final heat in the series. Just before the start *Constitution* nosed out on *Reliance,* securing the weather position. As the gun fired, the race committee called *Constitution* over early, forcing Rhodes to tack around and restart. In doing so, he fouled *Columbia,* which protested. While the two older yachts tussled, Barr extended his lead, holding it throughout the race and finishing twenty-five minutes ahead of *Constitution* and more than two hours ahead of the fumbling *Columbia.*

Immediately following the Glen Cove series, *Reliance* and *Constitution,* like horses to the trough, returned to Bristol. The Herreshoff loft commenced recutting sails. Although the last alteration to the mainsail had been successful in firming the leech, in the light winds of Long Island Sound, some thought it too tight. Most of the sails had also stretched during the series, requiring alterations. In addition to having her sails tailored, *Constitution* received a new set of steel standing rigging. Tied to the Herreshoff piers, the two yachts stripped of all sails looked like giant building cranes.

When Captain Nat had tuned his yachts, *Reliance* and *Constitution* left Narragansett Bay, sailing up Long Island Sound to New Rochelle. On June 5, *Columbia* was towed into a smoke-clogged Bristol Harbor, a forest fire to the east having lowered visibility to a few hundred feet.[56] Towed through the haze to the Herreshoff piers, *Columbia* received new plating and reinforcement around her bowsprit. When completed, she and her crew began the long tow to Sandy Hook east of the Verrazano Narrows where the final Cup races with *Shamrock III* would be held and where, for the next week, the American ninety-footers would race in the second series of defender trials.

On the morning of June 9, the three yachts were towed from their moorings in Sandy Hook's Horseshoe Harbor, but upon raising their sails, an impenetrable fog bank enveloped them. The race committee cancelled races for the day, and the crews lowered their water-soaked sails. Entrenched, the mist stalled racing for two more days, threatening to blanket the series. On June 11 a single turning mark was set fifteen miles to windward, the yachts required to sail out and back. At the start the three yachts lined up closely, *Reliance* in the middle and *Constitution* to weather. As they crossed the starting line, Barr footed, steering his yacht slightly to leeward, his sails eased and full. When *Constitution* tacked to port, the other two followed. After some time *Columbia* tacked back onto starboard. When the two leaders had established separation from *Columbia*, the wind shifted south, allowing *Reliance* and *Constitution* to fetch the mark and leaving *Columbia* helplessly to leeward. *Reliance* charged around the mark five minutes ahead of *Constitution*. They both carried spinnakers until the wind shifted again, allowing them to reach to the finish. *Reliance* beat *Constitution* by six minutes and *Columbia* by nearly thirteen.

Shamrock III had sailed only five times after the accident. On one of those days *Shamrock I* was unable to sail as a trial horse and on another, there was barely enough wind to fill her sails. She had sailed only fourteen times since launching. And with an unseasonably wet spring and early summer in Scotland and southern England, the prospects for productive practice looked bleak. With hopes to tune up on their American racecourse on May 18, both yachts were towed to the James Watt Dock in Greenock where Messrs. Scott & Co. began preparing them to cross the Atlantic.

According to the Deed of Gift a yacht challenging for the America's Cup had to travel to the racecourse on her own hull, just as the Cup's namesake *America* had done in 1851 when she defeated the Royal Yacht Squadron fleet around the Isle of Wight. This had always been a bone of contention, for a challenger was forced to build a yacht strong enough to withstand an Atlantic crossing, whereas defenders could build their yachts much lighter, knowing they would rarely sail in anything but flat water and light to moderate winds. In 1901, the New York Yacht Club had allowed Lipton to tow his yacht across. The same held true in 1903. With ample wind, *Shamrock I* and *III* would also sail on their way to New York, so to hasten the trip and save coal on the tugs. But because the rigs and sails on such yachts were so enormous, requiring scores of crewmen to tend them, smaller rigs were installed for the crossing. *Shamrock* was rigged as yawl, a smaller mast installed into the main mast gate and a second even smaller mast installed behind her rudderpost. *Shamrock III* was simply rigged with a smaller mast and sails built specifically for the Atlantic crossing, including a jib, staysail, and a main. The mainsail was raised on a gaff, but was loose-footed, meaning it had no boom, the clew or aft corner of the sail simply trimmed to the deck. Steel wire lifelines—a temporary safety fence—had been rigged around the deck's edge to protect the crew from falling overboard during the ocean passage. Although the yacht had been built to withstand the Atlantic, her shape was designed to race around buoys. With an extremely low freeboard, waves were expected to frequently wash down the deck. To seal both yachts water tight, the crew fastened special canvas hatch and companionway covers. The racing sails and spars were packed on board the Anchor Liner *Ethiopia*.[57]

On May 28, crowds of spectators from nearby towns and Glasgow poured into Gourock. Scores of steam and sailing yachts circled off the docks, many decorated for the occasion. "Flags flew from nearly every building ashore," wrote the *Glasgow Evening News*. "Right up till the moment of the fleet's departure spectators continued to arrive at the pier, which was a moving mass of expectant visitors. The tops of gangways, lorries, ladders, and household furniture lying at the pier . . . were utilized."[58] The *Shamrock*s would make the 3,644-mile passage from Gourock to Sandy Hook with two escorts, Lipton's *Erin* and his chartered oceangoing tug *Cruizer*. On board *Erin* were Lipton's Irish Terrier mascots, Pat and Mike, as well as a green parrot and five canaries, one of which (Fifi) had been trained to ring a bell and haul up a tiny bucket of seeds upon command.[59] All told, Lipton's armada comprised 159 sailors.

At 1:15 P.M. in bright sunshine, the first spell of good weather they'd had in weeks, *Cruizer* and *Erin* towed the yachts from the Gourock pier. As *Shamrock III* passed the landing, the crowd erupted in cheers. Nearby on the turbine steamer *Queen Alexandra,* "packed from stem to stern with interested sightseers" the Greenock Artillery Band struck up "The Dear Little Shamrock."[60] The yachts, flying the green and yellow Royal Ulster burgees, glided out the Firth of Clyde, a fleet of spectator boats following. After traveling south through the Irish Sea, the four yachts headed south-southwest toward the Azores.

John Brown Herreshoff, Nat's blind, domineering older brother, at age 40 in 1881. *(Courtesy Herreshoff Marine Museum/America's Cup Hall of Fame, Bristol, Rhode Island, www.herreshoff.org.)*

Known as Captain Nat and sometimes as the Wizard of Bristol, the naval architect Nathanael Greene Herreshoff in a 1920 Bachrach portrait. *(Courtesy Herreshoff Marine Museum/America's Cup Hall of Fame, Bristol, Rhode Island, www.herreshoff.org.)*

Captain Nat Herreshoff (top left) steams out to watch the America's Cup races of 1899, in which *Columbia* swept Lipton's first challenger, *Shamrock*. *(Courtesy Herreshoff Marine Museum/America's Cup Hall of Fame, Bristol, Rhode Island, www.herreshoff.org.)*

On April 11, 1903 thousands gather at the Herreshoff Manufacturing Company in Bristol, Rhode Island, to watch the launch of *Reliance*. Her polished bronze hull "glisten[ed] like the back of a new watch," wrote the *New York Herald*. (*Courtesy Herreshoff Marine Museum/America's Cup Hall of Fame, Bristol, Rhode Island, www.herreshoff.org.*)

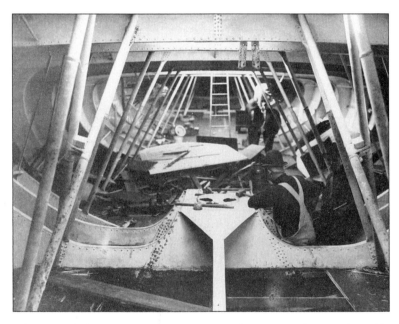

Reliance belowdecks during construction. Captain Nat designed her hull with a ribcage-like system of web frames strengthened by a lightweight system of longitudinal frames. (*Courtesy Herreshoff Marine Museum /America's Cup Hall of Fame, Bristol, Rhode Island, www.herreshoff.org.*)

Herreshoff's drafting and model room on the third floor of his Bristol home. His hand-carved models, hundreds of them lining the walls, mapped the evolution of yacht design. (*Courtesy Herreshoff Marine Museum/America's Cup Hall of Fame, Bristol, Rhode Island,, www.herreshoff.org.*)

Charles Oliver Iselin was a skilled yachtsman, sailing as crew aboard *Volunteer* in 1887, and a master manager for *Vigilant* in 1893, *Defender* in 1895, *Columbia* in 1899, and *Reliance* in 1903. (© *Mystic Seaport, Mystic, Connecticut*)

The three American ninety-footers, *Reliance, Columbia,* and *Constitution,* race upwind during the 1903 America's Cup defender trials. *(© Mystic Seaport, Mystic, Connecticut).*

Shamrock III and *Reliance* jockey for position during the 1903 America's Cup races. *Shamrock III* carried 14,337.7 square feet of sail to *Reliance*'s 16,169.67. *(© Mystic Seaport, Rosenfeld Collection, Mystic, Connecticut, James Burton, Photographer).*

Sir Thomas Lipton, the self-made tea and grocery merchant and America's Cup challenger from Glasgow, Scotland, stands on the deck of his steamyacht *Erin* in 1903. (© *Mystic Seaport, Rosenfeld Collection, Mystic, Connecticut*)

Reliance's foredeck crew douses headsails. With a 126-foot-long luff (forward edge), *Reliance*'s jib was equipped with a 3/4-inch plow steel luff rope capable of withstanding loads of up to 25 tons. (© *Mystic Seaport, Mystic, Connecticut, James Burton, Photographer*).

Reliance after being hauled at the Jacobs Yard in City Island, New York. Once afloat, her keel extended 19 feet below the waterline and held 102.3 tons of lead. (© *Mystic Seaport, Rosenfeld Collection, Mystic, Connecticut, James Burton, Photographer*).

Captain Charlie Barr drives *Reliance* upwind. His officers and afterguard—those advising him on tactical choices and his opponent's progress—stand by. *(© Mystic Seaport, Rosenfeld Collection, Mystic, Connecticut, James Burton, Photographer).*

Reliance blasts upwind, heeling to her rails. The crew of 64 men shifts its weight to windward to counteract the yacht's tendency to heel. *(© Mystic Seaport, Rosenfeld Collection, Mystic, Connecticut, James Burton, Photographer).*

Reliance sails downwind under full spinnaker, while crewmen prepare for a maneuver. The spinnaker pole was 83.75 feet long and weighed 1,000 pounds. *(© Mystic Seaport, Rosenfeld Collection, Mystic, Connecticut, James Burton, Photographer).*

Reliance charges upwind under full sail in 1903. Although she was 89.66 feet long on the waterline, from bowsprit to boom end, her sails stretched 201.76 feet overall. (© *Mystic Seaport, Rosenfeld Collection, Mystic, Connecticut, James Burton, Photographer*).

It must have been a great relief to finally pull away from shore. There had been weeks of preparation. Packing food, water, and coal and preparing the yachts for the crossing was no small task. Below decks *Shamrock I* and *III* were merely shells, without designated storage space or living quarters. Although pipe berths—lightweight canvas cots with one side bolted to a wall and the other tethered to the ceiling—had already been installed, provisions had to be organized and lashed down. Removing the rigging from such a yacht was a harrowing job, back-breaking for the crewmen and a logistical nightmare for the officers. Every part had to be labeled and properly stowed so that when they arrived in New York the rig could be stepped without error or delay. And working on the docks in Greenock would have drawn hundreds of spectators per day. Visiting a yacht like *Shamrock III* was a family event. As the crewmen scurried around on deck, prying eyes watched their every move. So once they'd cleared the coast and had reached open ocean, 159 men likely gasped a sigh of relief. Although they were still on Lipton's payroll and living on his boats, the boss was far away. He'd made plans to travel separately on a comfortable steamliner weeks later. The officers kept tight reigns on their crew, but offshore, as the pictures from the voyage attest, everyone relaxed. They brought musical instruments. Once over the horizon dress was informal. Lipton's photo album from this 1903 Atlantic crossing shows men wearing sailor berets and British navy-style middy blouses, others wearing undershirts and suspenders. Many clutched pipes between their teeth. After months of toiling in a grimy shipyard, they were finally at sea.

The four yachts first sailed south to the Azores to re-coal. After a week at sea, the yachts anchored inside the Faial breakwater, the officers and a few crewmen rowing ashore to purchase fuel and refill their water barrels from a community well. Although we don't know the exact details of the trip, the onboard photographer recorded a visual account of the Atlantic crossing. The photographer, a man in his mid-forties identified in Lipton's album simply as "our photographer," spent most of the trip on board *Erin*. His photos show crewmen laboring under the weight of sacks of coal and the yachts' captains on Faial wearing suits and yachting caps joy-riding on a mule cart. The photos seem particularly staged to please the boss. One picture shows *Erin's* galley staff on deck dressed in spotless white chef uniforms and hats, their mustaches trimmed, and the terrier, Pat, lying beside them. Another shows an officer on *Erin* raising signal flags, which the yachts used to communicate. The flags show a steady wind blowing, which would have prompted the *Shamrocks* to cast off their painters and raise their sails, a welcomed change of scenery after hours of inhaling coal exhaust from their tenders. When the wind died, *Erin* and *Cruizer* would refasten the *Shamrocks* and resume. On June 10, a particularly calm day in the middle Atlantic, a photo shows two officers and several crewmen from *Cruizer* rowing to *Erin* to, as the caption indicates, replenish their stores of fresh meat.

Expecting the fleet to arrive by Friday, June 12, Sir Thomas Lipton's American representative, Mr. H. H. Davies, had chartered the tug *Charles E. Matthews* on which he waited near the Sandy Hook Lightship. Early on Sunday morning, June 14, the four yachts loomed on the horizon. With a bevy of journalists on board and flying a shamrock flag off the stern, the *Charles E. Matthews* greeted *Shamrock III* at 5:30 A.M., the challenger lowering her sails and passing a towline. Soon after the pilot steamer *New Jersey* arrived to guide the fleet into the harbor. Commodore Robert E. Tod of the Atlantic Yacht Club intercepted the fleet at 6:30 A.M. on his schooner yacht *Thistle*. Flying a shamrock flag, Commodore Tod fired a gun salute, and *Cruizer* and *Erin* returned the honor, sounding their steam whistles. Escorted to quarantine, the fleet was surrounded by well-wishing pleasure craft. "Launches filled with pretty girls crowded about the yacht as [*Shamrock III*] dropped anchor," reported the *New York Herald*, "and with a hearty good will the bluejackets on her deck gave a rousing three times three and waved their caps at the girls, whose handkerchiefs were waving gayly at them."[61]

Towed through the Narrows, the yachts proceeded to Tompkinsville on the north shore of Staten Island where the crew passed through quarantine. After spending the night at anchor *Shamrock I* and *III* were towed to Erie Basin in Redhook, Brooklyn, where they were united with *Shamrock II*, which had remained in New York upon the completion of the 1901 Cup races. The crews immediately began removing the extra gear and ocean rigs. The racing spars were installed and the hulls cleaned and polished. After taking a train from London to Liverpool, on June 17, Sir Thomas Lipton and William Fife Jr. boarded the White Star Liner *Oceanic,* the same steamship on which Lipton had sent his official Cup challenge nine months earlier. As he boarded, Lipton was handed a telegram from the King: "As you are just about leaving for America," the King wrote, "let me wish you a prosperous journey and all possible good luck for the great race in August." And Lipton dispatched his sycophantic reply: "Your Majesty's gracious message has delighted us all" he wrote. "[I]t gives us encouragement and hope, and will make us do our utmost to try to bring back the Cup to England."[62]

While Lipton steamed west that day, the three American ninety-footers began their third series of trial races. The first race was hosted by Larchmont Yacht Club on Long Island Sound just west of Rye Neck and across the sound from Glen Cove. But two minutes and twenty seconds after the starting gun, while reaching under full sail including balloon jib, *Reliance* groaned, her topmast snapped, and a snarl of rigging came crashing down. The balloon jib hit the water and dragged alongside. The topsail gaff snapped. The wind had been blowing only three miles per hour. No one was hurt. Barr steered *Reliance* into the wind while the masthead man and other crewmen climbed into the fray and cleared the wreckage. *Constitution* continued on and beat *Columbia* by just under ten minutes.

Once towed to her mooring in New Rochelle, repairs began immediately. Iselin called the Herreshoff yard and ordered a new topsail gaff. A spare topmast was delivered to New Rochelle the following morning, and by the next day *Reliance* was on the starting line. That the riggers had effected repairs so quickly was a credit to their skill. *Reliance's* telescoping topmast was highly complex. As he had done with *Columbia* and *Constitution*, Captain Nat had installed a system in which the hollow, wooden, cylindrical spar could be raised and lowered by an internally lead wire rope wound from a winch below decks. Although construction plans show a system in which *Reliance's* topmast was held in place with a pin inserted by the masthead man (the same system used by his predecessors), L. Francis Herreshoff, who sailed on board *Reliance*, described a setup in which the base of the topmast was equipped with a steel ferrule and ratchet system that automatically locked the fully extended spar into place without requiring a masthead man to climb aloft.[63] With the hardware removed from the wreckage, refastened to the new topmast, and the repaired system hauled aloft and dropped into place, races resumed without delay.

On June 19 at Indian Harbor Yacht Club in Greenwich—through light, patchy winds with occasional rainsqualls—Barr controlled the start. Poised, he held the wheel gingerly, watching his competitors, steering with confidence, his crew anticipating each move and executing maneuvers with precision. As the yachts made the final approach to the starting line, trimming their sails and heeling to their rails, *Reliance* established a small lead. As the gun fired, *Constitution,* with Rhodes at the helm, pulled ahead. By the first mark the older boat held a five-second lead. After rounding, Barr and *Reliance* with her towering rig accelerated, leaving *Constitution* behind and rounding the second mark a minute and a half ahead. By the race's end *Reliance* beat *Constitution* by nearly two minutes and *Columbia* by twelve and a half.

Sailing south across the Sound, the three prepared for one final match in docile waters. On Saturday, June 20, at Seawanhaka Corinthian Yacht Club in Oyster Bay, the birthplace of the Seawanhaka Rule that had shaped Nat's vision for all three ninety-footers, *Reliance, Constitution,* and *Columbia* loped off the line in a light northeasterly wind. *Columbia* established a one-second lead over *Reliance* at the start, but Barr and his bigger boat quickly pulled away. While the two older boats, vying for position, busied themselves in a luffing duel—*Columbia,* defending her position using the right-of-way rules to drive *Constitution* into the wind—*Reliance* secured a formidable lead, rounding the first mark two minutes ahead. With puffs blowing in from the northeast, Barr, positioned farther up the Sound and aligned with the freshening breeze, stretched his lead. By the end of the second and final lap, he had defeated *Constitution* by more than four minutes and *Columbia* by seven and a half.

Reliance had won eight of nine trial races. The one loss was attributed to her failing topmast. *Reliance* had proven herself incredibly fast in light air. In addition, *Constitution* had consistently trounced *Columbia,* vindicating Nat's belief that *Constitution* was the faster boat from 1901. Had Nat proved his critics wrong? Would his "brute" hold up over time? Only subsequent trials would tell.

12

THE NINETY-FOOTERS

June 1903–August 1903

Flying decorative signal flags from stem to stern, *Erin* and the American steamyacht *Privateer* met the *Oceanic* as she powered into New York Harbor on June 24, 1903. Avoiding steady rain, onlookers hid under awnings. On her mizzenmast *Oceanic* flew Lipton's private signal, a green clover on a yellow background. At noon after *Oceanic* had docked at quarantine, newspaper reporters surrounded Lipton. He was just as eager to hear news of his yachts as they were to hear his thoughts on the upcoming races. The day before, crewmen had completed outfitting *Shamrock I* and *III,* their racing rigs installed and sails bent on, and the Erie Basin dry docks flooded. "I shall have with me the best skipper in Great Britain, Captain Bob Wringe," announced Lipton, "and I shall have with me, besides, Mr. William Fife, the best amateur [tactical advisor] in the United Kingdom. Count in the new Shamrock, and you will have a combination hard to beat. Take my tip, it is a combination that will lift the cup. I hold in high esteem the skill of Herreshoff, but I believe I have with me now a boat that will outdo his best."[1] One of the last people to board *Oceanic,* General Corbin of the U.S. State Department, seeking Lipton, fought through the crowd and extended an invitation to dine with President Roosevelt.[2]

By the next morning, June 25, Lipton, Fife, and New York Yacht Club member Archibald Cary Smith, the naval architect cum marine painter, were at the White House. At 1:30 P.M. they retired to the dining room and sat for lunch, Lipton to the president's right, Fife to his left. Although Roosevelt didn't commit to Lipton's invitation to watch the Cup races on board *Erin,* he expressed his enthusiasm for the competition by capping the lunch with "green pistachio ices in the shape of a big sloop, surmounted by a shamrock flag."[3]

Both Fife and Watson had talked candidly about their collaboration. But by the end of May, Fife had asserted his position as principal architect.

(Watson was conspicuously absent from New York and the White House luncheon.) Nevertheless Watson, with his greater experience in building large sailing yachts, had earned the lion's share of press coverage. He had already designed four Cup challengers, including *Thistle, Valkyrie II* and *III,* and *Shamrock II,* as well as the King's yacht *Britannia,* which had been so successful in her racing battles that she garnered the same patriotic esteem as the USS *Constitution*—Old Ironsides—had in the United States. We don't know if Watson was ever offered the *Shamrock III* commission, but if he had been, it's likely he would have turned it down. In recent years, he had steered his design work toward steam and had earned a reputation as one of the finest steamyacht designers in the world. To take on the monumental task of another Cup defender would have diverted his attention.

Conversely, Fife had steered his business toward racing yachts and had, in recent years, produced some of the fastest British racers afloat. Although Watson had provided valuable information, Fife was, in fact, the principal designer. He had drawn the lines, tested the models, and seen his yacht to completion at the Denny Yard.

When at the end of May the *New York Herald* asked Watson about his involvement, he replied diplomatically, "I have been ready to give Mr. Fife the benefit of any assistance he might want, but the Shamrock III is entirely Mr. Fife's own design and the embodiment of his own ideas. My share has been merely to stand at his back and say I thought that he was doing very well."[4] We don't know how much influence Watson had on the design, but we do know that by the end of June, Watson was in England and Fife was in America fine-tuning his yacht and working with Captain Wringe in *Shamrock III*'s afterguard. We also know that Watson's *Shamrock II* had been left in America following the last Cup challenge, propped on blocks at Erie Basin and largely ignored. The Denny yard fire that had threatened *Shamrock III* had in fact destroyed *Shamrock II*'s sails and perhaps her viability as a cost-effective trial horse.[5] But it is odd that Lipton—a man for whom money was no object—would have deigned to use the faster *Shamrock II* as a trial horse because of a few suits of burnt sails. Why had he left Watson's yacht in America in the first place? Perhaps politics were involved. Or perhaps Fife simply wanted to use a trial horse that he had built, one he knew as intimately as his latest creation. Whatever the reason, Watson's role was ultimately pushed to the sidelines.

As crewmen made final adjustments to Lipton's fleet, all eyes turned on the American yachts and their ongoing defender trials. After the last race off Oyster Bay, *Reliance* was towed through pelting rain to Erie Basin, and after *Shamrock I* exited the flooded dry dock, *Reliance* entered. *Columbia* returned to Morse Iron Works in South Brooklyn to have her bottom scraped and burnished. On June 23 *Constitution* sailed for New London, where, postponing preparation for pageantry, all three American ninety-footers met the following day to watch the Harvard-Yale boat races.

Although the crews of both yachts had a day off, the Herreshoff sail loft continued working night and day on new sails for *Reliance*. When she arrived early morning on Saturday, June 27, workers removed the mainsail, ferrying it ashore, and returned with a new lighter one. A team of steel workers fastened some loosened hawser plates, while another team of workers made repairs to *Columbia's* interior and applied a new coat of paint to her topsides.[6]

Excitement built as final preparations were made for the upcoming trials in Newport. With typically windy conditions at the end of June, the yachts would meet on a new playing field. *Reliance* had clearly dominated the early American trials in breathy winds, but would she hold up in a blow? And if she did win the right to defend the Cup was she fast and strong enough to take on Fife's newest design? *Shamrock III* had been built to cross the Atlantic, a capability that Nat, much to his advantage, could ignore when crafting his own model. But Nat's newest yacht, with her overblown proportions, seemed almost precarious. And with a rig towering above her competition, she was burdened with a time penalty. Would *Reliance's* speed make up for the tax imposed on her mountain of sails? Nat's design had been so outlandish that many considered it grotesque. Could something so aesthetically "wrong" be functionally right? "The Shamrock III in every particular shows refinement of design rather than extreme dimensions," wrote naval architect Irving Cox in a *New York Herald* editorial, "and while all the modern racing boats are, when judged by non-racing eyes brutes and freaks, we can compare the Shamrock with the Reliance in this respect by saying that she is a beautiful freak, as normal as a freak can be, while the Reliance is an ugly and powerful one."[7] Already one person had died on that which Cox considered the more wholesome of the two. Perhaps his disdain for *Reliance* hailed from a sense of impending peril. "The impression of ugliness," wrote German philosopher Theodore Adorno, "stems from the principle of violence and destruction."[8]

On Monday, June 29, the three ninety-footers met in Rhode Island Sound off Newport. With eighteen-knot winds, the conditions were rougher than any of them had seen that season, green water pluming from their bows and wetting their decks. The starting line was set five miles southwest of Brenton Reef Lightship and a turning mark dropped fifteen miles northeast of it. Jockeying for position behind the starting line, marked by a buoy and the steamyacht *Riviera, Constitution* blanketed *Reliance* and crossed the line first when the gun sounded at 12:15. In the wake of the turbulence caused from *Constitution's* sails, *Reliance* tacked to port, splitting from the other two yachts. Once well clear, *Reliance* tacked back to starboard and slowly inched ahead, rounding the mark just under two hours later, two minutes ahead of *Columbia* and three and a half ahead of *Constitution,* which had sailed poorly upwind. On the run home, all three yachts cleanly hoisted their spinnakers. *Reliance,* testing a new cotton-silk blend spinnaker built at the Herreshoff loft, pulled away, beating *Columbia* by four minutes and *Constitution* by five.

With the wind holding at eighteen knots on the following day, *Reliance* shot off the line when the gun sounded at 11:45 A.M. Having problems with her mainsail, *Constitution* lagged behind, *Columbia* rivaling *Reliance* up the first beat. With all three yachts sailing fast on port tack, *Constitution,* to leeward of the other two, tacked first. *Columbia* followed, and having gained on *Reliance,* forced Barr to tack downwind of her. Once clear, Barr immediately swung the wheel and his yacht onto port tack. At the helm of *Columbia,* Lem Miller tacked again to cover, keeping Barr in the turbulent wake of his sails. Barr was trapped, and for the next thirty minutes, every time he attempted to tack and clear himself, Miller tacked on top of him.

But Barr, as cool as always, doled out instructions to his mates and they, in turn, relayed them to the crew. *Reliance* hummed along like clockwork. Capitalizing on his boat's bigger sail plan, Barr knew that if he could play the tacking duel cleaner than Miller, a window would open. Sure enough, with crisper tacks, *Reliance* pulled close enough to her windward adversary, just under *Columbia's* lee bow, to nose ahead into clear air. With sails pulling, *Reliance* shot out from under *Columbia.* In a freshening breeze, *Reliance* heeled to her rails and extended on the others, rounding the turning mark four and a half minutes ahead. While the other two yachts vied for second place, *Reliance* sailed downwind to the finish unencumbered. Barr beat *Constitution* by seven minutes and *Columbia* by eight.

On Wednesday, July 1, *Shamrock III* and *I,* circled for position at their first trial in U.S. waters, but as *Shamrock III* sailed across the starting line, a shot rang out from the mainsheet traveler. The galvanized steel bar fastening the mainsheet to the deck burst; the main boom flopped to leeward and *Shamrock III* slid to a stop. *Erin* towed *Shamrock III* to the Robbins Dry Dock at Erie Basin.[9] Told the repairs would take a full day, Lipton and Fife and Captains Wringe and Bevis boarded *Erin* and steamed to Newport to watch the American trials.

In about ten knots of wind the three American yachts circled. As they'd done throughout the other trial series, the race committee ran a starting sequence in which after the gun, the yachts had a two-minute grace period to start. Their handicap time was calculated from when they crossed the line. *Constitution,* sporting a new Herreshoff mainsail, shot off the line after the initial starting gun, with *Reliance* a minute behind and *Columbia* a minute after that. Sailing in clear air, the newer yacht reined in *Constitution*—overtaking her handily, rounding the turning mark three minutes ahead, and then charging downwind under spinnaker. *Reliance* won handily, five and half minutes ahead of *Constitution,* which beat *Columbia* by nineteen seconds. So definitive and clean was the victory that Iselin announced *Reliance* would not sail the next day. He'd seen enough. But that night, bowing to pressure from Belmont and Morgan, Iselin finally consented and agreed to continue the series.

Iselin was confident in his yacht and the likelihood she'd be chosen to defend by the New York Yacht Club Cup Committee, which triggered his impulse to withdraw from subsequent trials. *Reliance* was fast and her crew sharp. But he also knew she, like any race boat, could potentially break. He had, after all, pressed Herreshoff to build the most extreme craft possible. Every hour they spent on the water translated to wear on the sails and hardware and a greater chance of an accident. To Captain Nat's credit, *Reliance* had proven herself strong with few gear failures. Iselin knew this, but as manager, he had to balance his yacht's potential to falter with equipment testing and crew training. Even Barr's crack crew needed time to practice, the opportunity to run through maneuvers until every onboard job had been mastered and every possible mistake intercepted. Races were often won on the errors of the competition, and since errors could never be anticipated, the only way to obviate them was through repetition. If he didn't sail enough, *Reliance*'s crew might bungle a tack, jibe, or spinnaker set. But if he sailed too much, he'd need to recut stretched or ripped sails and replace frayed halyards, sheets, and worn winch gears. To prepare his crew without stressing his boat required not only a strong rapport with the captain, designer, and financial backers but also a keen sense of crew dynamics and the mechanical guts of the boat. No dilettante could juggle such intricate hardware with so many complex personalities. In his knowledge, organization, and tact, Iselin was exceptional. In the same way that Barr had an uncanny feel for wind on the water and Herreshoff for lines of a hull, Iselin intuited the needs of his campaign. And so it was likely with mild trepidation that he agreed to continue the trials.

The morning of July 2 met with heavy southwest winds driving steep waves across Rhode Island Sound. The race committee had set a thirty-mile triangular course, the first leg to windward. When the starting gun sounded at 12:30, *Columbia* charged off the line first, *Reliance* following, and *Constitution* twenty-seven seconds off her stern.[10] Pounding upwind, *Constitution* pointed higher and sailed faster than the others. Although the previous races had been windy compared to those on Long Island Sound, this race was the most challenging. All three had approached the starting line flying their smallest club topsails, but all had doused them before the start. Foaming water lapped their hatches and lines groaned around winch drums. The crews executed every maneuver at twice the speed, every line under twice the load. And as the three yachts bucked across the starting line through spitting surf, all eyes focused on *Reliance,* desperately trying to reel in *Columbia* while fending off *Constitution*.

Eight minutes up the beat with her leeward rail buried, a snap ricocheted through *Constitution*'s rigging. Flinching, the crew looked aloft. The jaws holding the giant mainsail gaff in place at the mast had snapped. Heavily loaded and unsupported, the gaff wrenched forward and then snapped in half, the loose spar crashing and shredding the mainsail as it fell. Rhodes quickly ordered the other sails doused. No one had been hurt, but *Constitution* was a mess. Taken in tow, she was dragged off the course.

For a full half hour, *Columbia* held *Reliance* in check. The two yachts tacked upwind, *Columbia* ahead at each crossing. Barr, sailing his yacht aggressively, finally gained the advantage and once ahead stretched a two-minute lead at the turning mark. In his final approach to the turn, Miller ordered his masthead man up the rig to set the topsail and his bowsprit men out to set the jib topsail in preparation for the downwind leg. First the topsail was set, the yacht heeling heavily with the enormous addition to her sail spread. As if a pallet of bricks had been hauled aloft, this huge triangular spread of canvas mounted above the mainsail sent the yacht skidding on her rails. Just then, the yacht bucked into an oncoming set of swells. The bow crew, six in all, was clipping the jib topsail hanks onto the forestay. The head bowsprit man was standing on the sprit holding the headstay with one hand and clipping the hanks on with the other. The second man along the sprit handed the loose hanks up to him, holding the sail and the sprit with one arm, his feet balanced on the footrope. The next four held the sail and sprit with both hands, both feet planted on the footrope. They felt the rise and plummeting fall of the sprit with an oncoming wave, the yacht traveling at ten knots, the wave barreling at them in the opposite direction at the same speed. *Columbia*'s bow launched up and then dug down, her javelin bowsprit plunging deep below the surface. Then the sprit emerged. The first bowsprit man held fast, clinging to the forestay. Another, arms wrapped around the bowsprit, had managed to hang on. Three had been lifted off the sprit and hurled into the boat, slamming violently into the foredeck hardware. The second man, Karl B. Olsen of Honefoss, Norway, who'd been handing the hanks to his mate, never surfaced. He'd been washed clean of the spar. With cries of man overboard, the crew dropped the sails. The *New York Herald* reported the steam yachts *Delaware, Riviera, Surf, Rambler,* the tender *Park City,* the tug *De Witt C. Ivins,* and the torpedo boat *Winslow* joined in the search.[11] Crewmen climbed the rigging for a better line of sight. Those who'd been on the bowsprit were sprawled on deck vomiting sea water. But Olsen was lost.

Reliance, sailing alone, crossed the finish line after three hours. Caught up in the tragedy, no one realized, as *Reliance* limped up Narragansett Bay to Bristol, her bow had been bashed in, the bronze plates caved like a dented oil can. "Two plates under the bow on the port side have been badly dented," wrote the *New York Sun.* "In one plate just above the forward end of the water line, there is a dent that extends half the width of the plate. It is at least five feet in length and is deep enough for a man to lay his arm in."[12] The success of Herreshoff's latest was overshadowed by the mounting sentiment that all the ninety-footers, Lipton's included, were veritable death traps, a scourge of excessiveness perverting the sport. E. D. Morgan, crushed over the loss of his crewmember, declined to finish the series.

While critics lambasted yachtsmen and designers for their dangerous fleet of freaks, Captain Nat maintained his studious schedule. But in addition to carving models, modifying drawings, and overseeing a thousand coeval undertakings in the shops, he had, since early 1902, been working on a series of calculations. And each night as he sat in his third-floor office surrounded by wooden half models darkened with age, he hashed out plans—not to further exploit the current racing rules, as he had done so aptly throughout his career, but to destroy them. On February 13, 1902, S. Nicholas Kane and George A. Cormack convened a meeting of prominent New York Yacht Club members with the intent of diffusing those variables of the Seawanhaka Rule that had lead naval architects to design yachts with such exaggerated proportions. Both yachtsmen and designers felt the trend had gone too far.

In his *Men Against the Rule,* for which Cormack wrote the forward, Charles Lane Poor explained letters were sent to leading designers in the United States, Canada, Australia, France, Germany, England, Denmark, Norway, and Sweden, with the hopes of soliciting advice and suggestions to develop a new design rule that would produce "a wholesome type of yacht." Poor notes the letter was answered enthusiastically, designers submitting drawings and test data, the vast majority concluding that in addition to length and sail area, displacement should be a factor in any new rule. The committee agreed, but including a speed inhibitor like displacement would have little effect if the equation were skewed. To successfully tame the equation they'd need to also balance its variables. The committee sent out another query, charging the naval architects of the world with creating a viable formula, a daunting proposition, for it required countless hours of mathematical computation without pay. "So unlimited are the possibilities of varying the lines of the hull and of changing the ratio be-

tween length and displacement," wrote Poor, "that it would require almost endless experiments and tank tests to find even an approximation
towards the relationship. . . ."[13]

For months designers presented their ideas to the committee, but
one after another they were rejected. In their quest to cull "unwholesome" characteristics, they often created other undesirable features.
Those rule proposals were dismissed. Some equations bowed to political pressure—for a rule that in fostering a more salubrious design made
others obsolete (especially extreme racers owned by prominent yachtsman) would never be agreed upon. While many designers anticipated
new materials and future technology in their computations, Nat, who
having turned fifty-five was now wearing wire-rimmed reading glasses,
worked backward.

To find a cure to the Seawanhaka Rule's ills—dangerously large sail
plans mounted on fragile, attenuated hulls—he looked to its precursor,
the first length and sail area rule devised by naval architect Dixon Kemp
in 1883. Kemp's rule, (L x SA)/4000, had proved too simple and was
abandoned after only a year. Captain Nat substituted Dixon's constant
with 5.5 times the cube root of displacement, and like the Seawanhaka
Rule, used the square root of the sail area. All told his formula read:

$$\frac{\text{Length x } \sqrt{\text{Sail Area}}}{5.5 \sqrt[3]{\text{Displacement}}} = \text{Rating Measurement}$$

It's likely other designers had proposed similar variants of this. In fact the
Seawanhaka Yacht Club had come up with a similar rule that year, but
dropped it after one season.[14] If taken at face value, his formula placed
relatively equal emphasis on each factor, which Poor argued would create chaos, allowing "designers complete freedom to play one factor
against the other two." In theory, this could magnify the problems
caused by the Seawanhaka Rule. Nat, however, redefined one of his
variables—length. He proposed that instead of measuring the load waterline when floating on an even keel, a parameter he'd beguiled with
his spoon-shaped bow and long overhangs, that sailing waterline be
measured. To do this, he advocated using what he termed the "quarter
beam" length. This was determined by dividing the widest beam at the
waterline by four. This means a yacht with a twelve-foot waterline beam
would have a quarter beam of three feet. Then, measuring three feet

from the yacht's centerline, both the overall and waterline lengths were measured. The mean of the two equaled L. Nat's formula met with enthusiasm, but not everyone agreed. Nat's rule would make winning more difficult for some yachts (making them appear theoretically faster than they had once been). Their owners protested. And so the long process of political wrangling began. Nat had voiced his opinion. It was now up to those who would employ the rules. Until then, he would continue designing and preparing his racers to the Seawanhaka Rule.

The New York Yacht Club's fleet rendezvoused for its annual cruise from Glen Cove on July 16. Prepared for more racing, the three ninety-footers lined up on July 18, *Constitution* beating *Reliance* over a thirty-seven-mile course by more than a minute corrected time. The next day, racing from Morris Cove to New London, *Reliance* won. On July 20, sailing east toward Newport, *Constitution* again beat *Reliance* in a race from Sarah's Ledge to Brenton Reef Lightship by a minute corrected time. On July 22, in a race from Brenton Reef Lightship off Newport to West Chop Buoy and back (leaving Vineyard Sound Lightship to port and Lucas Shoal and Middle Ground to starboard), Barr, reminiscent of his youth, ran *Reliance* aground. Acting quickly, he ordered the balloon jib topsail slacked and jibed her boom. The yacht pivoted through the sand. Slowly, she ground through the shallow bank and floated into deep water. Avoiding the obstruction, *Constitution* passed *Reliance. Columbia* wasn't so lucky. Belmont drove his yacht onto the shoal and stuck fast. His launch *Vanish* and the tender *Park City* tried in vain to pull her free. Finally, the tug *Ocean King* dragged her from the shoal. As if to exacerbate the day of folly, while racing alone to the finish, *Constitution* lost her topmast.

The final trials were set for Newport, beginning on July 27. Over a thirty-mile course, *Reliance* manhandled *Constitution* and *Columbia*. Directly after the first race, a meeting was held on Lewis Cass Ledyard's steamship *Rambler.* The Cup Committee, including former Commodore Ledyard, Secretary George Cormack, Fleet Captain C. L. F. Robinson, J. Malcolm Forbes, Charles Oliver Iselin, August Belmont, E. D. Morgan, former Commodore S. Nicholas Kane, Newbury D. Lawton, and Edward H. Wales sat in *Rambler's* main saloon. The meeting lasted an hour. When they adjourned, Cormack announced *Reliance* had been selected to defend. "We have selected the Reliance to defend the America's Cup," Commodore Bourne told the *New York Sun,* "because that yacht has shown that she is beyond doubt the best boat of the three. As I understand it, the Columbia will be laid up at once and the Constitution will be held in reserve. There will be no more racing now until the America's Cup races."[15]

Tenders towed *Constitution* and *Reliance* up Narragansett Bay to Bristol, where Herreshoff workmen effected minor repairs. *Reliance* had sustained damage to her rudder and several bow plates when she ran aground. In addition, *Constitution's* sails were removed from the yacht and made ready if *Reliance* should need them during the upcoming regatta with *Shamrock III.*

The races were a few weeks away, and Lipton's crews, like the Americans, worked tirelessly. *Shamrock III* was sailing well, but they'd been faced with what seemed like an endless stream of niggling mishaps. On July 30, the yacht broke a masthead runner block and had to head in. Then *Shamrock III's* sails needed alterations. On August 6, while working at the shipyard, a pier collapsed and both captains Wringe and Bevis crashed into the water. Swimming clear of the debris, Wringe dragged two nonswimmers to a nearby boat and Bevis crawled to shore. Ultimately, no one was injured, but the incident had usurped the better part of a day. Despite the hectic final preparations, Lipton wasn't much help. Accepting an invitation from the Lehigh Valley Railway to visit Buffalo, Niagara Falls, and Canada, he left the city the following Saturday.

During the final days of July *Columbia's* crew stripped the yacht of sails, lines, and hardware, preparing her to be hauled and covered at City Island. By the end of the first week in August *Reliance* and *Shamrock III* had completed their final spins and were towed to Redhook's Erie Basin to be hauled and cleaned. *Constitution* was hauled at the Thames Towboat Company in New London, the crew paid for the season and then discharged. That *Columbia* and *Constitution* had been decommissioned was likely a relief for Captain Nat. No longer would he be responsible for overseeing the details of all three yachts, fielding complaints from their managers and diverting his time and energy from *Reliance.* Although the burden had been lifted, Barr still detected problems in *Reliance's* steering system. Nat and Barr went to work, spending hours in the dry dock under *Reliance's* hull. Following their orders workmen labored to rectify the problem while the crew scraped and burnished the bronze hull. Both held by a lattice of long support poles, *Reliance* and *Shamrock III* sat in the Erie Basin dry docks side by side. While *Reliance's* hand-burnished hull took on its original golden shine, *Shamrock III*, scrubbed clean, received a fresh coat of white enamel. As the work progressed the two yachts attracted a constant crowd of roughly eight thousand fixated people.[16]

With the first races scheduled to begin on August 20, thousands flooded New York from both Britain and America. It was estimated that a half million people had attended the 1901 races, and more were expected to attend in 1903.[17] Fleets of excursion steamers had sold out tickets, and the race organizers had coordinated a fleet of revenue cutters to patrol the racecourse. In compliance with a request from the U.S. Attorney General, the New York Yacht Club had printed and bound two thousand blue booklets comprising the rules and regulations, including diagrams for excursion vessels watching the races. The preparations weren't limited to New York. The London Hippodrome had erected a large seascape on which was fixed models of the *Reliance* and *Shamrock III*. Receiving reports via Marconi Wireless, the models would be moved along in accordance with the yachts' progress around the racecourse.[18]

Such hype brought endless speculation. Meteorologists forecasted light to medium winds. Assessing the conditions, Wall Street financiers wagered on the defender. The *Paul Mall Gazette* quoted Lipton: "I am confident of victory in light winds." Fife agreed: "Not more than a ten-mile wind per hour for us." Of *Shamrock III* Barr responded, "She cannot win in any wind."[19]

On the morning of August 20, Charles D. Mower, the New York Yacht Club's official measurer, arrived at Erie Basin with his tapes. The official measurement would shed new light on which yacht had an advantage. Most were confident that immense *Reliance* would owe smaller *Shamrock III* a time allowance, but just how much would determine their chances of success. In designing *Reliance* Captain Nat, following Iselin's wishes, had built a yacht of extreme proportions, but in doing so Nat had used the loopholes of the design rules to make his yacht seem less extreme on paper. If he had succeeded, the time allowance would not be a factor, for his yacht, in her superior speed around the course, would more than make up for the time granted *Shamrock III*. If he had failed, *Shamrock III,* albeit slower, would use her more efficient rating to win on corrected time. The two yachts had not yet lined up on a race-course. The only comparisons had been made through their respective trial horses. *Shamrock III* had in fact trounced *Shamrock I* in their practice spins, winning consistently by ten to twelve minutes. Although *Reliance* had beaten the older *Constitution* throughout the summer, the time difference had been much smaller. Had Fife figured out a way to design a theoretically slow boat that sailed incredibly fast? The official measurements would provide some clues to the questions everyone was asking. Mower and his team arrived dressed in suits and silk hats; the sailors, reporters, and of course the delegates from the New York and Royal Ulster yacht clubs waited with consternation.

With dark hair neatly parted on the left, thin lips, and wire-rimmed glasses, Charles D. Mower had a boyish but serious face. The measurer was twenty-eight years old and had been a member of the New York Yacht Club for only nine months. Under the headline "Rapid Rise," the *Boston Globe* announced his nomination for the head measurer position in February 1903 after John Hyslop, a sixteen-year veteran measurer and a veritable institution of rule implementation in North America, had resigned from the post. With an unusually analytical mind, Mower, originally from Lynn, Massachusetts, started building small boats in his teens. After building a few successful daysailers, he landed a job designing yachts at the offices of Arthur Binney. He continued building and designing his own highly successful boats that dominated racing on Massachusetts Bay. In 1898 he left Binney's office and began working for Bowdoin Crowninshield, the 1901 designer of *Independence*.

The bookish Mower ran his tapes around the yachts, necessitating that he be hauled via halyard to the dizzying tops of both yachts' topmasts. He asked questions, checked and double checked his figures, and jotted notes into a small book. Under the watchful eyes of Captain Nat, Iselin, Barr, Fife, and Captain Wringe (Lipton was still touring Niagara Falls), Mower was official and veracious in executing the task. Returning to his office, Mower transcribed the measurements onto an official certificate. With her crew of sixty-four men on board, *Reliance* was 89.66 feet on the load waterline. From the aft end of the boom to the tip of the bowsprit, she was 201.76 feet long. With fifty-six men on board, *Shamrock III* was 89.81 feet long on the load waterline and from boom end to bowsprit end 187.54 feet. According to Mower's calculations, *Shamrock III* held 14,337.67 square feet; *Reliance* held 16,169.67 square feet of sail, the most ever piled onto a Cup racer and any single-masted vessel.[20] After calculating a number of deck and rigging measurements, Mower signed his name to the official measurement certificate and had it delivered to members of the *Reliance* syndicate who were dining at the Waldorf-Astoria that evening. Mower's results concluded that over a thirty-mile course *Reliance* would owe *Shamrock III* almost two minutes. If the two yachts sailed the course with an average speed of ten knots, the defender would have to cross the finish line one-third of a mile ahead of *Shamrock III*, a challenge if the yachts were evenly matched. Nat and the New York Yacht Club had hoped their yacht would owe *Shamrock III* less time, but they knew their bigger yacht was fast. Asserting confidence in the face of disappointing news, members of the *Reliance* syndicate offered to bet $10,000 to anyone willing to post $7,000 on *Shamrock III*. The bet was never matched.[21]

While waiting for the race, Lipton toured the Hudson River Valley by train, and upon each stop he was met by thousands of people. Photos from his personal scrapbook show throngs of well-wishers piled outside his private car. As the guest of Adjutant-General Corbin, Lipton visited West Point and was entertained by the officers. He even attended a burlesque show titled "Lifting the Cup" in which he was parodied.[22] Upon returning from his trip north, Lipton visited Theodore Roosevelt at Oyster Bay on the presidential yacht *Mayflower* where—along with representatives from Great Britain, Germany, Russia, and Japan—they reviewed the North Atlantic Naval Squadron in Long Island Sound. Although Roosevelt had to decline Lipton's repeated invitation to attend the Cup races aboard *Erin*, Roosevelt said he would watch the races from *Mayflower* and in everyone's presence toasted the Cup competition, announcing, "May the best boat win."[23]

With the official measurements acknowledged, excitement escalated. "During recent years the attempts made by British yachtsmen to gain possession of the America Cup," wrote the *North Star,* "have created almost as much interest as the international cricket contests between England and Australia."[24] In a series of official correspondence, the New York Yacht Club race committee made final preparations with press agencies, the Navy, and U.S. Treasury Department. The Associated Press requested permission to steam within the patrol lines during racing aboard the yacht *Chetolah*. The Publishers Press Association announced in a letter to Commodore S. Nicholas Kane that they had chartered the *Samuel E. Bouker* from the White Star Towing Co. and that their reports would be transmitted via DeForest Wireless Telegraphy.[25] W. B. Franklin, commander of the USS *New Hampshire,* wrote to Secretary of the Regatta Committee Edward H. Wales announcing, "I have the honor to acknowledge the receipt of your communication . . . relative to details of signalmen for service during the Cup races, and to inform you that the men will report uniformed, and equipped with signal flags, at the time and places as directed."[26] The Treasury Department wrote to the committee announcing they would provide a fleet of twelve revenue cutters under the command of Captain Thomas D. Walker stationed on board the USRC *Gresham.*[27] It seemed all of America was ready for the battle.

THE WIZARD'S WING

August 1903–September 1903

A t dawn on August 20, the crowded Horseshoe anchorage inside Sandy Hook sprang to life. The crews of *Shamrock III* and *Reliance* began at dawn, removing canvas sail covers, uncoiling sheets and halyards, and wiping the dew from metal fittings. Along the Manhattan waterfront, members of the New York Yacht Club race committee boarded the newly painted oceangoing tug *Navigator*. With washed and pressed uniforms, the crews of the ocean tug *John Scully* prepared lines and anchors for the turning marks. Navy tugs *Coastwise* and *Unique* were dispatched to monitor the marks in case their anchors dragged.[1] *Navigator* steamed from the harbor first. Excursion steamers overflowing with spectators followed close behind. In addition to numerous other private yachts and commercially run excursion steamers, New York Yacht Club members had the option to pay three dollars each, including lunch but not wine, to sail on the *Cepheus* of the Iron Steamboat Company. For those needing more comfortable accommodations the steamer *Monmouth* of the Sandy Hook Line had also been chartered and made available to New York and Eastern Yacht Club members. *Monmouth* was equipped with thirty private sitting rooms capable of holding ten to twelve people, a room costing twenty-five dollars per day. In addition members would pay six dollars each per day including lunch.[2] John Brown Herreshoff reserved a ticket for the races aboard *Monmouth*.

Navigator, with race committee members Commodore S. Nicholas Kane, Newbury D. Lawton, and Edward H. Wales on board, was the first yacht to arrive at Sandy Hook. They dropped anchor, *Navigator* marking one end of the starting line, the other marked by the Sandy Hook Lightship. Pulled behind *Cruizer*, *Shamrock III* arrived with Captain Wringe at the helm. Standing nearby were William Fife Jr., Sir Thomas Lipton's representative Sharman Crawford, vice commodore and Cup Committee chairman of the Royal Ulster Yacht Club, and

Robert Bacon, the official onboard representative of the New York Yacht Club. Towed behind the tug *Guiding Star*, *Reliance* arrived with her afterguard, Charles Oliver Iselin and his wife Hope Iselin, serving as timekeeper, as well as W. Butler Duncan Jr., Newberry Thorne, Herbert Leeds, Woodbury Kane, Captain Nat, and the Royal Ulster Yacht Club onboard representative H. M. McGildowney. Charlie Barr stood at the helm, his fitted suit resting neatly over his small frame. Barr had also employed Captain Lem Miller of *Columbia* to trim headsails during the Cup races. The yachts glided into the starting area like two prizefighters entering the ring.

The crews, dressed in white duck pants, middy blouses, and bucket hats, lined their decks and hoisted their two-ton mainsails in unison. After *Reliance* had dropped her towline, Barr, alert and silent, crooked his finger and shot glances at his mates Christiansen and Miller. The two acknowledged his desire to begin positioning *Reliance* for the start. The yachts pitched in a rolling chop, halyards clanking on steel masts. Both skippers hoisted topsails. "*Reliance's* mainsail had hardly a wrinkle," wrote the *Daily Graphic*, "and her topsail set like a board."[3] The mainsail was new, having been hoisted for the first time only three days earlier.

The *John Scully*, under the command of U.S. Navy Lieutenant Commander W. J. Sears, dropped the turning mark precisely fifteen miles to windward, making the first leg of the race a south-southwest course. At 10:45 A.M. *Navigator* fired a preparatory cannon blast. The patrol-boat fleet all flying official Revenue Service flags from their mastheads fell into formation, flanking the starting line extending to windward, each boat four hundred yards from the next. The precise boundaries set by the patrol boats were outlined in a blue pamphlet handed out to spectator boat captains. With the preparatory signal, both *Reliance* and *Shamrock III* set their jib topsails. With fifteen minutes to the start, both Wringe and Barr focused on the task of gaining an advantageous position over the other. Barr, quick to make the first move, sailed to windward of Wringe. With the clock counting down, both yachts luffed, drifting over the starting line, *Reliance* commanding the windward position.

The crew of *Reliance* crouched quietly on the deck, ducking so to maintain a clear line of sight for Barr and his mates. A summer's worth of preparation had come to a head, and although their opponent sailed a hundred yards away, they had no idea what to expect. The two yachts had never lined up against each other, and the only point of measure had been the wild speculation reported in the papers for the better part of the year. Would Fife's tank testing outdo Captain Nat's more intuitive approach to design? Could *Reliance* compensate for the rating time owed *Shamrock III?* On a more immediate level, had the giant spinnaker been stowed free of twists? Had the balloon jib been properly banded with yarn? Some version of these thoughts likely ran through their heads, for the countdown toward the starting gun had commenced and all eyes were on them. Was the scrutiny warranted? Wasn't it just a race? What was at stake?

For *Reliance's* crewmembers and officers, the race was a job. Winning was important, for it earned them bonuses and future commissions. It also validated months of hard work and time away from their families. But what about the others involved? For Iselin and his wife and friends in the afterguard, the Cup series was a pageant of pride. It was simply their duty as New York Yacht Club members to meet the challenge. Iselin had sailed for honor his entire life, the acceptance of his family contingent on his racecourse success. He had never worked, instead devoting his life to sport. Yachting had become his unpaid vocation and like a lawyer whose career was shaped by courtroom victories, Iselin predicated his faculty and reputation on the performance of his yachts. For Herreshoff, however, the stakes were higher.

Reliance would prove his worth as a naval architect. His career hinged on victory. Although he had built winning boats of all sizes, *Reliance,* the most powerful ever created, was sure to become the measure of his success. Most believed he failed with *Constitution* in 1901. Even he believed he had lost touch with his last design:"I feel and know that my best years for such work have passed,"[4] he wrote to Iselin in May 1902. But Nat had returned to his model room and created something totally wild—so exceptional, in fact, that during the following months he penned a rule that would render his massive vessel moot. To win the America's Cup would validate his inimitable ideas.

But what was at stake for the public at large? This was a time when papers like the *New York Herald* and *Times,* the *Washington Post,* and the *Times of London* ran multi-page coverage of each race. They ran full-page diagrams and described every tack and jibe. The 1901 races drew a half million spectators.[5] Through the papers, millions read about them. And why did they care? The America's Cup races had become more than just rich men wrangling over a gaudy silver ewer. In a world gripped by drastic flux, they projected the inveterate friction between the two most powerful nations.

At the turn of the century the United States had begun to establish itself as a world industrial and military power, expanding into Alaska, Hawaii, Puerto Rico, and the Pacific. In 1903 alone Henry Ford incorporated the Ford Motor Company and the Wright brothers made the first sustained powered flight. But the United States still remained in Great Britain's shadow. Although England's colonial ties in Africa and India were beginning to unravel, it was still the empire—its capital, London, still the nexus of world power. In 1903 King Edward VII ruled. His nephew was Emperor of Germany, his sister-in-law Empress of Russia, and the crowns of Greece, Romania, Sweden, Denmark, Norway, and Belgium were all worn by monarchs with blood ties to the British royal family.

In a competition between America and Britain, the New World and Old, millions of readers and thousands of spectators saw more than just two yachts. They saw symbols of tradition, technology, craftsmanship, and skill. For Americans, *Reliance* was the manifestation of an intrepid national consciousness, an opportunity to challenge and even defeat the British Empire and prove American mettle to the world.

The two yachts drifted on the course side of the line for what seemed like an eternity. Huddled on deck, the crewmen waited. The clock ticked down. With one minute until the start, Barr shot glances at Wringe, while careful to maintain a steady hand. In such light winds any extra movement of the helm would slow the boat. The mates trimmed their sheets, the sails cambered for light winds. Forty-five seconds. Barr, still to windward (the course side) of the line, sailed for the lightship end, *Reliance* accelerating slowly in the dying breeze.

Thirty seconds. *Reliance,* reaching on port tack, pulled ahead of *Shamrock III.* Twenty seconds. Flying their largest light-wind sails, the yachts crawled to leeward. Barr maintained a high angle, steering for the lightship. Wringe bore off and split the starting line. Ten seconds. Both yachts were still on the wrong side (to windward) of the line. Both Wringe and Barr sailed downwind to position themselves behind the line, careful not to sail too deep. Every time they bore off, their yachts slowed and a light chop shook the wind from their sails.

Five seconds. *Reliance* approached the line. Three, two, one, counted Hope Iselin aloud. A puff of smoke lifted from the mouth of *Navigator*'s cannon, and a split second later—the time for sound to travel the length of the line—the report. Barr jibed and headed for the line. Having sailed deeper, a more direct route, Wringe crossed first. Barr, behind, made a long sweeping turn to windward, his trimmers ordering the winch operators below deck to grind on their command. The sails tightened on their spars in unison. Barr carefully nudged the helm, *Reliance* nosing to windward. Accelerating on starboard tack, *Reliance* dipped her leeward rail.

Having tacked in haste in an attempt to wrest the windward position from Barr, Wringe stalled *Shamrock III* on the line. The yacht lost her headway. Wringe had also called for his jib topsail, which hung shapeless in the light breeze. While the bowsprit man rigged the lighter baby jib topsail, *Shamrock III* lost more ground. As isolated puffs washed down over the racecourse, Barr picked his way through the patches of wind. Having lost so much headway at the start, Wringe labored far astern. The two yachts clawed to windward through the flagging breeze. Barr finally rounded the turning mark at 3:37:30, just before the five-hour time limit expired. *Shamrock III* was still deep in her upwind leg. With no hope of finishing within the time limit *Reliance* sailed alongside *Shamrock III*. Barr hailed Wringe and the two agreed to retire.

As stipulated in the rules governing the 1903 Cup races, races would be held every other day. Both crews spent August 21 drying sails. That morning George Cormack received an official letter from measurer Charles D. Mower stating that *Shamrock III* had not been in proper trim while racing, for the crew had inadvertently removed the anchor and chain during the waterline measurements:

> I beg to inform you that the measurement of Shamrock III made on the 18th is void, it having been found that the yacht was not in racing trim as required by the conditions of agreement. I beg also to inform you that an appointment has been made for re-measurement at Erie Basin on Monday Aug. 24th at nine A.M. it having been found impracticable to make a remeasurement prior to Saturday's race.[6]

Fife had confirmed the omission. Because *Shamrock III* had measured 89.81 feet on the load waterline, barely within the 90-foot limit, they feared the added weight of anchor and chain would bump the British boat over the limit, disqualifying her. A series of notes and telegrams were sent between the race committee and Sharman Crawford aboard *Shamrock III*. Because of the time and preparation needed to thoroughly measure a yacht, the remeasurement was scheduled for Monday, August 24. "I beg to inform you," wrote Crawford on letterhead embossed with the Steam Yacht *Erin* seal, "that Shamrock III will sail today with anchor and chain on board, and I will personally see that she is in the same trim when measured in Erie Basin on Monday morning as she is when racing today."[7]

Despite the cancellation of the first race, Lipton had had a grand time aboard *Erin,* entertaining about two hundred people. The men wore suit coats, vests, ties, and yachting caps; the women wore sunhats and Victorian high-necked dresses with long sleeves. As was his scheduled plan for each day of racing, his guests had arrived on *Erin* via his electric launch. Lipton, wearing a suit, cap, and his customary blue with white polka dot bow tie, greeted each personally as they boarded. They spent the day, sunning themselves in deck chairs, watching the races, eating and, of course, drinking copious amounts of tea.

On Saturday, August 22, *Erin* steamed toward the Sandy Hook Lightship, her decks teeming with guests. Under blue skies in building southwesterly winds, the two yachts, mainsails flying, were towed to the racecourse. Because of the wind direction, the starting line could not be set properly off the lightship, so *Navigator* steamed five miles east and dropped anchor. Before casting *Reliance's* towline, Barr ordered the intermediate club topsail sent aloft. At 11:30 A.M. the race committee fired the preparatory gun, commencing the countdown to the start. At the shot of the gun, the crew fell silent and Barr crooked his finger, signaling to his mates. Hope Iselin monitored the stopwatch while Captain Nat and Iselin eyed Wringe. Barr had ordered his large club topsail doused, and a second smaller one hoisted in its place. The *John Scully* set a turning mark fifteen miles due southwest, a course requiring the yachts to beat to windward and run home.

The two yachts largely kept clear of each other during the starting maneuvers, each loosely keeping tabs on the other. "The jockeying for the start was neither close nor exciting," reported *The Rudder,* "as there was no quick or close work."[8] In the final seconds of the countdown, Wringe shot for the line, but too soon. He bore away quickly, burning speed, and then trimmed in hard, just clearing the *Navigator's* bow as he crossed the line. Four seconds behind, *Reliance* set her jib topsail upon crossing the line. Both yachts pounded into oncoming swells. "Reliance took them much less kindly than the Fife boat," wrote *The Rudder.* "Shamrock was doing fine work, both pointing high and footing fast, and was unquestionably pulling away from the big Herreshoff craft."[9]

Blanketed by turbulent air from Wringe's sails, Barr tacked to port and sailed free of his opponent. Now in clear wind, Barr ordered the jib topsail doused and at 12:40 tacked onto starboard. Wringe had since tacked to port and now the two yachts converged, *Shamrock III* sailing high and fast. Barr held the right-of-way, although it appeared Wringe would cross. But as the two boats charged toward each other, it became apparent that Wringe wouldn't cross, opting instead to tack onto Barr's lee bow. Although to leeward, *Shamrock III,* having tacked, was nose-out on *Reliance,* sailing in clear air and blasting the bigger boat with turbulent wind from her sails. In this advantageous position, Wringe pulled ahead. Having established a lead, Wringe then tacked to port, sailed a short distance, and then tacked again to starboard, gaining separation from *Reliance.* But Wringe's hard-won advantage was short lived. Despite his commanding tactical position, the wind lightened, and the choppy seas abated. *Reliance* was no longer bouncing through the waves, her hull now slipping smoothly through the water. And Barr, working with his trimmers, found *Reliance's* groove. The Americans accelerated.

Barr tacked, and having gained when the two met at their next crossing, tacked back under Wringe's lee bow. In this tactical power position, Barr pulled ahead. As they approached the mark, a west-southwest wind shift secured *Reliance's* lead. Barr rounded the turning mark at 1:55:17, more than three minutes ahead of Wringe. The crew rustled upon the final approach to the mark, each man carefully moving to his position. Upon Barr's command the downwind sails stored below decks snaked up through the hatches in their yarn stops. The mastman secured a topping lift to the spinnaker pole. A crewman clipped the inboard end of the pole to the mast. The trimming sheets were fastened to the sails, which were prepared for the hoist. The bowspritman, holding the final stops to the headsails, signaled the distances to the turning mark. The mates relayed the information back to Barr. Commencing his turn, Barr signaled and the headsails were eased on their winch drums. A crewman eased the break on the mainsail sheet clutch, and the line whipped from the deck fairlead, spinning off its spool (needed to prevent it from tangling) belowdecks. The winch drums groaned as the massive sails opened to the wind like giant barn doors. The ballooner, a billowing headsail made of 6¼-ounce Wamsutta twill, set smartly. The spinnaker, made of the same material, rotated around the bow with the choreographed movement of its control lines and filled like a parachute to port.

Rounding three minutes behind, *Shamrock III's* crew bungled their downwind sails, the ballooner having to be doused, untangled, and rehoisted. While Wringe's crew fixed its mistakes, Barr charged toward the finish unmolested. More than twenty thousand people on a fleet of 150 steamers watched *Reliance* swoop across the line. Barr won by nine minutes. *Reliance,* as noted in the log of Captain Nat's steamyacht *Roamer,* was welcomed by "great noise at the end of the race . . ."[10]

To have won the first race in a best-of-five series alleviated months of anxiety. Owing to a number of fortuitous events—a waning breeze, a helpful wind shift, and sloppy British boathandling—*Reliance* had dominated. Barr had seized every inch of opportunity, even when Wringe had pinned him to leeward on the upwind leg. So much of luck is being prepared to act upon unforeseen events, and Barr—with Captain Nat and Iselin's consul and his crew's punctilious execution of maneuvers—had maximized the smallest gains in the oncoming wind shifts. There is only a small window of opportunity when tacking under an opponent's lee bow. If the port-tack yacht tacks too late, the starboard tacker will sail past him, rolling over him to windward. If the port-tack yacht tacks too far from the starboard tacker's lee bow, her sails won't effectively pitch turbulent air onto her competitor, rendering the maneuver useless. In choppy, windy conditions, Wringe had successfully lee-bowed Barr, but as the wind died, Barr, sailing swiftly, had pulled far enough ahead—possibly only a half boatlength in relation to Wringe—to command the lee bow position at their next meeting. Ultimately, Barr's quick maneuvering earned him a slight advantage, which, characteristic of his exceptional skill, he stretched to an insurmountable lead.

Despite the praise befallen *Reliance,* Captain Nat made no public statements. To some *Shamrock III's* early performance was alarming. "To the yachtsmen who watched the performance of the boats closely," wrote *The Rudder,* "the fine work of the Fife challenger to windward, early in the race, gave good reason for believing that she had the ability to put up a hard fight, and that it was by no means certain that *Reliance* would have so easy a time defeating her under all conditions of wind and weather."[11] London's *Daily Telegraph* agreed: "Shamrock is perhaps the ablest craft that has crossed the ocean cup hunting. The single criticism of Sir Thomas Lipton and his friends is

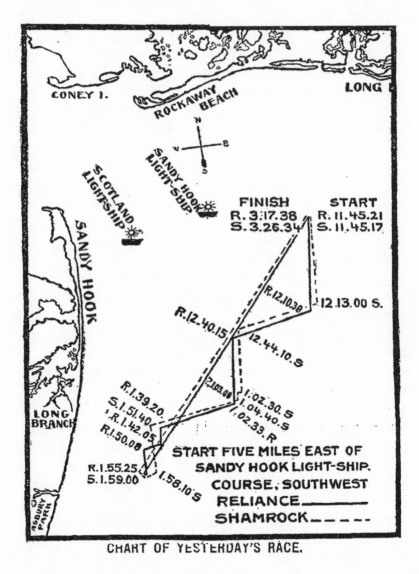

CHART OF YESTERDAY'S RACE.

August 23, 1903: Diagram showing the courses sailed by *Reliance* and *Shamrock III* in the first race of the 1903 America's Cup series. (Courtesy of the *New York Times*.)

that only a shift of wind insured the advantage of the defender."[12] News spread rapidly of the American victory both in New York and abroad. The Sunday *Times of London* reported:

> Evening papers were eagerly bought up ... the greatest interest being taken in the race ... and though the general disappointment was evident, the fact that the Reliance had won was received in a sportsmanlike manner. There was much enthusiasm at the Hotel Cecil and Carlton Hotel, where a large number of American visitors were staying, and many cheers were given for the Reliance. The result was immediately made known from the stages of the music-halls and other places of amusement. At the Earl's Court Exhibition the progress of the race was shown by red and green lights on the big wheel, and by a miniature course on the lake, where small yachts were placed representing Reliance and Shamrock, and their positions altered as messages were received from Sandy Hook. At the Crystal Palace three red bombs were sent up, and the same means of communication to the large crowd was adopted at the Alexandra Palace. At similar places the result was also posted up at various centers, whilst in different parts of London large crowds gathered to watch the lights which were sent up when the news reached London.[13]

On Monday morning, August 24, *Shamrock III* was towed to Erie Basin for remeasurement with anchor and chain. The misunderstanding was immediately cleared. Upon running his tapes, Mower found *Shamrock III* was actually shorter on the load waterline than before, measuring 89.78 feet compared to its previous 89.81. If the yacht had been too long, the rules allowed ballast to be removed, causing her to float higher and shortening the waterline length. Because of this, some believed the anchor ordeal was "another clever ruse on the part of Mr. Fife to increase the challenger's time allowance."[14] Without a doubt, Fife simply wanted to be forthright about the anchor omission so to avoid even the slightest grumblings of malfeasance. Ultimately, the time difference was negligible, the change in waterline length effecting only a fraction-of-a-second change. The time *Reliance* owed *Shamrock III* remained the same.

The next morning a south by east breeze wafted into the Horseshoe at Sandy Hook. The crews on both yachts started early. By 8 A.M.

Shamrock III's crew had hoisted her new Egyptian cotton mainsail, "fitting as tightly as wall paper in the usual Ratsey fashion."[15] Barr ordered *Reliance*'s mainsail and largest club topsail raised and at 9 A.M. they dropped their mooring pennant and sailed from the harbor with the wind off the port quarter. *Reliance* sported a new mainsail gaff—the one previously used, having been taken to Erie Basin to be strengthened with diagonal bracing.[16] Tossing a line to *Cruizer, Shamrock III* followed in tow. In flat seas and light winds the two yachts sailed for the Sandy Hook Lightship ahead of the spectator fleet steaming, en masse, toward the course. Although the crowds had somewhat diminished from the first day of racing, most of the excursion steamers were packed with "decks so crowded that from a distance they appeared like swarming beehives."[17]

Arriving an hour before the start, both yachts circled near the committee boat, *Navigator,* which flew flags indicating a triangular course had been set. At 10:45 the preparatory signal sounded, and the two yachts began circling. As he'd done in the previous race, Barr, gaining the weather position, stuck close to the British boat as they sailed parallel to the line and past the lightship. Wringe bore off, footing away from *Reliance* and the starting line, "showing an apparent dislike for working in close quarters with the crafty Barr."[18] Barr stuck with Wringe, sailing on his weather quarter. With two minutes to go until the warning signal, Wringe steered *Shamrock III* into the wind and Barr followed, their sails luffing "like impatient chargers shaking their manes."[19]

Forced into a tactical battle with Barr, Wringe showed reluctance. Challenging Barr in pre-start maneuvers was like entering murky, waist-deep waters to wrestle an alligator. Barr could sense the slightest weakness in his opponents—a scant loss of momentum or break in concentration—and then pounce, sailing aggressively and fast, securing the tactical advantage before his opponent realized what had happened. Winning the start was incredibly important, for it laid the tactical foundation of the entire race. When faced with a ferocious opponent like Barr, one might opt to avoid direct confrontation. It might be more prudent to steer clear, using the two-minute starting grace period as a cushion. Perhaps Wringe was still chafing from an alleged spat between he and Fife after the first race. The *Daily Telegraph* reported that Fife had hinted Captain Bevis "ought to be in charge of the challenger."[20] Although other reports discounted the slight on Wringe's performance, perhaps he was frazzled.

With visible trepidation, Wringe sailed *Shamrock III* eastward and Barr followed, sticking tight to Wringe's weather quarter. With three minutes until the start, the two yachts split around the lightship, tacked, and sailed back along the line to the committee boat, *Reliance* now on *Shamrock III's* weather bow. Barr set a course south of the committee boat, Wringe sailing to leeward. Accelerating, Barr left enough room to dive to leeward in front of *Shamrock III*. As the gun sounded, Barr carefully steered into position. Barr crooked his finger. Christiansen acknowledged. Upon the mate's command, below-deck trimmers wound the jib and forestaysail sheets. Another below-deck crewman winched in the slack from the lower leeward running backstay while a crewman on deck hauled in the slack from the upper leeward runner. The mainsheet ran from the boom to the traveler (at the stern) and seventy-five feet forward to the crew lining the windward rail. Using brute force, they hauled the four-inch-diameter mainsheet (which tapered at the ends) in unison. The slack was taken up below decks, the sheet running through a series of ratchets and breaks capable of holding the mainsail's full load. A below-deck crewman wound the mainsheet onto a lightweight drum so to prevent the massive, 800-foot length of line from tangling.[21] With his sails trimmed, Barr nudged *Reliance's* nose on the breeze. In their suits and yachting caps, Iselin and Herreshoff braced themselves calmly as *Reliance* crossed the line at 11:00:36 and heeled to her rails.

Avoiding *Reliance's* immense wind shadow—a patch of turbulent air caused by her sails—Wringe steered a course to the west; but miscalculating the time, he crossed the starting line nineteen seconds after the handicap gun and a half-mile behind Barr. Wringe had waded into the murky pool and received a thrashing. Barr had played the handicap gun perfectly, casting his immense wind shadow like an invisible blanket over his competitor.

Reliance had gained a formidable lead, but *Shamrock III* slowly closed the gap, Wringe footing fast while Barr pinched his yacht toward the mark. "The yachts heeled until their lee rails were well awash," wrote the *New York Times,* "and they went through the water, sending showers of spray over the bows and leaving broad trails of foam behind at a pace that strained the steamer to hold it."[22] As both yachts approached the first mark, the wind shifted to the west. *Reliance,* sailing a faster angle, pulled away from *Shamrock III*. In the final approach to the first mark Barr ordered the baby jib topsail doused and the reaching jibs hoisted in their stops. With the bowsprit man signaling the distances to the mark, the numbers relayed back to the helm, Barr began his sweeping turn, the giant mainsail groaning to leeward, and the reaching headsail sheets trimmed until the yarn ties popped and the sails billowed freely.

Wringe, still pounding to windward, ordered the big balloon jib, which was hauled on deck and clipped to its stay. Upon rounding, the giant sail was snaked aloft and made fast; the sheet was tended and the sail filled with a thump. *Shamrock III* shot ahead and closed the two-minute gap. She needed to finish within one minute of *Reliance* to win. Barr, seeing Wringe had made the correct sail call, ordered *Reliance's* ballooner set. Within a minute, the sail was on deck, the bowsprit crew fastening its hanks to the forestay. On Barr's call, the mountain of white cotton streamed skyward and filled.

Again, the wind hauled to the west. Barr ordered the spinnaker set. While the crew below deck handed up the giant sail and trimmers attached their sheets, crewmen unlashed the eighty-five-foot spinnaker pole from the deck—clipping an uphauler, or topping lift, halfway along its length and running the trimming line, or guy, through its outboard end. Another sheet was attached to the free end of the spinnaker. Several men wrestled the inboard end of the pole onto a mast-mounted fitting just above the deck while the topping lift was raised. The pole, made of solid wood, weighed 1,000 pounds. Christiansen ordered the halyard hoisted. The giant spinnaker flew up the mast. Once the halyard was made fast, the parachute of a sail was trimmed, the cotton yarn stops snapping as it filled with wind. *Reliance* jerked forward.

Barr wrestled the wheel, which had stiffened under the load of so much canvas. The afterguard looked aft for puffs—patches of dark water—as they drifted downwind toward them. With each puff, Barr braced the helm—a crewman, stationed at the second wheel, helping him maintain course. A minute after *Reliance*, *Shamrock III* hoisted her spinnaker, but "it was sheeted flatter," observed *The Rudder,* "and did not seem to do such good work as the sail on the Yankee craft."[23] While both yachts steered for the second mark the wind shifted to the south again, necessitating both boats to douse their spinnakers and rehoist their largest balloon jibs. That of *Reliance* was more than 180 feet long on the luff and 85 feet along the foot.[24] The work was exhausting, a series of successive sail changes requiring the below-decks crew to clear and reorganize the heaps of tangled sailcloth that had been tossed through the deck hatch from above. With each douse they aligned and banded (with yarn) the mountains of heavy canvas so that it could be rehoisted cleanly. Trapped inside a dimly lit steel cavern, the below-decks crew often worked in oppressively hot conditions. Sweating through their shirts, they worked quickly to organize the course cloth, often battering hands and skinning knuckles. When Barr called for a sail change, any delay was reprehensible. When the hatch opened and an officer called for a sail it was their job to make sure it was ready to go.

In the lead, *Reliance* rounded the second turning mark at 1:18:07, three minutes, fifty-seven seconds ahead of *Shamrock III*. Because of the wind shift, Barr was unable to hold his balloon jib and ordered it lowered and the working headsails hoisted. Capitalizing on Barr's mistake, Wringe called for the working headsails before rounding, making a cleaner turn and gaining on the Americans. As the breeze freshened, Wringe charged ahead, closing the gap, and chasing the clock. If he could finish within two minutes and fifty-one seconds of *Reliance* (the sum of one minute, fifty-seven seconds of corrected time and the one-minute, thirty-six-second difference in their official start times), he'd take the race and tie the series.

Yet another wind shift washed over the yachts, and both doused their baby jib topsails and hoisted their reaching jib topsails. Sailing one behind the other, the two yachts charged toward the finish. But as *Reliance* closed in, she slid into a windless patch. Although moving forward, her progress slowed, while *Shamrock III*, still in fresh winds, closed the gap. The excursion yachts listed as spectators crowded the rails with binoculars. Adjusting properly for the light winds, Barr sailed a hotter, or higher, angle toward the finish. *Reliance* slipped through the water, the crew sitting to leeward, artificially heeling the yacht so to help maintain shape in the sails. Barr held the helm lightly, steering with barely imperceptible movements. At 2:15:30 *Reliance* crossed the finish line. Once Barr had finished, all eyes turned to *Shamrock III* and the clock. Hope Iselin counted the seconds from the gun marking their finish time.

With sails pulling, Wringe had no choice but to sail through the same patch of light wind that had hindered Barr. *Shamrock III* lost momentum. The crowd watched the clock patiently as the yacht ghosted along. Because *Shamrock III* had started at the handicap gun, she had a window of three minutes and twenty-one seconds after *Reliance* in which she had to finish to win. With spectator boats crowding the revenue cutter patrol lines, and *Reliance* drifting quietly under mainsail alone, the seconds ticked away. The clock wound down. When the three-minute, twenty-one-second mark passed and *Shamrock III* had not crossed the line, a roar went up across the water. *Reliance* had won the second race.

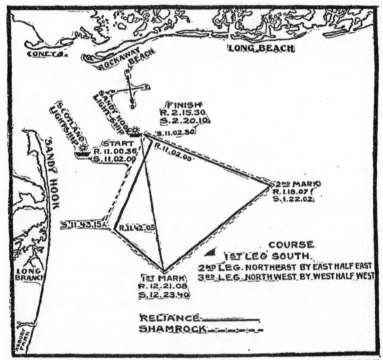

HOW THE YACHTS SAILED IN YESTERDAY'S TRIANGULAR RACE.

August 26, 1903: Diagram showing the courses sailed by *Reliance* and *Shamrock III* in the second race of the 1903 America's Cup series. (Courtesy of the *New York Times*.)

In almost any other racing sport, the drama of victory is staged in the final lunges to the finish. Even in clock-dependent sports, such as skiing, the competitors vie for the fastest time, posted clearly for all to see. In the America's Cup matches, however, yachts competed against one another as well as their theoretical boat speeds. A strange sight it was for the uninitiated to see the final protracted drama unfold: one boat crawled through glassy water as another bobbed listlessly, her crew cleaning up for the day, while twenty thousand people in their finest Sunday dress stared at their watches. When the time differential had elapsed—even though the yachts had barely moved—the crowd erupted. When *Shamrock III* finally crossed the finish line at 2:20:10, the crowd mustered a perfunctory cheer. The Americans had won by one minute and nineteen seconds corrected time. Nineteen seconds were attributed to Wringe's starting error. *Reliance* led the best-of-five series, two–nil.

Once the yachts had returned to the Horseshoe Harbor inside Sandy Hook, a black squall rolled in from the northwest. The sky "took on a deep coppery tint, almost the same that precedes the advent of the destroying twisting storms in the Western countries."[25] The temperature dropped twenty degrees, and driving rain accompanied by thunder, lightning, and fifty-five-mile-per-hour winds ripped through the harbor. Although *Shamrock III* and *Reliance* held fast to their moorings, Captain Nat's yacht *Roamer* broke loose and slammed into *Reliance's* tender *Sunbeam*. Still underway, J. P. Morgan's massive steamyacht *Corsair* was blown off course and her bowsprit "raked the side of the [excursion steamer] *Monmouth*." As the wind abated, *Cruizer*, one of Lipton's tenders, stood guard over *Shamrock III*, fending off two interlocked and drifting steamyachts.[26]

With racing scheduled for every other day, the crews spent the following morning and the afternoon of August 26 effecting repairs, combing the yachts' rigging, hull, and hardware for any signs of stress or damage. With so many thousands of pieces comprising a yacht of Cup-racing complexity, and the cataclysmic repercussions of even one small pin breaking (such as that holding the cap shroud of *Shamrock III* in Weymouth Bay), the crew made a special effort to ensure working order. If a small hairline fracture was detected, the fitting was replaced. If a splice had begun to chafe or unravel, crewmen made the repair. Because *Reliance* had raced the day before with a different gaff, the yacht was towed to Erie Basin and remeasured. Mower found that the new spar made no difference to the time allowance, confirming *Reliance's* victory from the day before.

Though brief, the passing squall portended a veritable plague of bad weather that had arrived and camped above New York. On Thursday, August 27, in light winds, the yachts started and then drifted for six hours off Sandy Hook, the time limit expiring with *Reliance* only six and a half minutes from the finish line. The racing was postponed until Saturday, and again the crews spent the day off preparing their yachts. But that morning another nor'easter slammed the East Coast and "kept the frail cup yachts cowering at their moorings."[27] The storm was so severe, that several ships sunk offshore. Charles Oliver Iselin and several New York Yacht Club members set out on board the race committee tug *Navigator* and saved nine men and two women on board the foundering yawl *Henry P. Mason.* The storm raged through Sunday and by Monday morning, August 31, with the gale subsiding, the yachts left the harbor.

The winds and seas were still high enough that Lipton advised some of his guests to stay home. Sailing under mainsails, the two yachts, wet with spray, bucked the residual rollers kicked up from the storm. As the two jockeyed for position at the start, Barr commanded the windward berth. As if releasing five days of pent-up aggression, in the final seconds before the starting gun "the British skipper . . . slipped away from him and whirled about on Reliance's weather bow. It was indeed a stirring sight as the two great seabirds, with their enormous wings outspread, slipped across the line, exactly at the same instant."[28] *Shamrock III* charged through the rolling swells easier than *Reliance,* which pushed spray off her bow like a plow through snow. *Shamrock III* footed fast in the favorable conditions. Despite the jostling ride, *Reliance,* with her powerful sails, bucked the waves, slowly reeling in *Shamrock III.* As the yachts approached the lee shore of Long Island and the sea state flattened, Barr shot ahead. After two hours of racing, *Reliance* was more than a mile in the lead and gaining. Herreshoff's yacht had simply pulled away.

Rounding the turning mark, *Reliance* cleanly set downwind sails and extended her lead. But again, the wind died and *Reliance,* drifting a half-mile short of the finish and three miles ahead of *Shamrock III,* simply waited, bobbing, until at 5:15 P.M. a gun signaled the time had expired. Although the weather had granted Lipton another chance, he was discouraged. "No one has any idea of how I have worried and fretted over this race," he told a *New York Herald* reporter.

No man was more confident of winning anything than I was when I came over. I didn't believe in gambling, but I would have been willing to bet the Erin that I would win. It is the greatest disappointment that I have ever had in all my life.

What can I do? I have tried my best. I cannot design a boat; I cannot sail one. I have common sense and I can see that the Reliance is the better boat. If I could design the challenger, then sail her, I might not be so blue to-day. There is no denying that I am sad and discouraged.

I have spent months of sleepless nights worrying over the challenger. It has been an awful strain. When the third Shamrock met with the accident off the hook—the time that she broke her mainsheet traveler—I simply collapsed. Every moment I have wondered what would happen to her. They tell me that I have a beautiful boat. I don't want a beautiful boat. What I want is a boat to lift the cup—a Reliance. Give me a homely boat, the homeliest boat that was ever designed, if she is like the Reliance.[29]

On September 1, the tenders towed their yachts to the starting line. "Both defender and challenger hung to their tugs, the *Guiding Star* and the *Cruizer*," wrote the *New York Times*, "as it was impossible to move about without their assistance. . . .There was not a breath of air about the Sandy Hook Lightship, and a thick fog hid the shore from view. . . .The surface of the gently heaving sea was smooth enough to reflect the tall masts and white and black hulls that rode its bosom."[30] Eager to resolve the series, Cup Committee members of the New York and Royal Ulster yacht clubs decided to attempt racing every day until a winner was decided. On September 2, the fleet of yachts traversed the glassy stretch of water between Sandy Hook and the lightship. "A mere shadow of the original excursion fleet went down the bay yesterday," observed the *New York Times*, "but undoubtedly it would have been larger had there been the slightest prospect of a race."

The picture around the lightship was ghostlike. The big yachts loomed up high, dimly outlined in the fog. There was no music or cheering as on the day before, and the silence was broken only by the regular warning of the lightship's foghorn. The only motion that ruffled the glassy surface of the waters was the quick, silent passage of a white steam yacht as it emerged from and vanished into the fog.[31]

Again, the race was postponed.

With each passing day anxiety escalated, the race committee eager to finish the series and the sailors eager to close the season. The sailors especially had grown tired of spending hours each day preparing their yachts for races that never happened. They uncoiled lines, removed heavy canvas sail covers, and then hauled headsails on deck and prepared them for hoisting. This was all done during the long nine-mile tow from Sandy Hook to the racecourse. Once the sails had been hoisted, they bobbed listlessly for hours waiting for wind. Once the race committee cancelled for the day, they doused and furled the sails and coiled the lines during the nine-mile tow home.

The same exasperation that plagued the crews had settled over Lipton. His yacht had faltered in the first two races. And now with day after day of inclement weather the guests that had previously streamed aboard his steamyacht *Erin* were gone. He and a handful of friends steamed out each day to no avail. Sanguine Jubilee Lipton grew melancholy. He had all but given up hope, ceding the patriotic rivalry to the Americans. Even after the second race, he praised American skill.

> I take my hat off to Mr. Herreshoff. He is a genius, and I take off my hat to Capt. Barr. They are too much for me.
>
> American brains and development have us beaten. If the day ever comes when England produces a Herreshoff then I will challenge for the cup again. It will not be until then. It is unpleasant to be compelled to admit it, but the brains in boat building are on this side of the water. Herreshoff is a wizard.[32]

At dawn on September 4, a light breeze picked up out of the south. By 8 A.M., the isolated puffs of wind had filled in and the race committee left the harbor, anchoring *Navigator* a quarter-mile west of Sandy Hook Lightship. The *John Scully* set a single turning mark fifteen miles south of the starting line, just east of Asbury Park. At 12:45 the preparatory signal sounded from *Navigator*. With both yachts sailing on starboard tack to the east, Barr held the windward berth by a third of a mile. The yachts ghosted through three mile-per-hour winds. Maintaining momentum was imperative. To lose speed and regain it would have been nearly impossible. The crews huddled on the leeward rail, inducing a false heel so to maintain shape in the sails. Both yachts carried their largest club topsails, *Reliance*'s the largest ever made.

The yachts tacked and stood westward parallel with the starting line, toward the *Navigator*. Barr tacked onto starboard. Halfway down the line, Wringe swung *Shamrock III* hard into the wind, coasting to windward on momentum alone. Having positioned his yacht farther to weather, Wringe bore off onto port tack and filled his sails. Behind, Barr tacked onto port and pursued Wringe. The second warning sounded at 12:55. *Shamrock III* soon tacked back onto starboard. The two yachts charged toward each other, gaining speed. Wringe held the right-of-way. As the two yachts converged, Barr swung *Reliance*'s bow hard under *Shamrock III*'s lee bow. "It looked as if Barr merely wanted to show his opponent how easily he could extricate himself from the worse position," wrote the *New York Times*, "for Reliance quickly reached to the front and out on Shamrock's weather bow."[33] Swinging a 202-footer into such a perfect lee bow position that one can sail ahead and to windward of one's opponent, all in three mile-per-hour winds, was like a perfect dive, where after a series of flips and turns the diver plunges gently into the water. Not only was this maneuver a testament to his virtuosity on the helm, but it also displayed the incredible efficiency of Herreshoff's design. With less power, *Reliance* would have simply stalled and lost momentum.

Holding a firm grip on *Shamrock III*'s weather bow, *Reliance* led both yachts to the west of the race committee boat. Attempting to free himself, Wringe bore off hard and jibed; Barr followed. After reaching speed, Barr turned toward the line, guarding the windward berth. The starting gun fired. "The smoke of the gun wrapped a veil about her sails," recalled the *Times* reporter.[34]

Instead of starting Barr maintained a windward hold on Wringe. Not wanting to start in Barr's turbulent air, Wringe held back, pinned by the Americans. Barr stalled until just before the handicap gun, starting at 1:01:56. Wringe, searching to no avail for a clear lane of wind, started late at 1:02:03, three seconds past the handicap gun. In crossing the line late, he carried three extra seconds of official sailing time, a strike against him. Barr had again manhandled him at the start.

Once *Shamrock III* had reached full speed Wringe tacked to port. Barr maintained his course. At 1:08:20 Barr tacked to port. The wind had built to five miles per hour. In the puffs, *Reliance* pointed higher than *Shamrock III*; in the lulls *Reliance* footed faster. Most of *Reliance*'s crew had shifted to windward, Herreshoff's giant wings drawing fully and the yacht heeling almost to her rails.

Both yachts sailed west toward Jersey Beach, *Reliance* gaining and establishing a clear lead. At 2:07:40 Wringe tacked onto starboard and thirty seconds later Barr tacked and covered him. *Shamrock III* sailed on port tack for half an hour. When Wringe tacked onto starboard at 2:31:30, Barr followed twenty seconds later and again covered him. In a building breeze both yachts heeled to their lines. Both doused their big jib topsails, *Shamrock III*'s crew taking a full minute longer than the Americans to set a baby jib topsail in its place.

Reliance tacked to starboard at 3:01:10 and then returned to port tack three minutes later. After sailing for 10 minutes, *Reliance* tacked again to starboard; *Shamrock III* followed, though considerably to leeward. At 3:36 *Reliance* reached the layline—the point at which after tacking she could "lay" or sail directly to the mark—and tacked to port, setting up for the final approach. Barr crooked his finger; Christiansen approached. He ordered the baby jib topsail doused and the ballooner hoisted bound in its yarn stops. As *Reliance* made her final approach to the mark, the bowsprit man signaled the closing distance. Barr started his turn.

As Barr eased the wheel to leeward, the trimmers eased their sails in unison, the giant boom and mainsail swinging open. *Reliance* carved through the turn. She rounded the mark at 3:40:39. Twenty-six seconds later the ballooner trimmer hauled his sheet and the stops popped up the length of the forestay, the sail filling. The foredeck crew hoisted the giant spinnaker pole, the sheets being led to their winches and the sail snaking up the mast on its halyard. And on Barr's command, the sheet was trimmed, the pole hauled back, and "in two minutes and six seconds after turning," reported *The Rudder*'s correspondent, "the big light sails were set and drawing nicely."[35]

Shamrock III rounded the turning mark cleanly eleven minutes, seven seconds behind at 3:51:46. Under the influence of a swell from the east, both yachts rolled under their colossal rigs. On the home stretch, Barr held a firm grasp on the lead. But a half hour after *Shamrock III* had rounded, Barr's afterguard, looking back to monitor Wringe's progress, watched as Wringe's trimmers continually eased the spinnaker pole forward, signaling a shifting breeze. Finally, Wringe ordered *Shamrock III*'s giant spinnaker doused, the foredeck crew working quickly to contain and pull through the forward hatch a mountain of sail. The wind shifted rapidly to the southeast. Wringe's afterguard looked aft with consternation. As was customary, he likely requested their consult while he steered *Shamrock III* to the fastest possible course. But his requests fell on deaf ears. The afterguard was baffled. The horizon suddenly loomed large, and within several minutes a wall of impenetrable fog engulfed them.

Reliance soon received the same wind shift from behind and within a few minutes Barr ordered the spinnaker dropped, the mainsheet trimmed, and the ballooner set. Captain Nat and Iselin peered aft into the mist but could not find *Shamrock III*. One way to predict the effects of oncoming weather was to monitor how it affected the yacht behind them. But *Shamrock III* had disappeared. With little information on which to base their next tactical move, Barr pointed his bow toward the finish and hoped for the best. In an instant the fog engulfed *Reliance*. "When I was about abreast of the 'Shamrock' the fog closed in on her," noted W. J. Sears aboard the mark tender *John Scully* in his summary statement to the race committee, "and, at the time, she appeared to be steering a course that should have taken her very close to the Light Ship. The same was true of the 'Reliance' when she was lost to my view on account of the fog."[36]

Soon after the yachts were consumed, the fog overran the spectator fleet. Horns and steam whistles rang out. Giant excursion steamers ghosted past each other, crewmen calling with bullhorns. They powered slowly, hovering in place as the southerly breeze and incoming tide set them askew. Boiler room attendants, on alert, fed their furnaces just enough coal to keep the engines warm and ready. Captains and crews maintained steady watch, peering into the fog, which had settled over them first as rolling mist, then as an impenetrable bank. Occasionally a whistle blew from nearby, and a captain returned the courtesy, announcing his location, lest they drift too close. When a ship loomed into view, whistles blew excitedly, sharp words were exchanged, and engines ground into gear. Holding the boats at bay, U.S. Navy ships and cutters from the Treasury Department patrolled what they blindly guessed was the racecourse boundary. The breeze grew cool. And the pell-mell fleet waited.

After an hour passed the excursion steamers were fully damp. "It was fortunate that the excursions fleet was very small," noted the *New York Time*'s correspondent, "because if a greater number of vessels had crowded the course, it would have been impossible to have prevented accidents in the thick fog . . ."[37] Unable to see the full length of the finish line, the race committee raised anchor and shortened it. And they waited.

Although *Shamrock III*'s progress was concealed, Lipton was hopeful. The fortuitous cloudbank afforded his yacht a fighting chance against *Reliance,* which when last seen held the lead. In yachts of such length, heavy fog made communication difficult between captain and crew, making mistakes, breakdowns, and injuries a distinct possibility. And there was always a chance a yacht could lose her way. Lipton could only hope the Americans would falter.

With her red Union Jack ensign hanging wet and limp off the stern, the 120-foot steamyacht *Erin,* allowed to pass through the patrol lines, hovered near a handful of New York Yacht Club steamyachts also exempt from the boundaries. The midday dinner had been served a few hours before and tea, breads, and deserts laid out for the guests. Lipton likely stood on *Erin*'s upper deck, forward of the main smoke stack. As was his custom onboard his yacht, he likely spoke casually with guests. But straying from his characteristic charm, he gazed passed them toward the finish line. If only there was a momentary break in the clouds, he could determine *Shamrock III*'s progress. As thick as the plumes of smoke from his London jam factory,[38] the fog dampened all hope of a glimpse. He had spent more than a year of dogged preparation, hiring the best designer, builder, captain, and crew in Europe, and spared no expense. His yacht, considered one of the most graceful ever built, shamed her gawky and overblown American competitor. Although he had praised the Americans' yachting prowess and had even sounded dejected in his public statements, he still held a glimmer of hope. Although the fog had provided a fighting chance, the lightship's groan was unnerving.

Following a compass course and unable to see his boat's bow, Barr, with Iselin and Captain Nat by his side, pressed on. They had likely agreed to a course before the fog settled in, and Barr stuck to it. The mates watched their sails and trimmed to accommodate the helmsman's course. His eyes glanced between the compass and the clouded canvases. Although we don't know what was said or done while rushing through the fog that day, we can guess that Herreshoff and Iselin were engrossed in the task of picking their way to the finish. Neither Captain Nat nor Iselin was likely to let down his guard. Although *Shamrock III* was behind them, they knew she would carry a new breeze first, a distinct advantage.

Hope Iselin counted down the time. By multiplying their time sailed with their speed through the water, and then factoring in their compass course, Captain Nat and Charles Oliver Iselin estimated their position. And with rapt determination they pushed toward the finish.

Heads turned to the sound of rushing water, groaning lines, and rustling sails, "as of the wings of some giant bird alighting from its lofty flight."[39] They heard the dull chime of halyards slapping a steel mast. High above the water a topsail dashed between clouds. The crowd peered into the brume. Then, from the race committee boat, an echoing shot signalling a yacht had finished ricocheted across the water. There had been no warning, no plodding final leg to the finish. Seemingly out of nowhere, the cannon shot had even startled some spectators. Carrying every possible sail, her hull veiled in mist, *Reliance,* like a billowing apparition, charged through the finish line. The bowsprit crew worked silently, wrestling the giant ballooner to the deck. With the sail down, Barr turned the yacht, sailing a higher angle and burying her rail in white foam. The masthead man, high in the rig, unfurled and hoisted to the topmast head a giant American yacht ensign. Crewmen set two more from the spreaders. The spectator fleet went wild. Cheers and a cacophony of steam whistles echoed through the haze. Spectators saluted *Reliance* as she ghosted through the fleet. And then, with a passing puff of wind and gentle plunge she "disappeared into the fog as mysteriously as she had risen out of it."[40] Once taken in tow by *Guiding Star, Reliance's* crew dropped the sails and raised one more ensign from the stern.

Watching their clocks, the crowd waited for *Shamrock III* to finish. Lipton hoped she could still win on corrected time. With his challenger veiled in fog, anything was possible. *Shamrock III* had to finish within two minutes of *Reliance* to win. Glancing from the fog to his watch, Lipton waited. The clock ticked down until finally two minutes had passed. They waited still longer for *Shamrock III* to appear, but nothing. After ten minutes, still nothing. Twenty minutes went by, then thirty—and all feared tragedy. But with a break in the fog *Shamrock III* appeared in the distance. Wringe, having lost his way, had steered so far east of the finish line that he was unable to hear the lightship's fog signal. Taken in tow, *Shamrock III* never completed the race. *Reliance* had won the America's Cup.

EPILOGUE

THE END OF AN ERA

September 1903–December 1944

Following the final race, the New York Yacht Club, Lipton, and members of the Royal Ulster Yacht Club, 150 people in all, met at the Waldorf-Astoria for a banquet hosted by the Pilgrims of the United States, an organization "to promote a better understanding between the two branches of the Anglo Saxon race, and to cement the tie of friendship between this country and Great Britain."[1] The dinner, held in the Astor Gallery, comprised a number of speeches, mostly congratulating Lipton for his sportsmanship and unflagging optimism in the face of defeat. Lipton, ever self-deprecating, vowed to return. "I am beginning to think there is some magic spell about that cruel old cup of yours," he told the reception hall.

> A few years ago it seemed to be within my grasp, but now it seems as far off as ever. I haven't even the consolation of that old Irish countryman of mine who, upon being asked if he could play a fiddle said he didn't know, for he'd never tired. I have, and I'll try again. I have made the proverbial three trials, but nevertheless I won't abide by the old decision of the third, and I hope I shall eventually succeed in capturing the famous trophy.
>
> However, you'll all agree with me in saying that I now seem somewhat astern. Unquestionably you have in Mr. Herreshoff the greatest designer of the age—but I want you distinctly to understand that you'll see that old cup on the other side yet.[2]

The next morning, *Reliance,* draped in decorative flags and American yacht ensigns, headed north under tow from the Sandy Hook Horseshoe through the Verrazano Narrows, past the Battery at the southern tip of Manhattan, under the Brooklyn Bridge, and north through Long Island Sound to Iselin's home at Premium Point. Remaining there for three days, *Reliance* was towed to City Island, where she was hauled at the Jacob's Yard, covered, and stored indefinitely. The crew was paid and discharged. In addition to his normal salary, Barr received a $1,000 bonus for winning the defender trials and another $1,300 for the successful Cup defense.

Rumors that Fife and Wringe had quarreled swirled. In an interview Wringe told a correspondent for the *New York Sun* that after the first race, Lipton had pulled him aside. Captain Wringe explained:

> That night, Sir Thomas sent for Capt. Bevis and myself, and he began talking about the results of the race, intimating that the Shamrock III should have won. I then said, "Why don't you send for Fife? He's the man. He knows how the boat was sailed, and surely he's got more at stake than I have and you should know it, Sir Thomas. We are not the men to be asked. See here, Sir Thomas, only one race has been sailed. You have other chances, and I tell you right here that I will step aside for any one and will do all I can to help him out, trim jib-sheet, haul on the mainsheet, do anything in my power to help *Shamrock III* to win.
>
> The facts are just these, as I saw them, and you can say right here that Barr in Shamrock III could no more beat me in the Reliance than I could him. The Reliance is the faster and better boat; that's all there is to it.[3]

Soon after returning to Osidge, his London mansion, Lipton expressed his intent to challenge again, sending an informal letter to George Cormack, the New York Yacht Club secretary. Lipton wanted to race smaller yachts; the New York Yacht Club didn't want to race at all. The string of biannual challenges had cost the Americans a lot of time and money—the *Reliance* defense alone was said to cost roughly a half million dollars—and they weren't keen on starting the laborious process of defending the Cup again. It seemed Iselin's plan to build a defender so extreme that it would dash all Lipton's hopes for future matches hadn't worked. But having trounced *Shamrock III, Reliance* served, at the very least, as a powerful deterrent from another challenge in ninety-footers. To dodge Lipton's request diplomatically, Cormack cited the America's Cup Deed of Gift, which stated if clubs should fail to agree on a measurement system, the terms of the match were "subject to the rules and sailing regulations" of the challenged club "but without any time allowance whatever."[4] This meant that if Lipton wanted to race a smaller seventy-foot boat—fine. But the New York Yacht Club would defend with whatever it wanted (most likely the bigger and faster *Reliance*) and the fastest boat would win—no clocks involved.

Lipton knew he couldn't win with a smaller yacht. Such a handicap was insurmountable. Even on an equal footing, Great Britain's finest designers, Watson and Fife, had bowed to the Americans. Since 1893 they'd taken five turns at Herreshoff and lost every time. Even after having pooled their knowledge in the early design stages of *Shamrock III*— considered the fastest challenger ever by both British and American critics—they failed miserably. To build and pit a smaller yacht against a larger was simply a waste of time and money. Herreshoff's behemoth, propped on wooden blocks at City Island, held Lipton at bay. *Reliance* had become the New York Yacht Club's loaded gun.

Cormack also stipulated that any discussion of changing measurement rules was out of the question until an official challenge had been delivered. "The New York Yacht Club," he wrote to Lipton, "does not feel that it can be asked to take a position upon such a question when no [official] challenge is pending or, so far as it is informed, even contemplated."[5] Lipton got the hint. They weren't going to change their minds.

During that same year, the New York Yacht Club officially adopted the design rule Nat had formulated. In his honor, they called it the Herreshoff Rule. Because of his unequivocal service to the club, a year earlier they'd also elected him an honorary member.[6] Also granting him honorary membership, the Seawanhaka Corinthian Yacht Club later adopted the new rule in 1904. On October 26, 1904, the New York Yacht Club gathered leaders of prominent American clubs at the Atlantic Coast Conference and further lobbied for the rule's adoption under the moniker "Universal Rule." At the same time, however, the club declared it was not bound by Nat's new formula. Although they had spearheaded a new design rule to discourage "unwholesome freaks," they maintained provisions that enabled them to pull *Reliance* off the shelf at any time to defend the Cup.[7]

But just as it appeared American yachtsmen had finally settled on a new rule, two of the design world's greatest practitioners met with tragedy. On November 12, 1904, George Lennox Watson died of a heart attack in Glasgow at age fifty-three. A year later, Captain Nat retreated from public life when his wife, Clara, died of cancer. He was crushed. She had raised their children and made his assiduous work schedule possible. Crippled by the loss, he grew reclusive and even more ornery. Without an outlet, he recoiled into his own impassivity. Upon the arrival of two tombstone sketches he'd ordered for his wife, he crossed out one and above the other wrote, as he'd done with every drawing he'd approved throughout his life, "This accepted . . . NGH."[8]

That year the New York Yacht Club received an invitation to send delegates to an international measurement conference in London, scheduled for January 15, 1906. Prior to the conference, Commodore Lewis Cass Ledyard, an attorney, notified the organizers that the United States would not attend, for it could not take part in the formation of an International Rule without seriously hurting the sport at home. One aversion stemmed from the fear that even if American delegates successfully argued for international adoption of Herreshoff's Universal Rule, the New York Yacht Club didn't want to be bound by it in the Cup arena. At that conference a new "International Rule" was formed and in subsequent years proliferated outside of the United States.

Despite the political wrangling over measurement rules, in 1907 Lipton officially challenged again, this time through the Royal Irish Yacht Club in Dublin. He proposed to race under the J Class or sixty-eight-foot rating rule. "I am animated solely," he wrote, "by a desire to see the famous America's Cup competed for by a more wholesome and seaworthy type of boat than that which has been adopted in recent contests."[9] The New York Yacht Club rejected it, reasoning that beyond the J Class stipulation Lipton and the Royal Irish Yacht Club had failed to provide the complete "dimensions of the challenging vessel."[10] They'd cited this finical pretense to mask the fact that they didn't have a designer. After probing Captain Nat on the efficacy of modifying a ninety-footer to face Lipton, he had flat out told them no. "It is necessary for me to say how distressed I was to hear of your decision not to build any more defenders," wrote E. D. Morgan upon receiving the refusal. "This will be a very serious matter for the Club . . . as soon as I had read your letter it occurred to me to ask you not to make known your decision for the immediate present as it might influence Lipton's plans."[11] Nat told no one and the New York Yacht Club rejected the challenge.

After overseeing the hauling and stowage of *Reliance* at City Island, he and Captain Lem Miller purchased *Shamrock II,* which later sold for scrap. Barr then assumed command of the 120-foot steel schooner *Ingomar* built by the Herreshoff brothers for Morton F. Plant. In April 1904, Barr sailed to Europe and dominated the English racing circuit. True to his aggressive style, when German skippers thought they could bully Barr he didn't flinch, twice slamming into rivals. In 1905, he commanded the three-masted schooner *Atlantic* in a race from New York to the Lizard in Cornwall, England. He finished in twelve days and four hours, winning the German Emperor's Cup, and setting a course record unbroken in formal competition until 2005—a hundred years later. For the next five years he dominated the seventy-foot class in America and in 1910 sailed Captain Nat's 136-foot steel schooner *Westward* to Europe, where again he was unstoppable. But in 1911, while in Southampton, England, Barr had a heart attack and died. He was forty-seven years old. "I was notified of Barr's death early this morning," George Cormack wrote to Captain Nat on January 24, the day Barr died, "and it caused me very much regret and sadness. He will be indeed difficult to replace—if we ever get another one as good."[12] At the funeral, the officers and crew of Lipton's steamyacht *Erin* served as pallbearers. His coffin was covered with both the Union Jack and the Stars and Stripes.[13] To the *New York Times,* Cormack avowed, "Captain Barr was the greatest skipper who ever lived."[14]

In 1913 Lipton challenged again. A series of correspondence crossed the Atlantic from February 28 to September 12. Lipton announced his intention to challenge in a seventy-five-foot waterline yacht. The New York Yacht Club rejected it. Lipton persisted, and finally the New York Yacht Club conceded, citing its right to defend with a ninety-footer. Lipton agreed and pressed on. Only later, after bowing to political pressure and charges of unsportsmanlike conduct, did the New York Yacht Club's Cup Committee agree to build a seventy-five-footer. "The financial conditions in America do not warrant such extravagant sums [as the last competition] being spent on pleasure," reported the *New York Times* in explaining the shift to smaller yachts, "even if it is to enable the United States to maintain the yachting supremacy of the world."[15] Once the challenge was accepted and the Cup committee decided not to defend with a ninety-footer, *Reliance,* which had waited dutifully in case of a challenge, was lowered down the ways at City Island and floated for the first time in ten years. Towed to the Robins Shipyard in South Brooklyn, she was dismantled. The stacked plates of bronze, angle bars of steel, giant lead keel, and crates of miscellaneous fittings and fasteners strewn slapdash around the yard marked the end of an era. The last of the behemoths was gone. Never again would boats so large and complex race for the Cup. A few months later her topmast crowned the 220-foot flagpole behind the centerfield scoreboard at Brooklyn's Washington Park near the Gowanus Canal, the home stadium for the Federal League's Brook-Feds. The lower section of the spar was stepped as the mainmast on the 162-foot steel schooner *Katoura,* the largest vessel the Herreshoff Manufacturing Company ever produced. *Constitution's* spar served as the foremast.

Ultimately, Captain Nat had agreed to one more defender, and at 6:30 P.M. on April 25, 1914, he gave a nod and *Resolute* slid down ways of the north construction shop. In August of that year World War I erupted in Europe and yachting halted, the Cup races uncompleted. Lipton stored *Shamrock IV* and converted *Erin* into a hospital ship, which he donated to the War effort. The yacht was later sunk by a German submarine. Captain Nat was sixty-six years old and with his increasingly severe bouts of rheumatism and other ailments, his doctors instructed him to have all his teeth removed, a painful procedure requiring months of rest. Having handed much of the designing work to his son Sidney, Captain Nat started wintering in Bermuda.

In 1915, while the War raged on, John Brown accepted a large order for torpedo boats from the Russian government. He had already deposited the check when Nat returned from Bermuda and quashed the lucrative contract. The commission would have lead to more deals with France and the United States, but Nat wanted nothing to do with it. Herreshoff biographer, Samuel Carter, contends Nat was reluctant "to contribute to a war that set America's friends against Germans."[16] We don't know if this is true. We do know that filling the rush orders would have required the brothers to expand the plant, a labor-intensive venture Nat was unwilling to enter. On July 15, the brothers entered a heated argument, but Nat wouldn't budge. Crushed, John Brown went home. Angry with Nat, he avoided the office for several days. Later that week he died in his sleep. "[T]he company lost something when J. B. died that was never regained," wrote L. Francis Herreshoff, "and the whole place seemed different after his death. After all J. B. was human even if N. G. was too busy to be."[17] Three months later, on October 7, Nat married forty-two-year-old

Ann Roebuck, who had come to Bristol to help nurse Clara in her final days.

When the war ended, Lipton's challenge was renewed on August 2, 1919. A year later *Resolute* and *Shamrock IV* met on the starting line marked by the Ambrose Channel Lightship off New York City. Although *Shamrock IV* won the first two races, *Resolute* bounced back and successfully defended the Cup. Captain Nat was seventy-two years old; *Resolute* was his last defender.

Without John Brown to manage the shop, the business lost all direction. Carving models, drawing plans, crunching numbers, and building complex machinery had been Nat's strong point. He'd never managed payrolls or vender accounts. Knowing this facet of business was beyond him, he had organized a few wealthy patrons mainly from the New York Yacht Club to form a stock-holding company. Although Nat, his son Sidney, and a new rising star in naval architecture, W. Starling Burgess (Edward Burgess's son), continued to produce viable designs, the company would never rebound. Yachting had been hit hard by the war. By 1924, Nat and his new board of directors decided to sell. When no one would buy, they auctioned the Herreshoff Manufacturing Company for a pittance.

Rudolph F. Haffenreffer, the owner of a prosperous Rhode Island brewery, purchased the business and vowed to continue the firm's good name. He asked Captain Nat and Sidney if they'd enter a partnership. Having sold most of his shares in the company before John Brown died, Nat earned a comfortable pension. He spent his winters in Florida and left most of the yard work to his son. Averse to entering a new business venture at seventy-six, Nat declined, agreeing only to consult. Sydney, however, stayed on as an employee. Although Nat spent more and more time in Florida, he and his son maintained a lively correspondence about design rules and construction techniques. They sent letters often, discussing professional ideas but rarely broaching personal subjects.

Even into his seventies, Lipton continued to be one of Britain's leading socialites, his name dotting newspapers on both sides of the Atlantic. He frequented theaters and rubbed shoulders with royalty and wealthy businessmen, most notably (although he was a lifelong teetotaler) the Scotch whiskey magnate Tom Dewer. At the end of the war

Congress passed the National Prohibition Act. Although his friend took a hit, the ban on alcohol spurred tea sales, and Lipton's North American business boomed. But in Britain, he was not prepared for a changed post-war business climate. Although his chain had grown to over six hundred branch stores, he ran them as he'd done in the 1890s, having neglected to modernize his machinery and accounting methods. In addition, he developed a debilitating sense of paranoia, installing listening devices in his London offices and goading managers to spy on each other. He continued to fire employees at the slightest provocation and hired replacements as he'd done in his youth, solely on intuition. His judgment, however, had dulled. In 1924, profits slipped. In 1925 they dove. After shareholders did not receive dividends that year, they organized an exhausting investigation of the accounts. When they unearthed a long list of shortcomings, the board of directors sacked him. Ceremoniously given the title of "life president and chairman," Lipton no longer filled a managerial role in the company's British holdings. Stripped of his authority, he turned to his American business over which he still held control.[18]

Basking in his American notoriety, Lipton soaked up everything the roaring twenties had to offer. He frequented clubs and shows and, of course, American yachting events, and the papers followed his every move. In 1929, the New York Yacht Club accepted Lipton's fifth challenge for the America's Cup and on his terms: yachts were to be built to the J Class rule without time allowance and races would begin with a single starting gun. Upon mutual agreement, they decided to hold a best-of-seven series in Newport, Rhode Island, the popular summer resort where many New York Yacht Club members had built luxurious mansions. And unlike Sandy Hook, Newport was blessed with consistent summer winds.

Harold Vanderbilt funded and skippered the defender *Enterprise*. The yacht had been designed by W. Starling Burgess (Nat's pupil and the son of Nat's Cup predecessor Edward Burgess), a Harvard-educated poet cum architect who'd spent the war designing combat planes for England. While building *Enterprise* at the Herreshoff yard, Burgess tapped Nat's vast library of drawings and employed many of Nat's inventions used on *Reliance* and *Resolute*. *Enterprise* integrated a number of technological breakthroughs, such as the Park Avenue boom, which allowed better control of sail shape and a duralumin (aluminum alloy) mast weighing roughly 1,200 pounds less than those made of steel. Charles E. Nicholson designed *Shamrock V*. Straying from the norms of construction, he built Lipton's newest yacht of wood, laying 3¼-inch teak planking over steal frames. He built the mast from wood. Lipton arrived in Newport with all the fanfare of past challenges, entertaining throngs of guests on his new steamyacht *Erin* (formerly the *Albion*). *Enterprise* won four straight races. Heartbroken, Lipton told reporters, "I can't win. I can't win." A few days later, his spirits having risen, Lipton left New York, vowing to challenge again.

In May 1931, Lipton turned eighty-three years old, although he claimed to be eighty-one. The Royal Yacht Squadron finally accepted his membership. That summer from the stern of *Erin* and *Shamrock V* he flew the white ensign, an honor bestowed only on members of the Royal Yacht Squadron and ships of the British Royal Navy. In September of that year while out for a drive, Lipton caught a cold. After spending a week in bed, he showed signs of improvement. He dressed, invited some friends for dinner. That night, however, he was found unconscious. He died the next day.

While the Universal Rule truncated extreme proportions on American racing yachts, the International Rule had the same effect in Britain. The era of big-boat racing had come to an end. There were still large yachts being designed and built, but they no longer formed the backbone of racing circuits. Despite the lack of these lucrative commissions, Fife met success designing the Meter classes, including the 6-, 8-, 12-, and 23-Meter yachts. Following the First World War, business ebbed. At that time Fife's America's Cup associate and friend Captain Robert Wringe died. Although business picked up again in the latter part of the decade, by the mid-1930s the Fairlie yard was forced to build boats on spec. In 1939 there were only three yachts built. After more than 140 years and 1,000 boats, upon the outbreak of the Second World War, William Fife & Son closed. On August 11, 1944, William Fife Jr. died. He was eighty-seven years old.

In 1903 the Denny yard built forty-four vessels, more than any other year in its history. The Denny Flow Tank continued to improve the world's understanding of fluid dynamics. In their power vessels, the Denny yard had garnered a superlative reputation and in 1905 they were placed on the Admiralty list. During the following years they built everything from torpedo boats and cargo ships to passenger vessels, barges, and submarines. They also parlayed their years of screw propeller data into a prototypical helicopter. With six propellers, each twenty-five feet in diameter and powered by a forty-horsepower gasoline engine, the contraption struggled to leave the ground. The first version was destroyed in a windstorm and a subsequent prototype was ultimately abandoned as military orders flooded the yard at the start of World War I.[19] The yard boomed through the Second World War, on average building one vessel per working fortnight.[20] But orders waned in the 1950s and the Denny yard struggled to make ends meet. The last of the family dynasty, Sir Maurice Denny, died in 1955, and in the early 1960s the company entered liquidation.

In early December 1931, flames reflected across Bristol Harbor. That evening townspeople watched as the Herreshoff-Brown estate, Nat's childhood home, the home built by Nathaniel Byfield, the town's colonial founder, burnt to the ground. A month later on New Year's Day, 1932, Nat's friend, the great yachtsman and manager Charles Oliver Iselin died in his country home at Brookville, Long Island, after battling years of illness. Nat was not there to see the house or his friend go. For the last few winters Love Rocks had remained dormant. Nat and Ann Roebuck had taken to spending all but summer in Coconut Grove, Florida, with Ralph Munroe, a friend they'd met while cruising in southern waters aboard *Helianthus,* their sixty-four-foot, gasoline-powered motoryacht. In their discussions of yachts and sailing, Nat and Munroe struck up a close friendship. On Munroe's property Nat built a small shack at the edge of Biscayne Bay. The two men, both in their eighties, spent their days in Munroe's boathouse, poring over old yacht photographs and discussing designs. Having grown too old to handle his own boats, Nat contented himself with building models, which he and Munroe tested with acute attention to detail. He also penned lines for the gaff-rigged Biscayne Bay Class and a number of other small daysailers. He had been designing boats for so long in his all-consuming way that without a drafting board, paper, and tools, without his vise, chisels, and plains, he was adrift, as if stripped of his identity. Since he was nine years old, he'd worked tirelessly so that the shapes of hulls, and sails, and their two-dimensional representation had become impulsive, reflexive, and so familiar they no longer represented a task but a comfort. He'd always been compelled to test his ideas, drafting sketches at the mere hint of an order, often with total disregard for contracts or the customer's wishes. For Nat, the need to design was so compulsive that he'd spend hours at his drafting table working, sketching his thoughts, even when he knew the boat would never be built.

In July 1924, just before the Herreshoff Manufacturing Company met the auction block, Nat received a letter from Mr. H. Wilmen Hanan of Brooklyn asking for a gasoline motoryacht. Nat didn't know the man personally, but sent him a multipage reply including profile and interior layout sketches. In the body of the letter he ran through the design particulars, providing dimensions for everything from the engine room and galley to the fish well and dining room: "Engine room is 11'4" long with average width of about 10'," he noted. "The aft part of the engine room will be about 7½' high and the forward part about 5½' high." After running through the specifications with incredible detail, he then explained:

> Perhaps you don't know the condition of our Works. Ever since the reorganization seven years ago it has been losing money and now the directors have decided to end up and sell the plant at auction. This auction sale is set for the 15th of next month. So we are in no condition at the present moment to consider taking on new work. My hope is that some interested yachtsman will buy the place and find a competent man to take charge of it so that it will not be a losing investment. My opinion is it will depend only on getting the right man. Personally, I gave up active control and most of the designing at the reorganization with intention of retiring entirely. I have been hanging around helping, part of the time, but with the coming sale I will be out of it altogether. I have worked up this little sketch simply for the love of designing.[21]

That a man harried with the pressure of selling his business while completing existing orders would spend hours designing a yacht with meticulous accuracy, knowing full well that he could not fill the order, exemplified the extent to which a life of drafting and carving models had framed his personality.

With the approach of winter 1936, Nat felt too weak to head south. He climbed the stairs to his third-floor drawing room, stooped over his desk, and penned the sketch of a bed in which he could bide the Bristol winter. The bed was equipped with mounts for drafting and writing tables and an eating tray, shelves for books and nautical charts, a wind-speed indicator, a barometer, and cubbies for drafting tools and reading glasses. In the spring he had workmen mount a mirror in the window so he could watch the comings and goings at the yard, in particular the J Class yacht *Ranger,* which was tuned there prior to the 1937 America's Cup races with *Endeavour II.*

He spent the next year in Bristol, his grandchildren and close relatives visiting often, especially on Sundays. During that time he notated his will, dividing his estate in equal portions among the family. He concluded an ongoing correspondence with the yachting writer W. P. Stephens[22] and also received his longtime benefactors J. P. and E. D. Morgan, Harold Vanderbilt, and upon his request, Charles E. Nicholson, who'd designed all the British Cup challengers since 1920. When W. Starling Burgess visited and broached the topic of religion, Nat balked. He later told his wife, "Sometimes I think Starling talks a little foolish."[23] Although Nat had never been a political man, Franklin Delano Roosevelt's Democratic platform spurred his ire. "If everyone worked hard, used his head, and saved," L. Francis recalled him saying, "he would be all right and the whole country would be prosperous." When his son asked him about the poor, he barked, "The only way to do away with the poor is to prevent the poor from having children."[24]

L. Francis, then working as a naval architect in Marblehead, visited his father on his birthday in March of 1938. "When I left him," he wrote, "he said I might never see him again, and while this proved true I had thought that he seemed so bright and was so mentally alert that he might last some time, but there came a time when he could no longer even get out of bed, and then he said that he would rather die than to become such a care and nuisance . . ."[25]

On June 2, 1938, Captain Nat's heart stopped. He died in bed. Less than four months later, with little warning, gusts of 186 miles per hour swept up Narragansett Bay. The Great Hurricane of 1938 left the Herreshoff Manufacturing Company in ruins. Half the south construction shop had been destroyed. Lifted off their blocks from the storm surge and high winds, many yachts at the yard were smashed. Some, only superficially damaged, weathered the storm. Others splintered. All told, across Southern New England, the storm destroyed 2,605 vessels and damaged 3,369.[26] *Riviera*, the skiff Nat and his brother had sailed across Europe in 1874, was never seen again.

After effecting repairs the Haffenreffers tried to sell, but there were no takers. On September 1, 1939, Hitler invaded Poland and within a year, with America on the brink of war, orders again stacked up at the Burnside Street office. Nat's son Sidney had become chief designer, and by the war's end they'd launched more than a hundred military vessels. But when the fighting stopped so did the orders. The Haffenreffers auctioned the land, buildings, tools, and machinery for $36,200.[27] The shops were razed, the piers dismantled, and soon after, all semblance of the Herreshoff working waterfront was gone.

In the century of Cup competition since *Reliance,* much has changed. Design formulae have evolved alongside construction methods, materials, and racing rules. After the ninety-footers, the America's Cup saw seventy-five-footers (1920), the J Class (1930 to 1937), the 12-Meter class (1958 to 1987), an aberrant ninety-footer versus a catamaran (1988), and the International America's Cup Class (IACC) yachts (1992 to present). And since 1983 when *Australia II* became the first syndicate ever to wrest the Cup from the New York Yacht Club, breaking the longest winning streak in sports history, the trophy has hopped from Australia to San Diego to New Zealand and onto its current home in Switzerland.

Although *Reliance* was the last of the giants, heralding a new, transformative era in Cup racing, she also canonized the themes now entrenched in modern Cup competition. That designers continue to produce lightweight yachts flirting with breakdown never fails to draw criticism. That foreign crews and outsourcing construction dilutes nationalism has been a reoccurring bone of contention. Litigious wrangling over the Deed of Gift has become a veritable institution. And design rule changes smolder in never-ending debate.

Despite these squabbles, the America's Cup is still sailing's most coveted trophy. There are other notable races, but the Cup reigns supreme. Why? Its longevity is certainly paramount. But perhaps its close association with wealth and power—those wielding considerable cultural influence—has established the America's Cup as something more, a competition that in each edition reifies the economic, political, and social climate of the times. In 1903, *Reliance* asserted America's efficacy as a world power; in the upcoming 2007 races, might syndicates backed by multinational corporations and crewed by sailors from around the world become the apotheosis of globalization?

Although caught in this tug-of-war between tradition and change, the America's Cup will evolve. Designers will use the latest and lightest materials. They will build boats that some consider ugly, and they will build boats that break. And grumbling over patriotism, escalating costs, rule changes, and the Cup's restive ancient charter will inevitably continue.

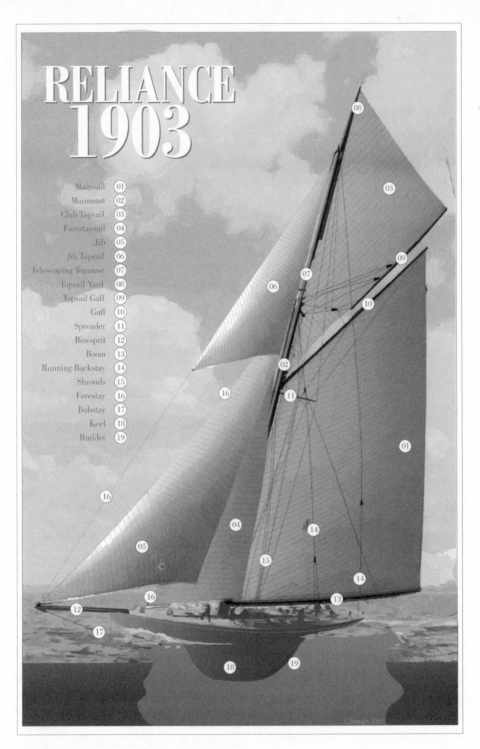

RELIANCE
1903

Mainsail 01
Mainmast 02
Club Topsail 03
Forestaysail 04
Jib 05
Jib Topsail 06
Telescoping Topmast 07
Topsail Yard 08
Topsail Gaff 09
Gaff 10
Spreader 11
Bowsprit 12
Boom 13
Running Backstay 14
Shrouds 15
Forestay 16
Bobstay 17
Keel 18
Rudder 19

(Illustration by C. Stauch)

aft. Behind the midpoint of a vessel when looking at a her lengthwise.

afterguard. Those sailors usually situated at the aft end of the boat designated to advise the helmsman on navigation, time, weather, and tactical decisions.

afterguy. A line used to control the windward spinnaker clew and the fore-and-aft movement of the spinnaker pole.

backstay. A wire rope supporting the mast from the aft end of the boat.

bad air. Air turbulence caused by another boat's sails.

balloon jib or ballooner. A giant headsail clipped to the forestay used for sailing across the wind or downwind.

beat. To sail toward the direction of the wind.

belaying cleat. A T-shaped fitting bolted to a deck or dock to which lines are fastened.

belowdecks. Any part of the space under a boat's deck.

bend. To fasten.

block. A pulley.

boom. The spar to which the foot of the mainsail is attached.

bow. The front of a vessel.

bowsprit. A spar projecting forward from the bow.

brigantine. A two-masted sailing vessel with a square-rigged sail on the foreward mast and a fore-and-aft set sail on the after mast.

capstan. A winch sitting vertically on its drum used for hauling heavy loads.

centerboard. A moveable keel capable of being raised to reduce drag while sailing downwind or lowered to increase lateral resistance when sailing upwind.

chain plate. Iron or steel fittings bolted internally to each side of a vessel to which the shrouds (supporting the mast) are attached.

clear ahead. A yacht that has no overlap with the yacht behind it.

clew. The aft-most corner of a three-sided sail.

coaming. A raised ridge built around a ship's hatches to prevent water from entering.

committee boat. A boat on which the principal race organizers reside. A flag posted on the committee boat marks one end of the starting line. A mark or another boat marks the other end of the line.

cover. To sail a course that mirrors one's opponent so to prevent him from passing.

deck line. The outline of the deck when viewing a vessel from above.

diagonals. The lines of a boat sweeping at an angle from stem or stern. In a design schematic, diagonals intersect sectional lines. A designer notes the distance between the points of intersection and the boat's centerline in his table of offsets.

downwind. Away from the direction of the wind. A downwind boat is farther from the direction of the wind than an upwind boat.

draft. The depth of a boat below the waterline.

ease. To let out.

fall off the wind. To steer a boat away from the direction of the wind.

feathering. When sailing upwind, the act of periodically steering a boat slightly into the wind so to maximize her upwind progress and spill excess wind from her sails.

foot (of sail). The bottom edge of a sail.

forestay. A wire rope supporting the mast from the bow.

foreguy. A line that secures the spinnaker pole to the bow.

foothold. An angled piece of wood secured to the deck to help crewmen brace themselves when the boat heels.

footing. When sailing upwind, the act of steering a boat slightly away from the wind so to fill her sails and maximize speed.

gaff. A spar supporting the top edge of a four-sided for-and-aft sail.

garboard. The first strake or plank laid next to a boat's keel.

halyard. A line used to haul a sail aloft. Halyards are also used to adjust sail shape.

hank. A ring or clip used to attach a headsail to a forestay.

head. The top corner of a three-sided sail.

header. A wind shift that forces a yacht to sail an angle farther from the windward mark when sailing upwind or allows a yacht to sail a closer angle to the leeward mark when sailing downwind.

headsail. Sails set in front of the mast.

heel. To lean or tilt on edge due to the force wind exerts on the sails.

hull. The body of a vessel, excluding her mast, sails, rigging, and hardware.

jackyard topsail. A three-sided sail hoisted above a gaff-rigged mainsail.

jib topsail. A three-sided headsail hoisted to the top of the outermost forestay.

jibe. Turning a vessel so that the wind crosses her stern. The opposite of tacking.

keel. The structural backbone of a sailing vessel running lengthwise along the ventral centerline from bow to stern. The keel usually contains the bulk of a vessel's ballast.

keelson. A load-bearing structural component mounted atop the keel that supports the mast.

knot. One nautical mile (6,076 feet) per hour.

lapstrake. Laid overlapping.

lee bow. In a crossing situation, this is a defensive maneuver in which the port-tack boat tacks to leeward and slightly in front of the starboard-tack boat in an attempt to cast turbulent air onto her opponent's sails.

leeward. Opposite from the direction of the wind. The leeward boat is farther from the direction of the wind than the windward boat.

lift. A wind shift that allows a yacht to sail an angle closer to the windward mark when sailing upwind or forces a yacht to sail an angle farther from the leeward mark when sailing downwind.

luff. To point a ship's bow into the wind, allowing her sails to flutter. The same effect can be accomplished by easing the sails beyond the point of proper trim.

mainsail. The large fore-and-aft sail fastened to the aft side of a sailing vessel's mainmast.

mainsheet. The line used to trim the mainsail.

mast. The tall vertical spar that supports a vessel's sails and rigging.

mast step. The area where the bottom of the mast attaches to the hull of a sailing vessel.

midships. The center of a vessel along her length or width.

port. The left side of a vessel when facing forward.

port tack. The condition of sailing with the wind blowing over the port side of the boat.

pinch. To steer a sailing vessel at an angle so close to the wind that her sails are not completely full.

prismatic coefficient. The extent to which a vessel's hull is narrow or full in shape. The larger the coefficient, the fuller the shape; the smaller the coefficient, the finer it is. If a yacht's prismatic coefficient is too big, the yacht will produce excessive drag. If the prismatic coefficient is too small, the yacht will produce an excessive quarter wave.

overhang. The portion of the forward or aft end of a boat that is not in the water.

overtaking yacht. A vessel that is passing another from behind.

race committee. A group of people designated to organize and run races. They manage the starts, time the races, and superintend judges who oversee rule disputes.

rail. The place where the deck line meets the topsides or side of the boat. While sailing upwind, a racing crew always sits or lays lined along the windward rail.

rake. The degree to which a mast leans backward toward the stern.

rating rule. A formula used to calculate a yachts theoretical speed potential.

reaching. Sailing across the wind.

reef and double reef. To reduce the size of a sail by partially lowering it and binding the excess cloth in stops. A double-reefed sail is shortened more than a single-reefed sail.

rig. The arrangement of spars, rigging, and sails.

rig tune. Like a violin, a rig can be tuned so that its spars, rigging, and sails work in harmony.

rigging. A combination of standing rigging, the stays and shrouds that hold the mast and other spars in place, and the running rigging, the myriad lines used to hoist and trim the sails.

right-of-way. The right of a vessel under the racing rules to pass in front of another.

ring bolt. Bolts equipped with fitted rings. These are sometimes used at the end of the chain plates.

rudder. A foil-shaped structure on the underside of a boat used for steering.

rudder post. A steel tube passing through the hull to which the rudder is attached.

running. Sailing with the wind.

running backstay or runner. Adjustable stays running from the mast to winches mounted on the starboard and port sides of the aft deck.

sandbagger. A type of centerboard sailing vessel with such a large sail area that crewmen used moveable bags of sand for ballast.

scow. A flat-bottomed boat.

sheave. The wheel inside a pulley.

shroud. Stays fastening the mast to the sides of the boat.

sheet. A line used to trim sails.

skylight. A piece of glass, usually in the shape of a prism, set into the deck of a vessel to allow light belowdecks.

sloop. A single-masted boat with one sail aft of the mast and one or more headsails.

spar. Any poles such as masts, booms, spinnaker poles, gaffs, or yards, that support sails on a sailing vessels.

spinnaker. A large parachute-like three-sided sail set forward of the mast and used when sailing downwind.

spreader. A load-bearing horizontal support used to hold the shrouds away from the mast.

starboard. The right side of a vessel when facing forward.

starboard tack. The condition of sailing with the wind blowing over the starboard side of the boat.

staysail. A lower headsail clipped to the innermost forestay.

stern. The aft end of a vessel.

tack. Turning a vessel so that the wind crosses her bow. The opposite of jibing.

taffrail. The rail that wraps around the stern of a vessel.

throat halyard. The halyard hauling the upper front corner of a four-sided mainsail.

topmast. A spar that extends upward from the mainmast. The topsail yard, jib topsail, and spinnaker are set from the topmast.

topping lift. A line used to lift the spinnaker pole off the deck.

topsail. See **jackyard topsail** and **jib topsail**.

traveler. A load-bearing metal bar mounted near the stern which the mainsheet runs from the boom. On *Reliance*, the mainsheet ran from the boom to the traveler and was then led forward to the crewmen lining the windward deck.

trim. To adjust the shape of a sail with control lines such as halyards and sheets so to maximize its efficiency.

upwind. Toward the direction of the wind. An upwind boat is closer to the wind than a downwind boat.

warning, preparatory signals. The canon blasts signaling the time during a race starting sequence.

weather. Toward the direction of the wind. The terms "weather" and "windward" are interchangeable.

wind shadow. The area of turbulent air caused by a yacht's sails.

windward. Toward the direction of the wind. The terms "windward" and "weather" are interchangeable.

windward advantage. In one-on-one match racing a yacht that holds the windward position at the start not only starts the race first but also maintains the ability to blanket her opponent with her sails.

windward mark. The turning mark on a racecourse located closest to the direction of the wind.

ACKNOWLEDGMENTS

I owe sincere thanks to Halsey and Nat Herreshoff III; they first clued me in to the importance of *Reliance* and, in my conversations with them, I came to realize what a unique character their grandfather, Nathanael Herreshoff, was. Halsey provided access to Captain Nat's personal letters and other uncatalogued material. Nat sent me numerous invaluable envelopes filled with photocopied packets of information, including his own ongoing research into his family's history. At the Herreshoff Museum I would also like to thank Museum Curator John Palmieri and Librarian Elizabeth Middleton, for generously lending their time and expert knowledge of the museum's collections. And thank you to Dave Ford for introducing me to them. Also, thank you to archivist and librarian Norene Rickson for letting me look over her shoulder as she catalogued boxes of Nathanael Herreshoff's original correspondence. And thank you to Halsey, John, and Norene for providing some wonderful photos.

I would like to thank Ed Kelly and John Rousmaniere for arranging access to the New York Yacht Club library. While conducting his own research, John often pulled relevant articles for me, fielded my questions, and always pointed me in the right direction. His knowledge of yachting history, the library, and the America's Cup archives is unparalleled. I would also like to thank Bill Watson, the former New York Yacht Club librarian. Thank you also to John Jay Iselin for providing valuable information about the life of Charles Oliver Iselin.

At the Mystic Seaport Museum G. W. Blunt White Library, I would like to thank Wendy Shnur and Paul O'Pecko for guiding me through the library's physical and digitized holdings. Also, thank you to Peggy Tate Smith for providing the wonderful *Reliance* photos from the Mystic Seaport Collection. I would like to thank Kurt Hasselbalch, curator of MIT's Hart Nautical Collection, for walking me through the *Reliance* design plans and answering my many questions about the plan list and Nathanael Herreshoff's academic record at MIT. Tom Nye, City Island historian and sailmaker at UK City Island, educated me on the history of City Island, its boatyards, and Ratsey's sail loft and spent the time to show me the City Island Maritime Museum's library and collection of photos.

In Glasgow, Scotland, I would like to thank Hazel McLatchie for helping me navigate Sir Thomas Lipton's eighty-five bound volumes of newspaper and magazine clippings and photos. At the Scottish Maritime Museum in Irvine, I would like to thank Mike Porter and May Fife McCallum for showing me the original plans for *Shamrock III* and providing background information about the Denny Shipyard in Dumbarton. Both Mike and May were incredibly generous with their time, Mike showing me around the museum in the off-season, and May, a Fife descendent and author of *Fast and Bonnie: A History of William Fife and Son Yachtbuilders,* providing invaluable information about the family. Anne Hoben, Director of the Denny Tank Museum in Dumbarton, gave me a detailed tour of the model production facility and test tank William Fife Jr. used to hone *Shamrock III*'s hull shape.

In Bangor, Northern Ireland, Royal Ulster Yacht Club Librarian Michael McKee gave me a wonderful tour of the club, discussing its history and how it meshed with that of Sir Thomas Lipton. In England, I would like to thank Royal Yacht Squadron Archivist Diana Harding for her tour of the Yacht Squadron clubhouse, for her suggestions and supply of source materials, and for her vast knowledge of yachting history, especially that dealing with the Isle of White.

I would like to thank the New York University interlibrary loan department for tracking down hundreds of obscure books and articles from libraries around the world. I would especially like to thank New School University librarians Carmen Hendershott and Desiree Vester, who tracked down numerous articles and electronic resources for me when I found myself landlocked in Prague. I would also like to thank Katie Richardson for her invaluable help scanning artwork for this volume as well as sending books and even lugging a few on the plane when visiting Prague, and Jared Kelly for reading the manuscript, interpreting design plans, and providing valuable insight on the interplay between naval architects and builders. Thank you to Kari Detwiler for tracking down the few source citations that slipped through the cracks. Also, thank you to Chris Stauch of Stauch Design in New York City, for his incredible illustration of *Reliance* accompanying the glossary. And thank you to Jacques Taglang and Francois Chevalier for their wonderful line drawings of *Reliance* and *Shamrock III* included in the endpapers.

Thank you to friends in the New School MFA program and especially Honor Moore for reading early drafts. I would also like to sincerely thank the National Arts Club for its 2003 Annual Award and Scholarship for Nonfiction. This generous award bestowed by Literary Committee Co-Chairs Marjory Bassett and Robert Kornfeld helped fund my research in the United Kingdom.

I would also like to thank my agent Dan Mandel at Sanford J. Greenberger Associates for making this book happen. At The Lyons Press, Ann Treistman was enthusiastic about the idea from the start, and my editor, Holly Rubino, provided valuable advice on how to shape the manuscript to its potential. Thank you to Cynthia Goss for her careful copyediting. And thank you to Jane Reilly for spreading the word.

I would also like to thank my parents for encouraging my passion for sailing and for reading drafts of the manuscript. Thank you to my sister, Cara Pastore of F22 Studio in Miami, for taking the jacket photo. And finally, I thank my wife Susan Detwiler for reading the manuscript multiple times in its entirety, providing invaluable advice, and for being so intelligent and supportive. And thanks, Susie, for sailing with me, too.

Chapter 1: The Block of Pine

1. Nathanael Herreshoff, letter to Charles Oliver Iselin, 23 May 1902, Coll. 85 Box 1 Folder 18, 25–26, Manuscripts Collection, G. W. Blunt White Library, Mystic Seaport Museum.
2. George A. Cormack, letter to C. O. Iselin, 1 September 1902, Coll. 85 Box 1 Folder 18, 26–34, Manuscripts Collection, G. W. Blunt White Library, Mystic Seaport Museum.
3. Nathanael Herreshoff, letter to C. O. Iselin, 5 September 1902, Coll. 85 Box 1 Folder 18, 4–9, Manuscripts Collection, G. W. Blunt White Library, Mystic Seaport Museum.
4. Ibid.
5. Ibid.
6. Nathanael Herreshoff, letter to C. O. Iselin, 25 September 1902, Coll. 85 Box 1 Folder 18, 10–15, Manuscripts Collection, G. W. Blunt White Library, Mystic Seaport Museum.
7. George A. Cormack, letter to C. O. Iselin, 25 September 1902, Coll. 85 Box 1 Folder 18, 26–34, Manuscripts Collection, G. W. Blunt White Library, Mystic Seaport Museum.
8. Gaston Bachelard, *The Poetics of Space: The Classic Look at How We Experience Intimate Places* (Boston: Beacon, 1994), 26.
9. L. Francis Herreshoff, *An L. Francis Herreshoff Reader* (Camden: International Marine, 1978), 225.
10. Ibid., 220–221.
11. L. Francis Herreshoff, *Captain Nat Herreshoff: The Wizard of Bristol* (Dobbs Ferry, New York: Sheridan House, 1953), 132.
12. L. Francis Herreshoff, *An L. Francis Herreshoff Reader* (Camden: International Marine, 1978), 231.
13. L. Francis Herreshoff, *Captain Nat Herreshoff: The Wizard of Bristol* (Dobbs Ferry, New York: Sheridan House, 1953), 133.

Chapter 2: The Town of Bristol

1. George Howe, *Mount Hope: A New England Chronicle* (New York: Viking, 1959), 64.

2. M. A. DeWolfe Howe, *Bristol, Rhode Island: A Town Biography* (Cambridge: Harvard University Press, 1930), 32.

3. Wilfred Harold Munro, *Tales of an Old Seaport* (Princeton: Princeton University Press, 1917).

4. Alexander Boyd Hawes, *Off Soundings: Aspects of the Maritime History of Rhode Island* (Chevy Chase: Posterity Press, 1999), 86, 97.

5. Munro, *Tales of an Old Seaport,* 222–223.

CHAPTER 3: THE WORLD OF WORK AND WAR

1. Steven M. Gillon and Cathy D. Matson, eds., *The American Experiment: A History of the United States* (New York: Houghton Mifflin, 2002), 510.

2. "The Yacht Club," *Times of London,* 18 August 1851.

3. Jack K. Bauer, *A Maritime History of the United States* (Columbia: University of South Carolina Press,1988), 72.

4. Nathanael Herreshoff, "The Old Tannery and My Brother John," 28 July 1933, in *Recollections and Other Writings By Nathanael G. Herreshoff,* ed. Calrton J. Pinheiro (Bristol: Herreshoff Marine Museum, 1998), 6.

5. Nathanael Herreshoff to W. P. Stephens, 31 August 1935, letter 13 of *Nathanael Greene Herreshoff and William Picard Stephens: Their Last Letters 1930–1938,* ed. John W. Streeter, (Bristol: Herreshoff Marine Museum, 1988), 71.

6. Ibid., 72.

7. Ibid.

8. Nathanael Herreshoff, diary notes, n.d., in *Captain Nat Herreshoff: The Wizard of Bristol,* L. Francis Herreshoff (Dobbs Ferry, NY: Sheridan House, 1953), 44.

9. Wilfred Harold Munro, *The History of Bristol, Rhode Island: The Story of the Mount Hope Lands* (Providence: J. A. & R. A. Reid, 1880), 359–362.

10. Gillon and Matson, *The American Experiment,* 592.

11. *New York Tribune,* 19 April 1866.

12. According to MIT's Alumni Directory, Nathanael Herreshoff is listed in the class year of 1870. He attended as a "special student" focused on mechanical engineering. He entering during the 1866–1867 school year and was registered through the

1869–1870 school year. About 26 students were enrolled as special students in 1866–1867. The annual course catalogs indicate that 1866–1867 was the only year in early MIT history that a special student category existed. None of the special students received degrees. Nat spent three years at MIT. Information courtesy Kurt Hasselbalch, Curator, Hart Nautical Library, MIT.

13. Nathanael Herreshoff to W. P. Stephens, letter 13 of *Nathanael Greene Herreshoff and William Picard Stephens,* ed. Streeter, 74.

14. Henry David Thoreau, *Walden,* 1854. Reprinted in *The Portable Thoreau,* ed. Carl Bode (New York: Viking-Penguin, 1982), 263.

CHAPTER 4: THE BUSINESS PLAN

1. James Mackay, *The Man Who Invented Himself: A Life of Sir Thomas Lipton* (Edinburgh: Mainstream, 1998), 71. Lipton claimed to be 21 when he opened his business, but Mackay's research uncovered that he was actually 23.

2. Thomas J. Lipton, *Leaves From the Lipton Logs* (London: Hutchinson, 1932), 89.

3. Clara DeWolf Herreshoff to James Brown Herreshoff, early 1870s, letter from *The Early Founding and Development of the Herreshoff Manufacturing Company,* Jeannette Brown Herreshoff (self-published, 1949), 45.

4. Nathanael Herreshoff diary, 13–14 February 1874, in *Captain Nat Herreshoff: The Wizard of Bristol,* L. Francis Herreshoff (Dobbs Ferry, New York: Sheridan House, 1953), 67.

5. Nathanael Herreshoff, "The Log of the Riviera," March 1932, in *Recollections and Other Writings By Nathanael G. Herreshoff,* ed. Pinheiro, 83.

6. Nathanael Herreshoff to W. P. Stephens, 9 July 1936, letter 23 of *Nathanael Greene Herreshoff and William Picard Stephens,* ed. Streeter, 146.

7. Ibid., 165.

8. Nathanael Herreshoff, "The Log of the Riviera," 14 July 1874, in *Recollections and Other Writings By Nathanael G. Herreshoff,* ed. Pinheiro, 84.

9. Ibid., 18 July 1874, 85.

10. Ibid., 24 July 1874, 87.

11. Ibid., 25 July 1874, 87.

12. Ibid., 5 August 1874, 89.

13. Ibid., 11 August 1874, 90.

14. Ibid., March 1932, 91.

15. Ibid., 92.

16. Ibid.

17. Ibid.

18. L. Francis Herreshoff, *Captain Nat Herreshoff: The Wizard of Bristol,* 54.

19. Nathanael Herreshoff "to W. P. Stephens," 31 Aug. 1935, letter 13 of *Nathanael Greene Herreshoff and William Picard Stephens,* ed. Streeter, 74.

20. Ibid., 73.

21. Anna F. Herreshoff to Jane Herreshoff, Fall 1876, letter from *The Early Founding and Development,* Jeannette Brown Herreshoff, 20–21.

22. Gillon and Matson, *The American Experiment,* 693.

23. Ibid., 694.

24. Nathanael Herreshoff to W. P. Stephens, 31 August 1935, letter 13 of *Nathanael Greene Herreshoff and William Picard Stephens,* ed. Streeter, 74.

25. A. Griswold Herreshoff, "On Catamarans," Herreshoff Marine Museum archives, Bristol.

26. L. Francis Herreshoff, *Captain Nat Herreshoff: The Wizard of Bristol,* 78.

27. Samuel Pepys diary, 16 July 1662, Bibliomania.com Ltd., 2000, www.bibliomania.com/2/1/59/106/frameset.html.

28. May Fife McCallum, *Fast and Bonnie: A History of William Fife and Son Yachtbuilders* (Edinburgh: John Donald Publishers, 2002), 15.

29. Nathanael Herreshoff, "Some of the Boats I Have Sailed In," 1934, *Recollections and Other Writings By Nathanael G. Herreshoff,* ed. Pinheiro, 51.

30. L. Francis Herreshoff, *Captain Nat Herreshoff: The Wizard of Bristol,* 76.

31. Nathanael Herreshoff, "The Old Tannery and My Brother John," 28 July 1933, *Recollections and Other Writings By Nathanael G. Herreshoff,* ed. Pinheiro, 28.

CHAPTER 5: THE STEAM ENGINE

1. Nathanael Herreshoff, "The Old Tannery and My Brother John," 28 July 1933, *Recollections and Other Writings By Nathanael G. Herreshoff*, ed. Pinheiro, 28.
2. Ibid., 29.
3. Bauer, *A Maritime History of the United States*, 288–289.
4. Mackay, *The Man Who Invented Himself*, 113.
5. Ibid., 75.
6. Samuel Carter III, *The Boatbuilders of Bristol* (Garden City: Doubleday, 1970), 70. Carter does not footnote this incident, but nevertheless includes it in his detailed Herreshoff family history. Because much of the information is based on informal conversations the author had while employed as a summer worker at the Herreshoff yard in the 1930s, as well as anecdotes from Herreshoff family members (including Louise DeWolf, John Brown Herreshoff's granddaughter; Norman Herreshoff, John Brown Francis's grandson; A. Sidney Herreshoff, Nathanael Herreshoff's son; and Natalie and Clara Herreshoff, Nathanael Herreshoff's great-granddaughters), I have noted the incident as a "rumor."
7. L. Francis Herreshoff, *Captain Nat Herreshoff: The Wizard of Bristol*, 115–116.
8. "Rules and Regulations of the Herreshoff Manufacturing Company," Herreshoff Marine Museum archives, Bristol.
9. Nathanael Herreshoff to W. P. Stephens, 26 March 1937, letter 27 of *Nathanael Greene Herreshoff and William Picard Stephens*, ed. Streeter, 166.
10. Clarence DeWolf Herreshoff, "Captain Nat Ignores a Bit of Horseplay," *Herreshoff Marine Museum Chronicle*, Fall 1980, 3.
11. Gillon and Matson, *The American Experiment*, 848.
12. "The Mary Powell Beaten," *New York Times*, 11 June 1885.
13. L. Francis Herreshoff, *Captain Nat Herreshoff: The Wizard of Bristol*, 105–106.
14. Nathanael Herreshoff diary, 6 January 1889, Manuscripts Collection, G. W. Blunt White Library, Mystic Seaport Museum.

CHAPTER 6: THE NEW AGE OF DESIGN

1. Alec Waugh, *The Lipton Story: A Centennial Biography of England's Great Merchant Sportsman* (Garden City: Doubleday, 1950), 53.
2. Ibid., 58.
3. Ibid., 69.
4. Mackay, *The Man Who Invented Himself,* 120.
5. Nathanael Herreshoff to W. P. Stephens, 19 June 1935, letter 6 of *Nathanael Greene Herreshoff and William Picard Stephens,* ed. Streeter, 38.
6. Edgar Kaufman, Jr., *The Rise of an American Architecture* (New York: Praeger, 1970), 149–150.
7. "A Yacht on New Lines," *New York Times,* 9 April 1891.
8. Nathanael Herreshoff, "Some of the Boats I Have Sailed In," 1934, *Recollections and Other Writings By Nathanael G. Herreshoff,* ed. Pinheiro, 56.
9. Charles Lane Poor, *Men Against the Rule: A Century of Progress in Yacht Design* (New York: Derrydale, 1937), 44.
10. Herreshoff, "Some of the Boats I have Sailed In," 58.
11. Ibid.
12. Ibid., 60.
13. "Why the Navahoe's Men Deserted," *New York Times,* 22 May 1893.
14. Ibid.
15. "Navahoe Is Badly Crippled," *New York Times,* 16 June 1893.
16. "Navahoe Causes Comment," *New York Times,* 13 August 1893.
17. Nathanael Herreshoff to W. P. Stephens, 31 August 1935, letter 13 of *Nathanael Greene Herreshoff and William Picard Stephens,* ed. Streeter, 79.
18. L. Francis Herreshoff, "Captain Charlie Barr," *The Rudder,* May and June 1948. Reprinted in *An L. Francis Herreshoff Reader,* L. Francis Herreshoff (Camden: International Marine, 1978), 97–99.
19. "Capt. Barr a Citizen," *New York Times,* 26 April 1893.
20. John Rousmaniere, address at Hank Haff Induction to America's Cup Hall of Fame, Rosecliff, Newport, 15 June 2004. Quote is from R. B. Burchard, "The Cup Champions and Their Crews," *Outing,* September 1895, 484.
21. John W. Streeter, ed., *Nathanael Greene Herreshoff and William Picard Stephens: Their Last Letters 1930-1938* (Bristol: Herreshoff Marine Museum, 1988), 14. In his annotation of letter No. 2

dated 26 May 1930 from Stephens to Herreshoff, Streeter surmises that this leak could have been attributed to *Defender* sitting lower in the water, which spurred Dunraven's indictment of malfeasance against the *Defender* syndicate.

22. Carter, *The Boatbuilders of Bristol,* 123.
23. Theodore Roosevelt, letter to Nathanael Herreshoff, 10 June 1897, from Herreshoff's personal letters, Herreshoff Marine Museum archives, Bristol.
24. Ibid.
25. Ibid., 16 June 1897.
26. Gillon and Matson, *The American Experiment,* 858.
27. Maynard Bray and Carlton Pinheiro, *Herreshoff of Bristol: A Photographic History of America's Greatest Yacht and Boatbuilders* (Brooklin: Woodenboat, 1989), 46.
28. Nathanael Herreshoff diary, 7 May 1898, Manuscripts Collection, G. W. Blunt White Library, Mystic Seaport Museum.

CHAPTER 7: THE TEA ENTERPRISE

1. Lipton, *Leaves From the Lipton Logs,* 135.
2. Fife McCallum, *Fast and Bonnie,* 65.
3. Ibid., 44.
4. "Topics of the Times," *New York Times,* 22 July 1899.
5. "First Yacht Race for Neither Boat," *New York Times,* 4 October 1899.

CHAPTER 8: THE FLOP

1. L. Francis Herreshoff, *An Introduction to Yachting* (New York: Sheridan House, 1963), 136.
2. Denny Ship Model Experiment Tank, Dumbarton, Scottish Maritime Museum. All information on the Denny Test Tank comes from museum information displays.
3. L. Francis Herreshoff, *An Introduction to Yachting,* 137.
4. Charles Oliver Iselin, letter to Officers and Crew of *Columbia,* November 1899, Coll. 85, Box 1 Folder 16:1, Manuscripts Collection, G. W. Blunt White Library, Mystic Seaport Museum.
5. E. D. Morgan, letter to Nathanael Herreshoff. 26 December 1900, Herreshoff Marine Museum archives, Bristol.

6. August Belmont, letter to Nathanael Herreshoff, 16 April 1900, Herreshoff Marine Museum archives, Bristol.

7. "Engineering in Yachts," *New York Times,* 19 May 1901.

8. "An Iron Constitution," *Science Siftings,* 9 April 1901.

9. E. D. Morgan, letter to Nathanael Herreshoff, 17 May 1903, Herreshoff Marine Museum archives, Bristol.

10. *Liverpool Echo,* September 4, 1901.

11. Clinton Crane, *Yachting Memories* (New York: D. Van Nostrand Company, Inc., 1952).

12. "Shamrock II Handicapped" (*The Field* article was excerpted), *New York Times,* April 6, 1901.

13. "Telescoping Masts and Monstrous Cutters," *Daily Graphic,* 5 June 1901.

14. *Daily News,* 5 June 1901.

15. "Constitution's Mishap," *New York Times,* 5 June 1901.

16. Winfield M. Thompson and Thomas W. Lawson, *The Lawson History of the America's Cup* (Boston: privately published, 1902).

17. Ibid. Although Thompson wrote the bulk of *The Lawson History of the America's Cup,* Lawson himself wrote the sections directly dealing with *Independence.*

18. Ibid.

19. W. B. Duncan, letter to C. O. Iselin, 18 January 1899, Coll. 85 Box 1 Folder 7, 29. Manuscripts Collection, G. W. Blunt White Library, Mystic Seaport Museum.

20. "The Handsomest Craft Ever Seen," *Paul Mall Gazette,* 9 September 1901.

21. " 'Constitution' Defeated," *Morning Post,* 9 September 1901.

22. A. B. C. Whipple, *The Racing Yachts* (Alexandria: Time-Life Books, 1980), 102.

23. Against *Columbia* in the 1899 races, she had lost the first race by 10m:08s corrected time, lost the second race because of a broken topmast, and then lost by 6m:34s corrected time in the final race. During the 1901 trials *Shamrock I* was consistently sailing a thirty-mile course 6 minutes faster than she had in 1899. She was therefore on par with *Columbia.*

24. *Dublin Express,* 6 September 1901.

25. "Boer Cause Theirs," *Washington Post,* 22 January 1900.

26. "Yacht Race Failed For Lack of Wind," *New York Times,* 27 September 1901.
27. "Says Columbia Crowded Shamrock II," *New York Times,* 28 September 1901.
28. "Columbia Wins by Narrow Margin," *New York Times,* 29 September 1901.
29. "Columbia Wins a Decisive Victory," *New York Times,* 4 October 1901.
30. L. Francis Herreshoff, *An Introduction to Yachting,* 143.
31. "Columbia Wins a Decisive Victory," *New York Times,* 4 October 1901.
32. Ibid.
33. Ibid.
34. "Sir Thomas Gives Up Hope," *New York Times,* 4 October 1901.

CHAPTER 9: THE TEMPLE TO THE WIND

1. Thomas J. Lipton, letter to New York Yacht Club, 7 October 1902, 1903 America's Cup Archives, New York Yacht Club Library, New York.
2. Charles Barr, letter to C. O. Iselin, 9 October 1902, Coll. 85, Manuscripts Collection, G. W. Blunt White Library, Mystic Seaport Museum.
3. "For the Defense of the Old Cup," *New York Herald,* 18 September 1903.
4. Kevin Phillips, *Wealth and Democracy: A Political History of the American Rich* (New York: Broadway, 2002), 33–41.
5. "America's Cup Challenge To Be Forwarded in a Fortnight from England," *New York Evening Post,* 8 September 1902.
6. *New York Times,* 9 October 1902.
7. Matthew Josephson, *The Robber Barons* (New York: Harcourt, 1934), 323.
8. Robert A. Scott, *The Gothic Enterprise: A Guide to Understanding the Medieval Cathedral* (Berkeley: University of California Press, 2003), 69.
9. Ibid., 92.
10. Thorstein Veblen, *The Theory of the Leisure Class* (Mineola: Dover, 1994), 5.

11. Ibid., 151.
12. Ibid., 87.

CHAPTER 10: THE BUILDING OF A GIANT

1. "No Word of Cup Challenge," *New York Herald,* 24 September 1902.
2. "Challenge Was Not On The Germanic," *New York Daily Tribune,* 3 October 1902.
3. W. B. Duncan, letter to C. O. Iselin, 20 October 1902, Coll. 85, Box 1 Folder 18, 42, Manuscripts Collection, G.W. Blunt White Library, Mystic Seaport Museum.
4. "Lipton Talks of New Boat," *New York Sun,* 9 October 1902.
5. George Lennox Watson, letter to William Fife Jr., 13 February 1902, Scottish Maritime Museum, Irvine.
6. Ibid.
7. *New York Herald,* 22 April 1902.
8. Mackay, *The Man Who Invented Himself,* 201.
9. William Denny & Brothers, *Denny Dumbarton* (London: ED. J. Burrow, 1932). This historical account of the William Denny & Brothers shipyard is largely based on this published history.
10. "The America Cup," *Dumbarton Herald,* 18 March 1903.
11. The letters between C. W. Post and Lipton ran in papers across the United States, 3 March to 5 March 1902. Among others, the article appeared in the *New York Herald, Press, Tribune, Sun, Evening Post, Commercial,* and *Morning Telegraph;* Boston *Globe, Herald;* St. Louis *Star,* Chicago *Record Herald, Chronicle,* and *Tribune;* Philadelphia *Public Ledger* and *Item;* Brooklyn *Times;* New Haven *Palladium; Washington Post;* Pittsburg *Dispatch;* Providence *News* and *Bulletin;* Baltimore *Sun* and *News;* Hartford *Times;* and the Milwaukee *Wisconsin.*
12. "Coronation Honors List," *Washington Post,* 26 June 1902.
13. "Cup Defender's Lead Keel," *New York Times,* 27 November 1902.
14. Nathanael Herreshoff to W. P. Stephens, 15 May 1930, letter 1 of *Nathanael Greene Herreshoff and William Picard Stephens.* ed. Streeter, 4. Streeter notes in his annotation that 102.3 tons was the largest keel ever poured for a single-masted vessel.

15. "New Yacht of Tobin Bronze," *New York Herald*, 29 November 1902.
16. "Still Believed that Defender Will be of Nickel Steel, in Spite of Reports," *Commercial Advisor*, 3 December 1902.
17. Carter, *The Boatbuilders of Bristol*, 95.
18. "Work on Defender," *The Evening Sun*, 4 December 1902.
19. *New York Times*, 5 December 1902.
20. *New York Times*, 7 December 1902.
21. "Lipton Talks of His Plans," *New York Sun*, 28 December 1902.
22. "Lipton 'Enthuses' Over Boat," *New York Sun*, 8 December 1902.
23. "Slow Work on New Cup Craft," *New York Times*, 22 December 1902.
24. *New York Herald*, 11 January 1903.
25. Ibid.
26. "First of Cup Yacht's Plates in Position," *New York Herald*, 25 January 1903.
27. *New York Sun*, 29 January 1903.
28. "Defender and Challenger," *New York Sun*, 1 February 1903.
29. "Different Types in Cup Race," *New York Sun*, 15 February 1903
30. *New York Herald*, 8 February 1903.
31. "Defender's Wire Rigging Finished," *New York Herald*, 3 March 1903.
32. *Bristol Phoenix*, 13 March 1903.
33. Norman L. Skene, *Skene's Elements of Yacht Design*, ed. Francis S. Kinney, 8th ed. (New York: G.P. Putman Son's, 1973), 4.
34. W. P. Stephens, *Traditions & Memories of American Yachting* (Camden: International Marine, 1981), 221.
35. "Shamrock III's Light Spar," *New York Times*, 5 March 1903.
36. "First Wager on Races Made by NYYC Man with G. L. Watson," *New York Herald*, 8 March 1903.
37. *Mail and Express*, 28 March 1903.
38. "Shamrock III," *Glasgow Evening News*, 17 March 1903.
39. "The America Cup," *Dumbarton Herald*, 18 March 1903.
40. "The America's Cup," *Glasgow Citizen*, 17 March 1903.
41. "Description of Sir Thomas Lipton's Challenger for the America Cup," *London Evening News*, 17 March 1903.
42. "Shamrock III," *Glasgow Evening News*, 17 March 1903.
43. Mackay, *The Man Who Invented Himself*, 196.

44. "Launch of the British Challenger," *Dumbarton Herald*, 18 March 1903.
45. *Mail and Express*, 28 March 1903.
46. "The America Cup," *Dumbarton Herald*, 18 March 1903.
47. "Shamrock III," *Glasgow Evening News*, 17 March 1903.
48. L. Francis Herreshoff, *An Introduction to Yachting*, 77–79.

CHAPTER 11: THE FINAL PREPARATIONS

1. "Reliance's Men Arrive," *New York Times*, 30 March 1903.
2. *Columbia* and *Constitution* photo, Rosenfeld Collection, Mystic Seaport Museum, 1901, in *Nathanael Greene Herreshoff and William Picard Stephens*. ed. Streeter, 195.
3. John Leather, "The Men Behind the Racers," *Maritime Life and Traditions*, March 2000, 14–29.
4. Ibid.
5. "Tender for New Cup Yacht," *New York Herald*, 28 January 1903.
6. "Crew of Reliance Due at Bristol," *New York Herald*, 29 March 1903.
7. "Sailmaker Ratsey on his Way to America," *New York Journal*, 3 February 1902.
8. E. D. Morgan, letter to Nathanael Herreshoff, 26 March 1903, Herreshoff Marine Museum archives, Bristol.
9. E. D. Morgan, letter to Nathanael Herreshoff, 4 April 1903, Herreshoff Marine Museum archives, Bristol.
10. "Preparations for Launching," *Bristol Phoenix*, 7 April 1903.
11. "Herreshoffs Deny Firebug Story," *New York Herald*, 11 April 1903.
12. "New Cup Yacht Is Launched and Is Voted a Marvel," *New York Herald*, 12 April 1903.
13. Ibid.
14. Ibid.
15. Ibid.
16. Ibid.
17. "Shamrock III," *Sunday Times of London*, 4 April 1903.
18. "Accident to Shamrock III," *Standard*, 18 April 1903.
19. "Shamrock III" *Daily Chronicle*, 20 April 1903.
20. "Shamrock III," *Liverpool Mercury*, 22 April 1903.
21. "Work on Reliance Delayed," *New York Sun*, 16 April 1903.

22. "Reliance Spreads Its Wings," *New York Sun,* 26 April 1903.

23. "The New Cup Yacht 'Reliance'," *Scientific American,* 11 April 1903.

24. "The Reliance Severely Criticized," *Glasgow Evening News,* 28 April 1903. This was first reported in the *Paul Mall Gazette,* and then syndicated in the *Glasgow Evening News.*

25. William Collier, *Classic Sails: The Ratsey & Lapthorn Story* (Cowes: Ratsey and Lapthorn, 1998), 34.

26. "An International (?) Contest," *Yachting World,* 30 April 1903.

27. "The America Cup," *Standard,* 29 April 1903.

28. "Cup Defender Faulty," *Daily Express,* 27 April 1903.

29. "Reliance and Columbia Sail," *New York Sun,* 5 May 1903.

30. "Old Cup Defender Shows Her Heals to the Reliance," *New York Herald,* 6 May 1903.

31. E. D. Morgan, letter to Nathanael Herreshoff, 7 May 1903, Herreshoff Marine Museum archives, Bristol.

32. *New York Daily Tribune,* 7 May 1903.

33. August Belmont, letter to Nathanael Herreshoff, 15 May 1903, Herreshoff Marine Museum archives, Bristol.

34. E. D. Morgan, letter to Nathanael Herreshoff, 14 May 1903, Herreshoff Marine Museum archives, Bristol.

35. "The Shamrocks," *Yachtsman,* 14 May 1903.

36. Tom Nye, e-mail to author, 17 February 2005. Tom Nye, City Island historian and UK (Ulmer Kolius) sailmaker, contends the lifespan of a cotton cruising sail was largely dependent on its owner's care. In addition, cotton cruising sails were often built less for performance and more for durability. Although the lifespan of cruising sails were largely dependent on the owner's performance needs, Nye asserts that cotton cruising sails lasted, on average, two to two and half times longer than cotton racing sails. We can therefore deduce that cotton cruising sails lasted on average four to five seasons.

37. *Reliance* construction contract, 1902, 1903 America's Cup archives, New York Yacht Club Library, New York. The contract specified the Herreshoff Manufacturing Company provide *Reliance* a suit of 17 sails, including a mainsail, No. 1 fore staysail, No. 2 fore staysail, No. 1 jib, No. 2 jib, working or jib headed topsail, No. 1 club topsail, No. 2 club topsail, No. 3 club topsail, No. 1 jib topsail, No. 2 jib topsail, No. 3 jib topsail, No. 4 jib

topsail, balloon staysail, balloon jib topsail, No. 1 spinnaker, No. 2 spinnaker and trysail.

38. From notes taken by John Palmieri, Curator, Herreshoff Marine Museum, from Nathanael Herreshoff's *Test of Canvas* notebook, 28 March 2003.

39. Thomas Ratsey, letter of general introduction for George E. Ratsey, 16 January 1903, Manuscripts Collection, G. W. Blunt White Library, Mystic Seaport Museum.

40. Collier, *Classic Sails,* 48.

41. *New York Sun,* 13 May 1903.

42. L. Francis Herreshoff, *An Introduction to Yachting,* 150.

43. Nathanael G. Herreshoff "Reliance (#605) Plan List," (Bristol: 1902), Cambridge: Haffenreffer-Herreshoff Collection, Hart Nautical Collections, MIT Museum, n.d. Although this pump system has been identified in numerous accounts by L. Francis Herreshoff (who sailed aboard *Reliance*), the design is not included in the official *Reliance* plan list. In Nathanael Herreshoff's drawings for the rudder and sternpost (No. 86–86) this pump system is conspicuously missing.

44. *New York Herald,* 17 May 1903.

45. Thomas F. Day, "Some Remarks," *The Rudder,* May 1903, 356.

46. "Mr. Iselin Talks of the Reliance," *New York Herald,* 19 May 1903.

47. Collier, *Classic Sails,* 70. Here Collier cites letters between Iselin and Edwin W. Lapthorn housed at the Mystic Seaport Museum. Coll. 236, vol. 50, 232.

48. W. P. Stephens to Nathanael Greene Herreshoff, 21 July 1935, letter 7 of *Nathanael Greene Herreshoff and William Picard Stephens,* ed. Streeter, 42. In this letter Stephens apologizes to Herreshoff for incorrectly stating in a profile of Tom Ratsey (*Yachting,* May 1935) that *Reliance* had used Ratsey & Lapthorn sails during the America's Cup races. Herreshoff had, in fact, built the sails used on *Reliance*.

49. *New York Herald,* 20 May 1903.

50. *New York Herald,* 21 May 1903.

51. Thomas F. Day, "Early Trials of Reliance, Constitution, Columbia," *The Rudder,* July 1903, 375.

52. "Two Rivals Give Place as Queen to the Reliance," *New York Herald,* 24 May 1903.

53. Thomas F. Day, "Early Trials of Reliance, Constitution, Columbia," *The Rudder*, July 1903, 377.
54. "The Reliance, Hard Pressed, Wins from the Constitution," *New York Herald*, 27 May 1903.
55. Ibid.
56. *New York Sun*, 5 June 1903.
57. "America Cup: Departure of Shamrocks," *Glasgow Evening News*, 28 May 1903.
58. Ibid.
59. "Challenger Here: Sure of Victory," *New York Herald*, 15 June 1903.
60. "Departure of Shamrocks," *Glasgow Evening News*, 28 May 1903.
61. "Challenger Here: Sure of Victory," *New York Herald*, 15 June 1903.
62. "Departure of Sir T. Lipton and Mr. Pierpont Morgan," *Liverpool Post*, 18 June 1903.
63. L. Francis Herreshoff, *An Introduction to Yachting*, 150. Although L. Francis Herreshoff, who sailed aboard *Reliance*, describes this ferrule and ratchet system in detail, the construction drawings show a sysem in which the topmast is held in place with a fid or pin.

CHAPTER 12: THE NINETY-FOOTERS

1. *New York Herald*, 25 June 1903.
2. "Lipton Here, Full of Hope," *New York Sun*, 25 June 1903.
3. "President Wishes Luck to Lipton," *New York Herald*, 27 June 1903.
4. *New York Herald*, 26 May 1903.
5. "Sir Thomas Lipton's Shamrock III Launched," *New York Times*, 18 March 1903.
6. "President Wishes Luck to Lipton," *New York Herald*, 27 June 1903.
7. Irving Cox, editorial, *New York Herald*, 21 June 1903.
8. Theodor W. Adorno, *Aesthetic Theory*, trans. Robert Hullot-Kentor (Minneapolis: University of Minnesota Press, 1997), 46.
9. "Cup Challenger Disabled," *New York Herald*, 1 July 1903.
10. "The Ninety-Footers," *The Rudder*, August 1903, 447–451.
11. "Sailor Drowned as Yachts Raced," *New York Herald*, 3 July 1903.
12. "Repairing the Reliance," *New York Sun*, 4 July 1903.
13. Poor, *Men Against the Rule*, 59.
14. Stephens, *Traditions & Memories*, 138.

15. "Reliance Wins Trial Races," *New York Sun,* 28 July 1903.
16. "Tuesday's Cup Race," *Daily Mail,* 18 August 1902.
17. Ibid.
18. "Today's Great Race," *Cardiff Daily News,* 20 August 1903.
19. "Opinions and Prospects," *Cardiff Daily News,* 20 August 1903.
20. From the official measurement certificate, 1903 America's Cup Archives, New York Yacht Club Library, New York.
21. Central News Agency report, *Cardiff Daily News,* 20 August 1903.
22. "Quest of the America's Cup," *Glasgow Herald,* 8 August 1903.
23. "The America's Cup: Sir Thomas Lipton's Third Attempt," *Paul Mall Gazette,* 18 August 1903.
24. "The America Cup," *North Star,* 20 August 1903.
25. The Associated Press and Publishers Press Association, letters to the New York Yacht Club Race Committee, 12 August 1903 and 14 August 1903, America's Cup Archives, New York Yacht Club Library, New York.
26. W. B. Franklin, letter to New York Yacht Club Regatta Committee, 14 August 1903, America's Cup Archives, New York Yacht Club Library, New York.
27. U.S. Treasury Department, letter to New York Yacht Club Regatta Committee, 1 August 1903, America's Cup Archives, New York Yacht Club Library, New York.

CHAPTER 13: THE WIZARD'S WING

1. W. J. Sears, Lieutenant-Commander, U.S. Navy, letter to New York Yacht Club Regatta Committee, 8 September 1903, America's Cup Archives, New York Yacht Club Library, New York.
2. S. Nicholas Kane, Newbury D. Lawton, and Edward H. Wales, letter to New York Yacht Club members, 18 July 1903, America's Cup Archives, New York Yacht Club Library, New York.
3. "The America Cup," *Daily Graphic,* 21 August 1903. According to L. Francis Herreshoff, of the six mainsails built for *Reliance* during the season, two were made of four-O duck and four were made of triple-O duck.
4. Nathanael Herreshoff, letter to Charles Oliver Iselin, 23 May 1902, Coll. 85 Box 1 Folder 18, 25–26, Manuscripts Collection, G. W. Blunt White Library, Mystic Seaport Museum.

5. "Thursday's Cup Race," *London Daily Mail*, 18 August 1903.
6. Charles D. Mower, letter to George Cormack, 21 August 1903. America's Cup Archives, New York Yacht Club Library, New York.
7. Sharmon Crawford, letter to New York Yacht Club Race Committee, 22 August 1903, America's Cup Archives, New York Yacht Club Library, New York.
8. "America Cup Races," *The Rudder*, September 1903, 497.
9. Ibid.
10. J. M. Into, "Log book entry for Nathanael Herreshoff's steam-yacht *Roamer*," 22 August 1903, comp. John Palmieri, Herreshoff Marine Museum archives, Bristol.
11. "Second Race," *The Rudder*, September 1903, 499–501.
12. "Incidents of the Race," *Daily Telegraph*, 24 August 1903.
13. "Reception of the News in London," *Sunday Times*, 23 August 1903.
14. "Shamrock III In Dry Dock," *New York Times*, 24 August 1903.
15. "America Cup: The Second Race," *Daily Telegraph*, 26 August 1903.
16. "Reliance to be Remeasured," *New York Times*, 26 August 1903.
17. "With the Excursion Fleet," *New York Times*, 26 August 1903.
18. "Second Race," *The Rudder*, September 1903, 499–501.
19. "The Race In Detail," *New York Times*, 26 August 1903.
20. "America Cup: The Second Race," *New York Times*, 26 August 1903.
21. L. Francis Herreshoff, *An Introduction to Yachting*, 150.
22. "The Race In Detail" *New York Times*, 26 August 1903
23. "America Cup: The Second Race," *New York Times*, 26 August 1903.
24. William E. Simmons, "Sailing a Cup Defender," *Outing*, September 1903, 652.
25. "Storm Spreads Terror on Land and Water," *New York Times*. 26 August 1903.
26. Reuters report, "Gale at New York," *Daily Telegraph*, 26 August 1903.
27. "Fickle Wind Again Deserts the Yachts," *New York Times*, 1 September 1903.
28. Ibid.
29. "'I Was Deceived,' Says Sir Thomas," *New York Herald*, 29 August 1903.
30. "No Wind for the Yachts," *New York Times*, 2 September 1903.
31. "Race Again Postponed," *New York Times*, 3 September 1903.

32. "The Yacht Races," *Bristol Phoenix,* 1 September 1903.
33. "The Race in Detail," *New York Times,* 4 September 1903.
34. Ibid.
35. "Third Race," *The Rudder,* September 1903, 501–503.
36. W. J. Sears, Lieutenant-Commander, U.S. Navy, letter to New York Yacht Club Regatta Committee, 8 September 1903, America's Cup Archives, New York Yacht Club Library, New York.
37. "Swift Reliance Keeps Cup Here," *New York Times,* 4 September 1903.
38. Mackay, *The Man Who Invented Himself,* 170. On January 27, 1898, Lipton was fined ten shillings for excessive black smoke pumping from his jam factory.
39. "Swift Reliance Keeps Cup Here," *New York Times,* 4 September 1903.
40. Ibid.

EPILOGUE: THE END OF AN ERA

1. "Sir Thomas Toasted at Pilgrim's Banquet,"*New York Times,* 5 September 1903.
2. Ibid.
3. "When Wringe Found Out," *New York Sun,* 28 September 1903.
4. George Cormack, letter to Sir Thomas Lipton, 14 March 1904, America's Cup Archives, New York Yacht Club Library, New York.
5. Ibid.
6. George Cormack, letter to Nathanael Herreshoff, 28 March 1902, Herreshoff Marine Museum archives, Bristol. Nathanael G. Herreshoff was officially elected an honorary member of the New York Yacht Club on 27 March 1902.
7. W. P. Stephens, *Traditions & Memories,* 138.
8. From tombstone sketches in Nathanael Herreshoff's personal letters. Herreshoff Marine Museum archives, Bristol.
9. W. P. Stephens, *Traditions & Memories,* 226.
10. Ibid., 227.
11. E. D. Morgan, letter to Nathanael Herreshoff, 15 October 1906, Herreshoff Marine Museum archives, Bristol.

12. George Cormack, letter to Nathanael Herreshoff, 24 January 1911, Herreshoff Marine Museum archives, Bristol.

13. "Yachtsmen at Captain Barr's Funeral," *New York Times,* 29 January 1911.

14. "Capt. Charles Barr, Noted Skipper, Dead," *New York Times,* 25 January 1911.

15. "Yachtsmen Pleased at Race Prospects," *New York Times,* 8 June 1913.

16. Carter, *The Boatbuilders of Bristol,* 162.

17. L. Francis Herreshoff, *The Wizard of Bristol,* 154.

18. Mackay, *The Man Who Invented Himself,* 284–285.

19. Denny Ship Model Experiment Tank, Dumbarton, Scottish Maritime Museum. All information on the Denny Test Tank comes from museum information displays.

20. William Denny & Brothers, *Denny Dumbarton,* 33.

21. Nathanael Herreshoff, letter to H. Wilmen Hanan, 13 July 1924, Herreshoff Marine Museum archives, Bristol.

22. Streeter, ed., *Nathanael Greene Herreshoff and William Picard Stephens.* Nathanael Herreshoff's letters with William Picard Stephens were bound and annotated by John Streeter. Many of these letters provide valuable insight into Captain Nat's life and were referenced throughout this book.

23. L. Francis Herreshoff, *The Wizard of Bristol,* 321.

24. Ibid., 319.

25. Ibid., 321.

26. "The Great New England Hurricane of 1938," NOAA Report and statistics, www.erh.noaa.gov/box/hurricane1938.htm.

27. Bray and Pinheiro, *Herreshoff of Bristol,* 222.

Adorno, Theodor. *Aesthetic Theory*. Translated by Robert Hullot-Kentor. Minneapolis: University of Minnesota Press, 1997.

Aldridge, Arthur F. "International Races for Next Summer." *Yachting*, February 1907: 78.

Albion, Robert Greenhalgh. *The Rise of the New York Port, 1815–1860*. Hamden, CT: Archon Books, 1961.

"America Cup Races." *The Rudder*, September 1903: 496–503.

American Society of Mechanical Engineers. *Historic Engineering Record, Massachusetts and Rhode Island*. Portsmouth, NH: American Society of Mechanical Engineers, 1980.

Anderson, Henry H. and Robert C. MacArthur. *The Centennial History of the United States Sailing Association*. Portsmouth, RI: US Sailing Association, 1997.

Annan, Thomas. *Glasgow Victoriana: Classic Photographs*. Edited by James McCarroll. Ayr, UK: Fort Publishing, n.d.

Auden, W. H. *The Enchanted Flood or Iconography of the Sea*. Charlottesville: University of Virginia Press, 1950.

"Are We Going to Keep the Cup?" *Harper's Weekly*, 25 April 1903.

Bachelard, Gaston. *The Poetics of Space*. Translated by Maria Jolas. Boston: Beacon Books, 1964.

Bateman, Charles. *Sir Thomas Lipton and the America Cup*. Edinburgh: Oliphant Anderson & Ferrier, 1901.

Bauer, K. Jack. *A Maritime History of the United States: The Role of America's Seas and Waterways*. Columbia: University of South Carolina Press, 1988.

Beale, Howard K. *Theodore Roosevelt and the Rise of America to World Power*. New York: Collier, 1962.

Bicknell, Thomas W. *The History of the State of Rhode Island and Providence Plantations Biographical*. New York: American Historical Society. Vol. 2, 1920: 324–330.

Bleekman, George. "Viewing an International Yacht Race from the Erin." *The Rudder*, September 1903: 503.

Bourke, John. *The Sea as a Symbol in English Poetry*. Windsor, UK: Alden & Blackwell, 1954.

Bowman, W. Dodgson. *Yachting and Yachtsmen*. New York: Dodd, Mead and Company, 1927.

Bode, Carl, ed. *The Portable Thoreau*. 1947. Reprint, New York: Viking-Penguin, 1982.

Bray, Maynard and Carlton Pinheiro. *Herreshoff of Bristol: A Photographic History of America's Greatest Yacht Builders*. Brooklin, ME: Woodenboat Publications, 1989.

Brightman, Thomas P. "Thomas P. Brightman Recollections." *Herreshoff Marine Museum Chronicle*. Spring 1989: 1, 4. An interview with Paul A. Darling.

British Yachts and Yachtsmen: A Complete History of British Yachting from the Middle of the Sixteenth Century to the Present Day. London: Yachtsmen Publishing, 1907.

Brooks, Jerome, E. *The 30,000,000 Cup: The Stormy History of the Defense of the America's Cup*. New York: Simon and Schuster, 1958.

Brown, Terence. *Ireland: A Social and Cultural History, 1922 to the Present*. 1985. Reprint, Ithaca, NY: Cornell University Press, 1990.

Burnett, Constance Buel. *Let the Best Boat Win: The Story of America's Greatest Yacht Designer*. Cambridge: Houghton, 1957.

Carter, Samuel III. *The Boatbuilders of Bristol: The Story of the Amazing Herreshoff Family of Rhode Island, Inventors, Individualists, Yacht Designers, and America's Cup Defenders*. Garden City, NY: Doubleday, 1970.

Chevalier, Francois and Jacques Taglang. *America's Cup Yacht Designs 1851–1986*. Paris: self-published, 1987.

Clark, William H. *Ships and Sailors: The Story of our Merchant Marine*. Boston: L.C. Page, 1938.

Collier, William. *Classic Sails: The Ratsey and Lapthorn Story*. Cowes, UK: Ratsey & Lapthorn, Ltd., 1998.

Conner, Dennis and Michael Levitt. *The America's Cup: The History of Sailing's Greatest Competition in the Twentieth Century*. New York: St. Martin's Press, 1998.

Constable, George, ed. *The Classic Boat*. Alexandria, VA: Time-Life Books, 1977.

Cookman, Scott. *Atlantic: The Last Great Race of Princes*. New York: John Wiley & Sons, 2002.

Crampsey, Bob. *The King's Grocer: The Life of Sir Thomas Lipton*. Glasgow: Glasgow City Libraries, 1995.

Day, Thomas Fleming, ed. "Early Trials of Reliance, Constitution, Columbia." *The Rudder,* July 1903: 375–383.

———. "Some Remarks." *The Rudder,* May 1903: 356–358.

Dear, Ian. *The Royal Yacht Squadron, 1815–1985.* London: Stanley Paul, 1985.

Denison, Archibald Campbell. *America's Maritime History.* New York: G.P. Putnam's Sons, 1944.

DeWolf, Katherine Herreshoff. *The Story of the America's Cup.* North Plymouth, MA: Plymouth Cordage Company, 1930.

DeWolf, Louise Henry. "A Boy's Will is the Wind's Will." *Herreshoff Marine Museum Chronicle,* Fall 1983: 1–2.

"The Dismasting of Shamrock III." *The Rudder.* May 1903.

Dunlap, G. D. *America's Cup Defenders.* New York: American Heritage Press, 1970.

Eastland, Jonathan. *Great Yachts and their Designers.* New York: Rizzoli International Publications, 1987.

Fanta, J. Julius. *Winning the America's Cup: Twenty Challenges 1870–1970.* New York: Sea Lore Publishing Company, 1969.

Fox, Uffa. *Sail and Power.* New York: Charles Scribner's Sons, 1936.

Gardner, William. "Uniform Rule Not Perfect." *Yachting,* February 1907: 77.

Gifford, Don. *The Literature of Architecture: The Evolution of Architectural Theory and Practice in Nineteenth-Century America.* New York: Dutton, 1966.

Gillon, Steven M., and Cathy D. Matson, eds. *The American Experiment: A History of the United States.* Boston: Houghton, 2002.

Guild, Reuben Aldridge. *Early History of Brown University: Including the Life, Times, and Correspondence of President Manning, 1756–1791.* Providence: Snow and Farnham, 1897.

Gutelle, Pierre. *The Design of Sailing Yachts.* Camden, ME: International Marine Publishing, 1979.

Haffenreffer, R. F. *The Herreshoff Manufacturing Company: Designers and Builders of Sailing and Power Craft Since 1861.* Bristol, RI: Herreshoff Marine Manufacturing Company, 1941.

Hall, Charles H. "The Three Shamrocks." *Yachting,* June 1920: 250–254, 266.

Hansen, Hans Jurgen. *Art and the Seafarer: A Historical Survey of the Arts and Crafts of Sailors and Shipwrights.* Translated by James and Inge Moore. New York: Viking, 1968.

Harding, Diana. "Cowes Castle." Information Leaflet No. 2, Royal Yacht Squadron, 21 February 2001.

———. "Robert Stephenson, *Titania* and That Other Race of 1851." Information Leaflet No. 6, Royal Yacht Squadron, 30 August 2001.

———. "The Royal Yacht Squadron." Information Leaflet No. 3, Royal Yacht Squadron, 21 February 2001.

———. "White Ensign." Unpublished notes, n.d.

———. "The Yacht America and the Race of 1851." Information Leaflet No. 4, Royal Yacht Squadron, n.d.

———. "Yacht Crew." Information Leaflet No. 7, Royal Yacht Squadron, n.d.

Hawes, Alexander Boyd. *Off Soundings: Aspects of the Maritime History of Rhode Island.* Chevy Chase, MD: Posterity Press, 1999.

Heckman, Richard. *Yankees Under Sail: The Age of Sail Brought to Life in a Collection the Best Sea Stories.* Dublin, NH: Yankee Publishing, 1968.

Herreshoff, A. Griswold. "The Herreshoff Shop." *Herreshoff Marine Museum Chronicle,* Spring 1984: 1–2.

———. "Reliance-80th Anniversary." *Herreshoff Marine Museum Chronicle,* Spring 1983: 1, 4.

Herreshoff, Clarence DeWolf. "Captain Nat Ignores a Bit of Horseplay." *Herreshoff Marine Museum Chronicle,* Fall 1980: 3.

———"J. B. Herreshoff's Cost Estimates." *Herreshoff Marine Museum Chronicle,* Spring 1981: 3.

Herreshoff, Jeannette Brown. *The Early Founding and Development of the Herreshoff Manufacturing Company.* Tampa, FL: self-published, 1949.

Herreshoff, Halsey C. "Herreshoff Name and Origins: An Excerpt from a Letter to the Providence Journal." *Herreshoff Marine Museum Chronicle,* Fall 1997: 2.

———. "Now Then and Say When." *Herreshoff Marine Museum Chronicle,* Spring 1987: 3.

———"The Reliance Coin." *Herreshoff Marine Museum Chronicle,* Winter 2001: 3.

————. "Seven Brothers." *Herreshoff Marine Museum Chronicle*, Fall 1982: 1.

[Herreshoff, Lewis]. "Catamaran Chronicle." *Spirit of the Times*, 24 November 1877. *Nathanael Greene Herreshoff and William Picard Stephens: Their Last Letters 1930-1938*, ed. John W. Streeter. Bristol: Herreshoff Marine Museum, 1988, 227-233.

Herreshoff, L. Francis. *An Introduction to Yachting*. Dobbs Ferry, NY: Sheridan House, 1963.

————. *Capt. Nat Herreshoff: The Wizard of Bristol*. Dobbs Ferry, NY: Sheridan House, 1953.

————. *Common Sense of Yacht Design*. Vol. 2. New York: Thomson, 1948.

————. Correspondence, 1925–1971, Coll. 138, Manuscripts Collection, G. W. Blunt White Library, Mystic Seaport Museum.

————. *An L. Francis Herreshoff Reader*. Camden, ME: International Marine Publishing, 1978.

————. *Nathanael Greene Herreshoff: 1848–1938: A Life and Appreciation of his Work*. Hartford: Wadsworth Atheneum, 1944.

————. *The Writings of L. Francis Herreshoff*. New York: Rudder Publishing, 1946.

Herreshoff, Nathanael G. Diary. Manuscripts Collection, G. W. Blunt White Library, Mystic Seaport Museum.

————. "Letter to Mr. Foster." 6 March 1932. *Herreshoff Maritime Museum Chronicle*, Spring 1982: 3.

————. Personal letters, Herreshoff Marine Museum Archive, Bristol, RI.

————. *Recollections and Other Writings*. Edited by Carlton J. Pinheiro. Bristol, RI: Herreshoff Marine Museum, 1998.

Herreshoff, Nathanael G. III. "Before the Boatyard: The Herreshoff Family." Lecture presented on 30 October 2000 at the Bristol Historical and Preservation Society Headquarters, Bristol, RI..

————. "The Herreshoff Family in the 19th Century." Lecture presented on 9 September 2003 at the Herreshoff Marine Museum, Bristol, RI.

"Herreshoffs of Bristol." *Harper's Weekly*, 26 August 1899.

"The Herreshoff Plant at Bristol." *Yachting*, December 1924, 45–62.

Hitchcock, Henry-Russell. *Rhode Island Architecture*. Cambridge: Massachusetts Institute of Technology Press, 1939.

Hitchcock, Henry-Russell, Albert Fein, Winston Weisman, and Vincent Scully. *The Rise of an American Architecture*. New York: Praeger Publishers, 1970.

Hobsbawm, Eric. *The Age of Empire, 1875–1914*. New York: Vintage Books, 1987.

Holm, Ed. *Yachting's Golden Age, 1880–1905*. New York: Knopf, 1999.

Howe, George. *Mount Hope: A New England Chronicle*. New York: Viking Press, 1959.

Howe, M. A. DeWolfe. *Bristol, Rhode Island: A Town Biography*. Cambridge: Harvard University Press, 1930.

Iselin, Charles Oliver. Correspondence, Coll. 85, Manuscripts Collection, G. W. Blunt White Library, Mystic Seaport Museum.

Jobson, Gary. *An America's Cup Treasury: The Lost Levick Photographs, 1893–1937*. Newport News, VA: The Mariner's Museum, 1999.

Josephson, Matthew. *The Robber Barons: The Classic Account of the Influential Captialists Who Transformed America's Future*. San Diego: Harcourt, 1934.

Knapp, Bettina L. *Machine Metaphor and the Writer: A Jungian View*. University Park: Pennsylvania State University Press, 1989.

Lane, Joshua Wheaton. *Commodore Vanderbilt: An Epic of the Steam Age*. New York: Knopf, 1942.

"Launch of Shamrock III." *The Rudder*, May 1903: 293–299.

Leather, John. "The Men Behind the Racers," *Maritime Life and Traditions*, March 2000: 14–29.

Levine, George R., ed. *Harp on the Shore: Thoreau and the Sea*. Albany: State University of New York, 1985.

Lipton, Sir Thomas J. *Leaves from the Lipton Logs*. London: Hutchinson, 1932.

Lowry, Philip J. *Green Cathedrals*. Cooperstown, NY: Society for American Baseball Research, 1986.

Mackay, James. *The Man Who Invented Himself: A Life of Sir Thomas Lipton*. Edinburgh: Mainstream Publishing, 1998.

Mason, H. B. "George Lennox Watson (1851-1904)." *Encyclopedia of Ships and Shipping*. n.p., 1908.

McCallum, May Fife. *Fast and Bonnie: A History of William Fife and Son Yachtbuilders*. Edinburgh: John Donald Publishers, 2002.

Metzger, Charles R. *Thoreau and Whitman: A Study of their Esthetics.*
Seattle: University of Washington Press, 1961.

Miller, William Jones. *Celebration of the Two Hundredth Anniversary of the Settlement of the Town of Bristol.* Providence: Providence Press, 1881.

Minningerode, Meade. *Certain Rich Men: Stephen Girard, John Jacob Astor, Jay Cooke, Daniel Drew, Cornelius Vanderbilt, Jay Gould, Jim Fisk.* Freeport, NY: Books for Libraries Press, 1970.

Mower, C. D. "The First Trials of Reliance." *The Rudder,* June 1903: 359–360.

———. "Launch of Reliance." *The Rudder,* June 1903: 300–301.

Munro, Wilfred Harold. *The History of Bristol, R.I.: The Story of the Mount Hope Lands.* Providence: J. A. & R. A. Reid, 1880.

———. *Tales of an Old Sea Port.* Princeton: Princeton University Press, 1917.

The National Cyclopaedia of American Biography. "Charles Oliver Iselin." Volume 26. New York: James T. White & Co., 1937: 330–331.

"The Ninety-Footers." *The Rudder,* August 1903: 447–451.

Palmer, Henry Robinson. "The Herreshoffs and Their Boats." *New England Magazine,* July 1895: 343–360.

Palmieri, John. "Reliance Centenary Talk." Lecture presented on 30 March 2003 at Herreshoff Marine Museum Annual Meeting. Herreshoff Marine Museum, Bristol, RI.

Papa, James A. Jr. "Water Signs: Place and Metaphor in Dillard and Thoreau." In *Thoreau's Sense of Place: Essays in American Environmental Writing.* Edited by Richard J. Schneider. Iowa City: University of Iowa Press, 2000.

Parkinson, John. *The History of the New York Yacht Club: From Its Founding Through 1973.* Edited by Robert W. Carrick. New York: New York Yacht Club, 1975.

Pease, George C. "Another Herreshoff Success." *Harper's Weekly,* 13 June 1903.

———. "The Cup Yachts and the Season's Problems." *Harper's Weekly.* 30 May 1903.

Peck, John. *Maritime Fiction: Sailors and the Sea in British and American Novels, 1719–1917.* Houndmills, UK: Palgrave, 2001.

Pendlebury, Katherine DeWolf. "J.B. Herreshoff." *Herreshoff Marine Museum Chronicle,* Fall 1980: 3.

Phillips, Kevin. *Wealth and Democracy: A Political History of the American Rich*. New York: Broadway Books, 2002.

Pinheiro, Carlton J. "Columbia's Launching Accompanied by Shocking Accident." *Herreshoff Marine Museum Chronicle,* Fall 1999: 1–2.

———. "Gloriana: Alone in Her Class." n.v. 21 (1991): 1, 4.

———. "NC-4 Anniversary." *Herreshoff Marine Museum Chronicle,* Spring 1979: 3.

———. "Herreshoff Catamarans—Amaryllis." *Herreshoff Marine Museum Chronicle,* Spring 1980: 1.

Poor, Charles Lane, PhD. *Men Against the Rule: A Century of Progress in Yacht Design*. New York: Derrydale Press, 1937.

Pringle, Henry F. *Theodore Roosevelt*. San Diego: Harcourt, 1984.

Report to the New York Yacht Club of the Committee on Challenge of the Royal Ulster Yacht Club: Reliance vs. Shamrock III, 1902–1903. New York Yacht Club Library.

Robinson, Bill, ed. *The Great American Yacht Designers*. New York: Alfred A. Knopf. 1974.

Robinson, W. E. "Bristol and the Herreshoffs." *The Rudder,* March 1899: 65–70.

Rousmaniere, John. *The Golden Pastime: A New History of Yachting*. New York: W.W. Norton, 1986.

Scott, Robert A. *The Gothic Enterprise: A Guide to Understanding the Medieval Cathedral*. Berkeley: University of California Press, 2003.

Shaw, David. *America's Victory*. New York: Free Press, 2002.

Simmons, William E. "The Evolution of the Racing Yacht." *Harper's Weekly,* 7 September 1901: 900–901.

———. "Sailing a Cup Defender." *Outing,* September 1903: 644–653.

Simpson, Richard V. *Bristol: Montaup to Poppasquash*. Charleston: Arcadia, 2002.

———. *Images of America: The America's Cup, The Rhode Island Connection*. Charleston: Arcadia, 1999.

Skene, Norman L. *Skene's Elements of Yacht Design*. Revised by Francis S. Kinney. 8th ed. New York: G.P. Putnam Son's, 1973.

Smallwood, Robert Bartly. *Sir Thomas Lipton, England's Great Merchant Sportsman, 1850–1931*. New York: Newcomen Society of North America, 1953.

Smith, Howden D. *Commodore Vanderbilt: An Epic of American Achievement*. New York: R. M. McBride, 1927.

Stephens, Olin J. *All This and Sailing, Too.* Mystic, CT: Mystic Seaport, 1999.

Stephens, W. P. "The Evolution of the Yacht Designer, First Paper–English Designers." *Outing,* October 1901: 49–53.

————. "The Evolution of the Yacht Designer, Part II–The American Designers." *Outing,* November 1901: 223–228.

————. "Reliance." *The Rudder,* June 1903: 333–334.

————. *The Seawanhaka Corinthian Yacht Club: Origins and Early History 1871–1896.* New York: n.p., 1963.

————. *Traditions & Memories of American Yachting.* Camden, ME: International Marine Publishing, 1981.

Stone, Herbert L. *The America's Cup Races.* New York: Macmillan, 1930.

Stone, Herbert L., William H. Taylor, and William W. Robinson. *The America's Cup Races by the Editors of Yachting.* New York: Norton, 1970.

Streeter, John W., ed. *Nathanael Greene Herreshoff and William Picard Stephens: Their Last Letters, 1930-1938.* Bristol, RI: Herreshoff Marine Museum, 1988.

Sutcliffe, Andrea. *Steam: The Untold Story of America's First Great Invention.* New York: Palgrave MacMillan, 2004.

Swan, William. "The Fate of the Cup Defender." *Yachting,* March 1936, 117.

Tea Fortunes. Directed by Sue Clayton, Jonathan Curling, and Allister Goulding. First Run Icarus Films, 1985.

Thomas, Barry. *Building the Herreshoff Dinghy: The Manufacturer's Method.* Mystic, CT: Mystic Seaport Museum, 1977.

Thompson, Winfield Martin and Thomas William Lawson. *The Lawson History of the America's Cup: A Record of Fifty Years.* Boston: n.p., 1902.

Tobin, James. *To Conquer the Air: The Wright Brothers and the Great Race for Flight.* New York: Free Press, 2003.

Trevelyan, G. M. *History of England.* 6th ed. Vol. 3. Garden City, NY: Doubleday, 1953.

Veblen, Thorstein. *The Theory of the Leisure Class.* Mineola: Dover, 1994.

"Voyage of the Shamrocks." *The Rudder,* July 1903: 384–385.

Walker, Fred M. *Song of the Clyde.* Edinburgh: John Donald, 2001.

Ward, Baldwin H., ed. *Flight: A Pictorial History of Aviation*. New York: Simon, 1953.

Waugh, Alec. *The Lipton Story*. Garden City, NY: Doubleday, 1950.

Wescott, Lynanne and Paula Degen. *Wind and Sand: The Story of the Wright Brothers at Kitty Hawk*. New York: Harry N. Abrams, 1983.

Who Was Who in America. A component volume of *Who's Who in American History*. "Charles Oliver Iselin." Volume 1, 1897–1942. Chicago: A.N. Marquis Co., 1943.

Whipple, A. B. C. *The Racing Yachts*. Alexandria, VA: Time-Life Books, 1980.

William Denny & Brothers. *Denny Dumbarton, 1844–1932*. London: Ed. J. Burrow, 1932.

"The Yachting Season of 1901." *Harper's Weekly*, 1 June 1901.

INDEX

A page number followed by an "n" refers to an endnote found in the Notes section of this book.

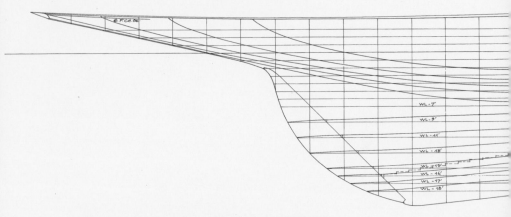

© F. CH. 86

SHA

WL - 7'
WL - 9'
WL - 11'
WL - 13'
WL - 15'
WL - 16'
WL - 17'
WL - 18'

LOA	134'-8¾"	DRAFT	19'-10½"
LWL	89'-10"	DISPL.	1666 T.
BEAM	24'-10¾"	SAIL AREA	14154 Sq.Fᵉ.

RE-DRAWN FROM ORIGINAL LINES Nᵒ D685 B,
THE NATIONAL MARITIME MUSEUM, GREENWICH,
BY COURTESY OF DAVID J. LYON AND A. J. VINER,
BY
F. CHEVALIER
1986

WILL

WILLIAM

1 0 1
SCALE

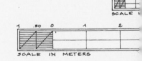

1 .50 0 1 2
SCALE IN METERS

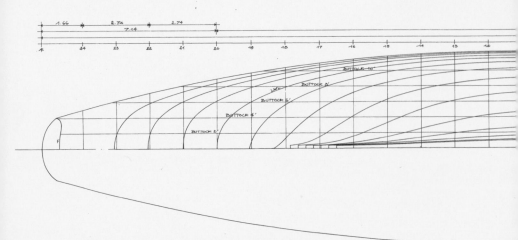

1.66   2.74   2.74
7.14

4   24   23   22   20   19   18   17   16   15   14   13   12

BUTTOCK 10'
BUTTOCK 8'
LWL
BUTTOCK 6'
BUTTOCK 4'
BUTTOCK 2'